"Alexandra Wenman is a wonderful messenger for the Angels, and her book *Archangel Alchemy Healing* is a comprehensive read covering so many different aspects and facets of working with the angelic kingdom. This book is for anyone interested in calling on the Angels for world service or if you want to know how to open inner doorways to experience the angelic kingdom."

—**Steve Ahnael Nobel**, former director of Alternatives, London; creator of Soul Matrix Healing; and author of *Freeing the Spirit*

"Alexandra Wenman's *Archangel Alchemy Healing* is a timely contribution to the evolution of humanity. The book sheds light and clarity on the three titular themes (Archangels, alchemy, and healing) while guiding the reader along the experience of the sometimes narrow path of light, accompanied by the heavens but also fraught with challenges. Wenman does not shy away from the more difficult task of recognizing 'false light' both without and within and helps the reader strengthen inner knowing and discernment at a time when it could not be more important: these times of great change and the efforts of lower energies to obfuscate the light and love that are here to support us. The channeled messages of this book offer hope, uplifting and carrying the reader beyond doubt to the loving accompaniment of the angelic realm, and the exercises allow the anchoring of that hope in direct experience. A guide for the path!"

—**Kathryn Hudson**, certified Angel Therapy and Crystal Healing practitioner and teacher; author of *Inviting Angels into Your Life* and *Discover Your Crystal Family*

"*Archangel Alchemy Healing* is a masterpiece. It is probably one of the most comprehensive books ever found in regard to the Archangels and all things associated with them. Not only is it a font of knowledge, but it also shows how people can connect and use the powerful energy of the Archangels to heal and help make a positive difference in the world. Alexandra lives, breathes, and walks the path of the Archangel Alchemist—leaving a trail of magic behind her wherever she goes. This is definitely a book not to be missed."·

—**Lorraine Flaherty**, founder of Inner Freedom Therapy and author of *Healing with Past Life Therapy*

"A divine read, packed full of insight, wisdom, and knowledge to help us connect to the angelic realms. In her relatable manner, Alexandra has written a book that can truly empower those of us open to healing and who are on a spiritual pathway to self-realization. Highly recommended."

—**Claire Broad**, medium, spiritual teacher, and author of
What the Dead Are Dying to Teach Us

"Alexandra Wenman's *Archangel Alchemy Healing* leads us seekers through imaginal portals of light as her angelic beings—like the alchemical images of old—carry us into the inner realm brimming with messages of empowerment, loving support, and guidance. Drawing on angelic iconography, this beautifully written text opens to an imaginal realm, taking the reader on a journey of discovery, beyond the territory defined by word or form into the inner landscape of the soul. *Archangel Alchemy Healing* is sure to be warmly welcomed by spiritual seekers everywhere."

—**Janet Piedilato, Ph.D.**, author of
The Mystical Dream Tarot and *The Dream Gate*

"Alexandra Wenman's book *Archangel Alchemy Healing* is a transformative guidebook to the mystical, angelic realm that exists all around and within us. If you are seeking to understand your true spiritual nature and navigate the unfolding process of divine energy in your life, this is the book you need. You will discover the profound message that we are all 'Earth Angels' and that love is our only task."

—**Karen Wyatt, M.D.**, author of *7 Lessons for Living from the Dying*

"Alexandra Wenman offers a bridge between the seen and unseen with such clarity, grace, and eloquence. *Archangel Alchemy Healing* is a book for the Quantum Age and beyond, with the Archangels providing leading-edge guidance to create a new way of integrated healing and well-being. Thank you, Alexandra, for bringing forth their genius and love so powerfully to help us through these transformational times."

—**Stephanie Lodge**, "The Hug Angel," peace ambassador, founder of
Angelic Academy, and author of *Soul Scars*

ARCHANGEL ALCHEMY HEALING

The Celestial Science in the Vibration of the Universe

Alexandra Wenman

FINDHORN PRESS

Findhorn Press
One Park Street
Rochester, Vermont 05767
www.findhornpress.com

Findhorn Press is a division of Inner Traditions International

---

Disclaimer

The information in this book is given in good faith and is neither intended to diagnose any physical or mental condition nor to serve as a substitute for informed medical advice or care. Please contact your health professional for medical advice and treatment. Neither author nor publisher can be held liable by any person for any loss or damage whatsoever which may arise from the use of this book or any of the information therein.

Cataloging-in-Publication data for this title is available from the Library of Congress

ISBN 978-1-64411-562-6 (print)
ISBN 978-1-64411-563-3 (ebook)

Printed and bound in the United States by Lake Book Manufacturing, Inc. The text stock is SFI certified. The Sustainable Forestry Initiative® program promotes sustainable forest management.

10 9 8 7 6 5 4 3 2 1

Edited by Nicky Leach
Cover logo by Viktorija Medina
Text design and layout by Richard Crookes
This book was typeset in Adobe Garamond Pro and HelveticaNeue

To send correspondence to the author of this book, mail a first-class letter to the author c/o Inner Traditions • Bear & Company, One Park Street, Rochester, VT 05767, USA and we will forward the communication, or contact the author directly at **www.alexandrawenman.com**.

This book is dedicated to love.

May it ever envelop you in its wings,
inspiring you to become the most
divine version of yourself
it is possible to be in human form.

Contents

◆ ◆ ◆

◆

PART ONE

How to Become an Archangel Messenger

PART TWO

Guardians of the Non-physical Worlds

PART THREE

Archangels and Our Ascension

PART FOUR

The Archangel Alchemy Healing System

Angelus

We are beautiful
And we are bold
We are brave
And we are gold

We are magical
And we are might
We are the day
We own the night

Ruffle no feather
Out of spite
We are the bells
That peel back plight

Raising the
Sword of truth
We lift our pens
To write
To right!

We are the Angels
Of the light.

Foreword

When Alexandra invited me to write this foreword to her magnificent book, I was filled with a sense of honour that she would trust me with the task and, in the same moment, overcome with doubt that I was not up to the job. That mixture of honour and doubt led me to read Alexandra's book again and hope to find reassurance from the Angels she so eruditely portrays so that I could indeed introduce her inspired work.

I did not have to read far beyond her introduction to feel instantly reassured. It was then I realized that what Alexandra and I both share is an unshakable and foundational belief in the power of unconditional love. Sadly, what I don't share with Alexandra is a lifelong awareness of Angels in my psychic sphere—until recently. And I want to tell that story.

Someone close to me, whom I love dearly, experienced a miscarriage in the second trimester. I was eagerly waiting to welcome the new baby girl into the world, and I was to be part of her wider circle of love, nurture, and upbringing. So, the loss of this life was a real blow to my hopes and dreams. She was named Angel, and after her passing, I began my first relationship with a soul who still received all my unconditional love and, to my complete surprise, became as real to me as if she had lived.

Angel's first gift to me was a deeper discovery of my unconscious self—a realm she seemed to inhabit—and she encouraged me to connect with new realms of wisdom and love that had previously been dormant. I now depend on her for comfort, inspiration, and magic on a daily basis.

She encouraged me to write my book *The Secret of the Alchemist*, because "it will be good for you and you have important things to share with the world."

"What do I have to share with the world that it does not already know?" I asked.

Her reply was simple and unequivocal: "The power of unconditional love!"

By following the wisdom that the Angel in my life has brought, I now feel free to open the rest of my heart to receive what the host of Angels offers.

In her book, Alexandra reveals the unlimited realm of angelic beings that all share the same mission—to point us to the greatest and most fundamental force to enable each of us to live a truly empowered life, whatever obstacles, setbacks, and disadvantages we experience. That force is, of course, love—in the context of Alchemy. As Alexandra says, "The purpose of Archangel Alchemy is to restore your purity and awaken the divine child that lives within you. Your true essence is pure love."

15

This is where Alchemy comes into the mix; to combine with love to form what, in my experience, can only be described as magic. Many of us struggle to believe we are worthy of love, or we have a confused image of what love is, and misunderstand that it is actually the currency of relationships—with ourselves and others. We think, mistakenly, that we first need to either earn the love of the universe, or we retreat into denial about our true self. The absence of love will always lead us away from what is good for our whole being and away from the truth of who we really are.

Alchemy provides an inner laboratory for us to apply the real essence of the *prima materia* of the human soul to transform what we consider to be the base and dark matter of our psyche, the parts we have rejected, and turn them into the very gold of life—our real treasure.

In this transformative book, Alexandra guides us to receive all the help we need from the Angels of the celestial and earthly spheres to facilitate a new empowerment, free from the shackles of our fears and doubts. This book and its author are your gateway to the world of the Angels of light. Whether, like me, you are a novice, or even if you are an experienced light worker, *Archangel Alchemy Healing* will bring you and your world into new realms of wholeness.

I recommend this book to you because it is so much more than words on a page; it is filled with all the intent of unconditional love that permeates from Alexandra's gift.

As someone once said of old, "Just say the word, and I will be healed!"

Colm Holland
Glastonbury 2022

The original publisher of Paolo Coelho's *The Alchemist*, Colm Holland is author of *The Secret of the Alchemist* and founder of The School of Alchemy Transformation.

Channelled Message
from the Angelic Hierarchies of Light

Question: What are Angels, and how can you explain people's different experiences of them?

Like you, we are multidimensional in nature. Angels exist at every level of creation and so, too, we can appear to you at every level of your being. We are part of you, and you have experienced us as such, but here, in this third dimension, we appear as separate guardians of light, guides to assist you through unconditional love on your path to reunite with your soul's true calling. That calling is simply love.

You will experience us and feel our energy differently depending on what level of consciousness you are tuning into and how high your vibration is at the time. Many believe we come from the fifth dimension, and some say we are from the seventh, but we are present in every dimension of reality. We are the properties of creation. The divine archetypes and building blocks your universe is created on.

Every cell, molecule, and atom has, at some level of its being, an angelic consciousness, for we are the consciousness of love. Each individual Angel is a part of the divine whole, so we are like the cells, molecules, and atoms of God—the elements that come together to make the whole. You are part of this. Every one of you has angelic qualities. As each one of you is just as divine as the next. Some of you have just forgotten this, and we are making ourselves known at this time to help you remember.

When people first encounter us, they need to believe we are something separate from them, as they are in the frame of mind that they are searching for something or someone to help or rescue them. They don't believe in their own inner divine power, and so they call on us to assist. At first, they may ask for help with little everyday things, but as they learn to work with our energies they discover there is so much more to the world and who they really are. We are here to help you discover

that what you think you want may not be what you want at the highest
level of your being.

We are like a ladder. We help you on your path by providing
necessary steps back to the divine. The stairway to heaven is just a
stairway in your own consciousness, and we angels are the fabric that
makes up each step. We are the building blocks of creation. We are like
the individual facets that make up the infinite diamond of your divine
soul and spirit. Every aspect of your divinity you connect with, every step
you take, every lesson you learn is part of the divine whole, drawing you
closer and closer to divine oneness—to the truth of your divinity.

Each of you is a shimmering diamond of divine love, light, and
potential. We are here to lovingly assist you in fulfilling the deepest and
most magnificent potential you hold within you.

We are the light codes and filaments within your very cells, yet
we are also beings of pure light that surround your physical being and
world. We are internal and external. We are within and without. Like
the universe, all is above and below. All is within and without. We are
you, yet we surround you as separate beings. It is one and the same
thing.

If you feel overwhelmed with this information, or with any spiritual
concept, just remember that all is love. All comes back to love. Love is
the answer.

Live a life of love for self first, and the rest will fall into line. All that
is not aligned with your purpose and path will begin to drop away. Let
it go with love. Do not struggle against love. Allow yourself to flow with
love. Go into freefall. Stop fighting against the tide.

Many changes are afoot on this planet right now. We angels are on
the rise because the level of love on this planet and the vibration of your
hearts are on the rise. We have not appeared out of nowhere. There are
no more of us than there used to be—we are infinite. We always were,
and always will be. You were just not so willing or able to see us before.

As more light penetrates the dark corners of your shadow, your
angelic and divine qualities will rise and rise and you shall know us,
within and without. We are within you and we surround you. We are the
manifestation of your love and the essence of your creation.

If you love the Angels, then surely you must love yourselves.

Divine ones, you are truly blessed, for you are built on love, and nothing you could ever say, do, think, or feel will ever change that. Our increased presence in your awareness is proof that the world is rising in love. There is no turning back from this process. This is the evolution of your soul and the Ascension of your planet.

At your core is love. Love is the balance. Love is the key. Love is the pivotal point. Come back to love in every moment. Return to love. Remember love. Breathe love, see love, spread love, feel love, choose love, give love, live love.

Come home to love.

Living With Angels – A Prologue

I have experienced Angels and spirit for as long as I can remember and, indeed, ever since I was a small child. I say "experienced", because Angels do not always reveal themselves in a way that can be "seen" as such. Although I do see them—both with my physical and inner sight—I have also experienced their wondrous presence in many different forms. I will talk about some of the miraculous and beautiful ways you, too, may experience angelic energy and receive their messages throughout this book.

I believe that everyone is psychic and everyone possesses healing abilities. In my experience it is our birthright to be able to access vaster realms of awareness than we have been taught we are able to and that our societal constraints would have us believe.

Like many other seers, mystics, and healers, I came into this world psychically open. I died at birth. I was turned around the wrong way (I believe I had perhaps regretted my decision to come to Earth and was trying to climb back out). My mother was told to expect a stillborn, but I was delivered by high forceps and miraculously resuscitated by my father's best friend, who was the anaesthetist on hand in case they needed to deliver me by caesarean. In the end, there was not enough time, and they had to get me out fast. Both my mother and I stared death in the face that day, and I believe that I, quite literally, came into the world with one foot in this world and one foot in the realms beyond.

Many years later, when I underwent sessions in both regression hypnosis and rebirthing breathwork, I remembered my birth. I was told by my Angels and guides that if I had not survived, neither would my mother, as we had a soul contract to fulfil together in this lifetime. It seemed I had come here with important work to do, and she would need to keep me on the straight and narrow. Ever determined, she went on to have three more children after me and, together with my older sister, there are five of us Wenman kids. So my parents more than had their hands full.

Because I could "see" as a child, I would have many mystical experiences that I just assumed everyone else had, too. Lying awake at night, I would see faces staring at me in the dark. Bizarre creatures, star beings, elementals and animal spirits would all make their way into my awareness—some of them friendly, and some not quite so comforting to have around.

My mother raised us as Catholics—despite my dad being a non-practising Anglican, a doctor, and a self-professed "man of science"—and whenever I was scared at night, Mum would show me how to pray to the Angels for protection. One such prayer I had in a book and knew by heart as a child was:

Angel of God, my guardian dear,

To whom God's love commits me here,

Ever this "day" (or "night" at bedtime),

Be at my side,

To light and guard,

To rule and guide,

Amen.[1]

I suffered terribly from sleep paralysis, where I would wake up in the middle of the night, terrified and unable to move my body. But whenever I said the Angel prayer, the paralysis would lift and then I could see arcs of brilliant diamond light, like starlight, streaking across my bedroom. The arcs had a particular shape, like that of the top of a church arch. I will talk more about the significance of this shape later, as it is not random.

Where these lights came from is anyone's guess, as we lived 20 minutes outside a country town in the Australian bush. With no street lights, it was often so dark at night you could not see your hand, even when you held it right in front of your face. One source of light that was brighter than I have seen in most other places in the world was the light of the stars. They glistened like diamonds against the huge canopy of that big New South Wales open sky.

Sometimes, as a child, I would climb into bed with my mum and dad and lie awake staring at the ceiling. In the dancing, curving lights above me, a huge lioness would appear, and I would feel immediately safe. I now know that lioness was the Archangel Ariel, Lioness of God and the Angel of Courage, watching over me.

In my angelic visitations, I would also sometimes hear very soft, exquisite music and gentle voices inside my mind telling me not to be afraid and that it was all going to be okay. I still hear those same voices today. Sometimes, they are as ethereal as a whisper, and sometimes, they are louder and more insistent when they need to get my attention, but they have always been there, even when, at times, I have forgotten or refused to listen to their guidance.

I communicate with many different guides and groups of beings, but these particular voices I know to be the collective chorus of the Angelic Kingdom of Light. How do I know this? I suppose in many ways I have just always known it. My mother is psychic and, although she was invested in Catholicism when I was young, she was part of a women's healing group. She and some of her friends would meet in circle regularly to pray the rosary (a beautiful prayer to Mother Mary, which is known by many to invoke miracles) and request healing for the world and whoever needed it.

When I was about 11 years old, I remember one of my mother's friends looking at me and saying to my mother: "Alex has the gift. She's got Angels all around her."

I had no idea what she was talking about at the time because, to me, I was just me, and I didn't think that I was different from anyone else. That same woman still tells me almost every time I see her that when I was born, I came in with an army of Angels. She says when I was a baby and she would visit and hold me, she would be covered from head to toe in goosebumps.

Another byproduct of my death-at-birth is that I have an exceedingly long memory. As a baby, I was aware of my surroundings. I remember breast-feeding with my mother and seeing vivid lights and colours around people, which I now know to be the aura.

I have a particular memory of a day at the seaside, when I was left on my own as my parents walked up the beach to greet friends. I thought they were leaving me and became terrified. All of a sudden, a large dragonfly appeared and began to circle above me. At first I thought it might sting me but then I realized that it was there to protect me. Angels can also show up in the form of winged insects and birds. I remember having a strong feeling of calm in the presence of the dragonfly in that moment. It was as though I recognized it and felt instantly safe.

Years later, I told my mother about this memory. She was surprised I could remember the event. "But you were only an infant. You can't have been much more than a year old," she said.

I was always interested in the tiny details of life and had a fascination with bugs and insects and their worlds. Another memory I have from when I was around the age of four is of sitting in our garden for what seemed like hours, telepathically talking to a cricket in the palm of my hand about the fact that we are all one because we are all God. As the other kids played together at school, I would go off alone and sit under the pine trees, talking to the beetles. To me, they were full of wisdom to share. I knew these creatures as my friends, and, in some ways, I felt they understood me more than people did.

I always knew myself to be somehow connected to all things and part of all life. It wasn't until I was around that same age of four and hit my head on a bookcase and needed stitches that I started to realize I was "separate" from the rest of the world. My dad held me up to look at my stitches in a mirror, and I burst into tears, because I suddenly realized I was in a body—and a tiny one at that.

During my first ride on the school bus I experienced something similar. I caught a glimpse of myself in the rearview mirror and the face looking back at me didn't feel at all like mine—only I couldn't recall what my face was supposed to look like. It was as though I was wearing a different body to the one I usually had. I had a faint memory of being much, much taller, but couldn't fully bring up the memory to the surface of my mind. In any case, I didn't feel like "me", whoever this other "me" was.

In whatever form they have shown up, I have always recognized the presence of the Angels—in the same way you recognize a person you know very well and can sense their energy when they walk into a room, even if you aren't facing in their direction.

There is a certain quality of light and a feeling in the air when I sense Angels are near. Sometimes, I can smell a beautiful perfume, such as rose, jasmine, frangipani, orange blossom, or gardenia. Usually, it is a fragrance I would associate with white flowers. I will see flashes, sparkles, or orbs of light in my peripheral vision. As a natural clairvoyant (seer), I see them most often as clear pictures inside my own mind; however, nothing quite compares to the out-of-this-world visitations I have had, when an angelic being, usually an Archangel, has stepped into my body and shown me the vast holographic and infinite nature of our universe and existence.

A few times over the years, I have even seen the Angels with my physical sight as a shimmering apparition. Sometimes, the Angel is standing nearby when this happens, and sometimes the Angel is standing directly in my energy field and I can see it from all angles. It's as though I am the Angel and am looking at it simultaneously, like a projection coming from my own being.

Two days before writing this chapter, I watched in awe as a single orb of pure white light dropped through the ceiling of my office at home and formed into a tall, shimmering figure with a feminine angelic outline. The day before, I had done a big spring clean, turning that corner of my room into an altar, with a framed image of the cover of my *Archangel Fire Oracle* deck proudly displayed on a little white table.

I took this visitation as confirmation that the Angels were very happy I had tidied up. When I finished work that evening I was overcome with the need to dance, and my office became a one-woman disco, complete with a starlight strobe lamp a friend had given me for Christmas.

How you relate to and experience the Angels and angelic energies may be totally different from how I experience them, so in this book, I want to show you how to establish your own relationship with them. When you invite the Angels into your life, things will never be quite the same again. Be prepared to change and grow in unexpected and miraculous ways, but be warned: Angels are not always light and fluffy. If you find yourself heading in the wrong direction, or making a decision that may not be for your highest good, they may take swift action to put you back on track.

This may not always feel comfortable, but with the Angels by your side, although you may be tested and go through lessons, you can be sure that it will always be for your highest good and, if you listen to them and heed their call, you will never put a foot wrong.

For many years, I shut down my spiritual side to try to fit in. It didn't help that I was often told I just had a vivid imagination. At Catholic school, I was also taught that being psychic was the "work of the devil", and so my vibrant little mind was gradually narrowed to fit their view of what the world should look like.

At 14 years old, I had an experience where my bedroom filled with many beings; most of them, the spirits of my ancestors. I couldn't see or hear them, but I knew there were many beings in the room and that I was somehow being called to communicate with them. I refused. I told them that, while it would be nice to be psychic to pass my exams, I did not want to see dead people. I guess I had seen one too many scary movies.

I still dabbled in spiritual subjects over the years. I loved crystals and would sleep with a rose quartz and amethyst under my pillow. I also got hold of a copy of *The Spiral Dance* by Starhawk and began to learn about subjects like candle gazing. I would carry it everywhere I went in my school backpack. I never delved too deeply, though. I would explore the world of spirituality, but then get scared and close myself down again, afraid of what I might see if I let myself go too deep.

When I moved to London in my early twenties, my gifts started to open up again, almost too rapidly. It was like I couldn't hold back the floodgates. I was doing my best to fit in and be "normal" but soon fell into a deep depression, and on my first visit home to Australia, at the end of 2001, after years of repressing my true nature, I finally exploded.

Once I was back in the company of my family, all my pent-up emotions flooded out of me, and I came clean to my mum about how low and helpless I was feeling. She simply said: "Have you asked your Angels for help?"

Despite how silly I felt, I was at rock bottom, and something in me knew she was right. I called out silently with my whole heart: "If you really are there, I need to know you are real, and I need help."

From that day on, the Angels showed up again in my life in ways that were unmistakable. Everywhere I looked, I would see the word "Angel". It would be written on the T-shirts of people I walked past in the street. I would open a book, and there it was, on the page in front of me. On another day, I was in a supermarket, and a voice came over the loudspeaker saying: "Would Angel please come to the checkout . . ."

A few days after the conversation with my mum, my then boyfriend and I drove up to my hometown of Coffs Harbour from Sydney. I wanted to show him a nature spot called The Promised Land near a beautiful little village called Bellingen. The area has freshwater swimming holes and is on the way to Dorrigo National Park's waterfalls. When we pulled up to park the car, a wooden sign directly in front of us read: ANGEL GABRIEL CAPARARO RESERVE. Although Angel Gabriel Capararo was an actual person who lived in the area, the only part of the sign that was visible to me above the dashboard was the part that read: ANGEL GABRIEL . . .

Angels will often reveal their presence in the form of physical signs like this. The people around you may not even notice, but it will feel as though you are having your own private joke with the universe. When you ask the Angels for a sign, it may come in the form of a white feather, shiny coins on your path or, in the same way it happened for me, the word "Angel" may pop up again and again, to the point where you will not be able to ignore it or explain it away. You can also ask for specific signs.

On that trip home, I began to explore my connection with Angels more. I found a book on Angels, and during an exercise to connect with your Guardian Angel, I was given the name Ariel. I soon learnt that Ariel is one of the Archangels.

As I further developed my own connection with the Angels, I discovered that I had a specific connection with the Archangels. Before I even met my Guardian Angel, every time I asked who my Guardian Angel was, I kept getting the name Ariel. Pretty soon, I realized that every time I called on the Angels, the first ones to show up were the Archangels.

Over the years, I became familiar with the Archangels and their individual personalities and qualities. When I became the editor of *Prediction* magazine, I wrote a column called "Archangel Alchemy", and my relationship with these powerful beings kept developing and growing from there. So it seemed only natural that they were to become the subject of my first Angel healing card deck, *Archangel Fire Oracle*, and now this book, *Archangel Alchemy Healing*.

PART ONE

How to Become
an Archangel Messenger

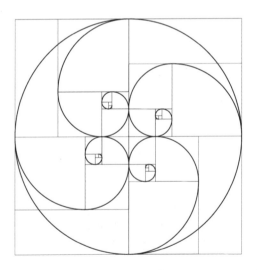

CHAPTER 1

The Purpose of Archangel Alchemy

Archangels are leader Angels that assist humanity with our evolution by helping us to access the divine through our higher wisdom and knowledge.

They differ in relation to other Angels, which help us with more practical day-to-day things (there are Angels for everything, such as Guardian Angels, Parking Angels, Sleep Angels, and even Angels in charge of buildings and cities). The Archangels have more to do with our Ascension and attainment of enlightenment, as they are specifically charged with connecting us directly to God and our own inherent divine nature. The Archangels, in my view, act as doorways to our own divinity.

The purpose of Archangel Alchemy is to restore your purity and awaken the divine child that lives within you. Your true essence is pure love.

Gifted by the Archangels of the Angelic Kingdom of Light, the attunements, meditations, and processes in this book will help you harmonize and align with your true state of innocence. This is the state of grace that resides within the soul of every human and activates when each person realizes they are a divine soul in an earthly form.

The diamond frequency is the restorer of the sacred crystalline birthright that all humans have access to, without exception. You are born of the pure light of Source, and to that light you will return. As humanity returns to this state of original innocence, we are helping to raise the vibration and frequency of the whole, and collectively anchoring in the Diamond Earth Ascension Blueprint to awaken the next Golden Age.

Our Evolution and Becoming Human Angels

In this time of global awakening, there are more Angels than ever before at our disposal. The reason for this is that humanity is expanding in awareness and, as we raise our individual and collective consciousness, we are able to perceive and access information that was previously unavailable to us. Along with more people becoming aware of the existence of Angels and other high-frequency light guides, as a collective, we are also becoming more aware of our innate gifts and angelic qualities. As we open our hearts to higher love and soften into deeper compassion, we awaken to a much greater truth—the truth that we ourselves are divine, and we are all connected through a unified field of unconditional love.

Love is the very fabric our universe is built on, and it is visible in the patterns of nature. Sacred geometry, as shown by the Fibonacci sequence and equations such as the Golden Mean (see chapter 23 for a more in-depth explanation of the mathematics), is revealed to us in the unfolding petals of a rose, the seeds of a sunflower, and the spiral of a pine cone. The blossoming rose is also a beautiful symbol of the opening heart of humanity, the divine feminine and the ever-expanding universe, which is reflected in our ever-evolving search for greater knowledge and wisdom.

The Ascension, otherwise known as "The Quickening", is a rapid acceleration in our collective evolution. It is bringing with it a remembering and reawakening of our lost or forgotten knowledge, practices, and abilities, all of which are part of our original blueprint. Gifts of telepathy, clairvoyance (inner sight), clairaudience (the ability to hear messages from spirit and our higher self) and clairsentience (tuning into the feelings of others or sensing the energy of a place with our emotions) are just some of the byproducts of this raising of our collective vibration.

The Angels want us to know that the way to access our divinity is through opening our hearts and following our own unique calling and desires. No two human beings are the same, and we were not all created to fit into the same box. The unified divine mind of humanity is like a beautiful crystal or diamond, with each individual a unique shining facet of that diamond. If all the faces were the same, the light wouldn't fractal in the same way and the diamond would be lacklustre indeed.

You become more angelic and access your true god-self when you say yes to the calling of your heart and follow your own will, authority, and guidance over and above the advice, viewpoints, or agendas of another. So long as we do no harm, we are meant to be free to experience our own unique version of heaven on this earth. The more we say yes to that inner calling, the more we inspire others to do the same.

What sets one person's heart on fire may seem boring to someone else. We have been conditioned to ignore that calling in favour of trying to fit in and, as a result, many of us have kept ourselves small. What a shame it would have been if the likes of Mozart or Beethoven hadn't chosen to share their gifts!

When we throw caution to the wind and have the courage to spread our proverbial wings, we don't just benefit ourselves. Like Olympic athletes who are constantly besting their last performance and that of their competitors, as a human race, we are inspiring each other and pushing ourselves to new capabilities, accessing our inner genius and achieving incredible feats of mastery. Look at how rapidly we have moved forward in terms of technology alone in the past one hundred years. Video calling was once something we could only witness while watching sci-fi films and now we use it every day to contact our families and loved ones.

As we become aware of the angelic aspects of ourselves, we realize that we, too, are part of the angelic kingdom, and we help to create that kingdom right here in our daily, earthly lives. We are then able to know ourselves as divine, and we tap into our inner power of manifestation and co-creation. When you realize that every bit of your life, the world, and your experiences has been created by you on some level, you are no longer a passive bystander, seemingly without much influence in the way your life journey unfolds. This realization enables you to take back your power, so you can steer your life in the direction you choose it to go.

Earth Angels are naturally empathic people that want the best for themselves and everyone else. What is the best possible version of Earth you can imagine? Every time you do this, you help to steer the whole world towards our highest potential future.

What world, then, will you go forth and create?

How Does Archangel Alchemy Work?

Archangel Alchemy is different from most other forms of healing, in that it sparks an alchemical process. In this healing system, we use the symbolism of the diamond to refer to the multifaceted divine soul. Ancient alchemists knew that the soul was the Philosopher's Stone, and the closer one got to their own soul, the closer they got to the uncovering the fabled "elixir of youth" and attaining the secrets of life itself.

The ancient science of alchemy is said to be a process of transmutation, whereby an original substance is separated into its greater and lesser elements. Both elements are purified and then reunified into a more refined substance. The process is repeated until, eventually, the greater absorbs the lesser and the purification of the original substance is complete. For example, it is said that alchemists were once able to transform lead into gold via this method. The Philosopher's Stone was said to be the key magical ingredient needed to perform this function.

Alchemists worked with symbols to describe each aspect of the alchemical process. In terms of spiritual alchemy, symbolism takes you out of the logical mind and opens your imagination. When we think of the difference between a sign and a symbol, as Carl Jung pointed out, a sign represents something we already know the meaning of, such as a stop sign. However, symbols tend to refer to the unknown or something we may not already know the meaning of.[2]

Symbols, such as Egyptian hieroglyphs and our modern-day emojis, can also contain multiple meanings. They are not a linear language, with just one explanation for each image. Working with symbols can, thus, help to stretch your mind and get you thinking outside the box. Symbols compel you to wonder what they might mean and that, in turn, forces you to open your imagination to search for the answer or meaning. Your ability to imagine is exactly what you need to be able to step beyond the confines of 3D physical reality and into your true multidimensional magnificence. This is why I like to think of symbols as doorways or gateways that can help you connect more easily with your higher self.

In terms of alchemy as a spiritual process, the Archangels want to help us purify our lower or human self, so that it can be reunited with our higher or divine self. It is our human programming, with all of its hurts, traumas, judgements, and misconceptions, that prevents us from living our highest potential. We can think of the Philosopher's Stone as the essence of our own soul, which is unconditional love. If we embrace our hardships, misunderstandings, issues, and blocks with more and more love, and do it repeatedly, we move ever closer to the goal of oneness via enlightenment, and thus, move closer to achieving lasting harmony and peace for ourselves and our planet.

The attunements gifted you by each of the Archangels within this book aim to initiate a powerful alchemical process within you. Symbolism and visualization add a key element to the healing process as it helps you to witness your own metamorphosis. As you blaze with the holy diamond fire of the archangels, you embody their gifts and qualities and begin to shed all that is no longer serving you. Through working with Archangel Alchemy and performing the self-healing process regularly, you may find that old habits begin to shift and your preferences and tastes for certain things may change seemingly overnight.

How Archangel Alchemy Can Help in Your Daily Life

Archangel Alchemy can make a real difference in your day-to-day living. Working with the Archangels in this alchemical process can help you to:

◊ Connect to the truth of who you are so you can release what is no longer serving you and choose to direct your life towards your highest and most fulfilling and joyful purpose

◊ Heal and integrate multiple timelines and wounded aspects of the self

◊ Free yourself from negative thoughts and emotional patterns

◊ Improve physical health and well-being

◊ Stop apologizing for who you are and celebrate yourself

◊ Discover your true desires

◊ Connect to your own divine will and authority

◊ Transmute and alchemize lower or negative energies and influences

◊ Transcend karma, ancestral patterning, and adverse effects of astrology, Schumann resonance, EMF, geopathic stress, and so on

◊ Activate your diamond-rainbow DNA

◊ Harness key incoming Ascension frequencies and source codes to raise your vibration and access your genius through higher levels of consciousness and awareness

◊ Upgrade your light body and subtle body templates for increased health and vitality

◊ Know your core truth, and live according to your integrity

◊ Balance the left and right hemispheres of your brain and masculine and feminine sides

◊ Embrace your sacred creativity and sexuality

◊ Experience more grounding and stability in the midst of the extreme change and shifts currently occurring on the planet

◊ Learn to trust yourself more, so you may discern the best course of action for you in any moment or situation

◊ Step on to your highest potential divine timeline

◊ Return to unity love consciousness.

The Science of Archangel Alchemy

This book also covers scientific research into spiritual phenomena, including Angels. In my opinion, science is only just starting to catch up with what the mystics have known for eons, but there is some exciting research being done into topics such as channelling, precognition, the nature of consciousness, cosmic rays, astral travel, out-of-body experiences, and even spirit visitations.

Because of the very physical and tangible nature of my own visions and experiences with the Archangels, in particular, I wanted to try to go some way towards offering possible scientific explanations for what I know to be real occurrences. The scientific research I have included here is by no means definitive, and I only offer it as an invitation for you to keep an open mind and do your own research.

I have tried to explain the science—especially the mathematics, which describes the realms the Angels and Archangels inhabit—in layman's terms, and I could never hope to cover every topic on the subject, but I hope my findings and the research I am sharing here open a door for you to explore more of the links between the non-visible world of spirit and our everyday reality.

CHAPTER 2

The Beginnings of Archangel Alchemy

How Angels Can Exist Both within and around Us

For a long time as a child, I had an invisible friend called Rose, but I didn't see myself and Rose as separate. It was as though she was actually a part of me, and for a few years, when I was very little, I demanded that my mother call me Rose. Many years later, I learnt that my Guardian Angel's name is, in fact, Rose, so I must have somehow known my "invisible friend" was an Angel.

As I understand it, our Guardian Angels are an intrinsic part of ourselves; they are higher aspects of our own consciousness. If you have read the books or watched the TV series of Philip Pullman's trilogy *His Dark Materials*, the concept of each person having a daemon is a similar idea.

Along with my knowing that my Guardian Angel was a part of myself, a number of times in my life I have also had embodied experiences with the Archangels, where it has been impossible to distinguish where the angel ends and I begin.

Because of these potent experiences, I have developed a unique way of describing and working with Angels, Archangels in particular. To me, Angels are not figments of our imagination (although we do need our imagination to access and communicate with them), and they are not just Beings of Light or guides that exist outside us and around us. On some level, Angels are part of us. They exist within and around us, as we are part of the divine oneness that permeates all of existence, and so are they.

A Meeting with Archangel Metatron

During a healing workshop I attended in 2008, the teachers announced that we would be doing Angel readings.

As we began the exercise, I closed my eyes and asked which Angel was with me. All of a sudden, my skin felt like electricity and a surge of pure love shot through my body like a lightning bolt. It was as though this energy was actually inside me, and I could feel sparks of light all over me and around me. My eyes were closed, but the room filled with a beautiful, bright, golden light, and I could see a massive golden Angel with his feet on the Earth, while his head seemed be somewhere up in the universe amongst the stars. He looked like a giant golden Transformer and was all angular, as though he was made from geometric shapes. He resembled a huge angelic robot! Totally overwhelmed and shaking from head to toe with excitement, I asked his name.

"I am Metatron!" came an immense, booming voice that rippled through the very core of me. It was less of a voice and more of a frequency or resonance, and it was simultaneously silent yet louder than anything my human ears should've been capable of withstanding. Until this point, the only Angels I had ever really heard of were the ones mentioned in church. I knew of Michael, Gabriel, and Raphael, but who was this huge being with a name like a robot?

Metatron showed me how to bring a golden cube down through my body to cleanse my chakras and align my energy field. He gave me many messages about how I would be working with the Angels and he specifically spoke about "alchemy".

As I was coming out of the vision, an Angel healer who was assisting on the workshop crossed over from the other side of the room, which was full of around 50 people, and stood beside me.

She gently placed her hand on my shoulder and said: "My darling, I just saw that whole thing happen. I was guided to walk over here. The Angels want me to tell you that they have been waiting for you to work with them. They want you to write about them, and they want to work with you. It's very important that you start to work with them."

Both of us were staring at each other in amazement and then we simultaneously looked down. There on the floor, directly between our feet, was a perfectly formed, large, fluffy, white feather. Later that evening, I did an online search on Metatron and discovered that, amongst other things, he is known as the Angel of Sacred Geometry.

After that course, the messages from the angels started to get clearer and clearer.

A Meeting with Archangel Raphael

A few months later, I signed up to an Angel workshop being held at Mysteries, the crystal shop in Covent Garden, and during the class, I had yet another incredible experience with an Archangel. This time, while I was practising a healing exchange with a close friend also attending the workshop, Archangel Raphael appeared and casually sat down inside my body.

I could feel this amazing Angel infuse my whole being. I had no idea what he was doing in my energy field, but the palms of my hands were tingling, as though they were on fire. I could see my body completely lit up with the most beautiful emerald green aura. It was like I had become the Archangel Raphael and he had become me. There was no separation.

My friend let out an excited gasp: "Babe, he's just stepped into you!"

"I know" I laughed. "I can't believe you can see it, too!"

I needed to find out what he was showing me, but I had a feeling it was some kind of channelled energy healing that could be directed through the palms of my hands.

Several more times over the years, I had similar angelic experiences where these amazing celestial beings would infuse my energy with theirs and a powerful healing vibration would seem to come through my palms.

A Meeting with Lord Melchizedek

One of the most memorable of these experiences occurred in 2009, as I was travelling to work on the bus one morning. It was just a regular day like any other. I was quite tired, so I decided to close my eyes and do a bit of meditation. I centred my awareness in my heart chakra and started to send love out to everyone around me, as I had taught myself to do many times before. Suddenly, as the bus neared Bank station, only a few stops before London Bridge, where I had to alight, I felt an incredibly intense tingling sensation. A vibration of pure love rushed through my body, and I intuitively knew another huge being was about to appear. I waited for Archangel Metatron to show himself, but this time, something was different.

A massive golden-white Being of Light did indeed appear, and again, his energy was merged with my own. I could see him, but I simultaneously was him. He was absolutely massive, with feet on the earth and planets orbiting around his head. But I knew this wasn't Metatron because, instead of just golden light, this being was surrounded by a beautiful pearlescent diamond-white light that contained all the colours of the rainbow. This diamond-rainbow light was surrounded by a violet fire and the violet flame had a blazing and sparkling golden outline, and beyond that were thousands of stars.

My eyes were closed, yet I could see and feel this being so clearly. It was like I had stepped out of this reality into a totally different dimension. The space I now occupied with my energy field, which was fully merged with his energy field, was easily as a big as this universe. But, more than that, I could see that in that moment, I was as big as the universe. My body was running so much energy, I felt like I had been hooked into an entire electrical power grid, but the feeling was one of overwhelming love.

This magnificent figure looked like a giant wizard with a long white beard that appeared to be made from clouds. By this time, I had done a lot of research on the Angels and knew quite a few of the Archangels' names. At first I thought this being must be Archangel Zadkiel because of the appearance of the violet flame, but I soon realized that this was not a being that I was at all familiar with and I was not even sure he was an Angel. He was far bigger and more powerful than any Angel I'd ever encountered. Tentatively, as I was in quite a state of shock, I asked to know his name.

"I am Melchizedek!" boomed a voice louder even than that of Metatron many months before. I had never heard the name Melchizedek before, and was utterly overwhelmed by what was happening, but remembering my mother's advice to "Always ask for a message", I silently asked why he had appeared.

He spoke just two words to me: "Spiritual Alchemy."

Golden symbols, strange letters and shapes lit up in golden-white light, began to flood my vision, as though I was absorbing information that was beyond my comprehension. The vibration of love was immense. I was buzzing and tingling from head to toe. Again, as with Metatron, I felt as though I had put my finger straight into an electric power socket of divine love and all my circuits were being zapped with the most sublime force of energy. And then, I slowly started to come back to my senses and be aware of my human reality just as the bus was arriving at my bus stop.

By the time I got to work, I was understandably quite shaken, but I was also elated. Logging on to the internet, I soon discovered that, while there was quite limited information about this incredible being known as Lord Melchizedek online, he had been mentioned in the Bible. One website, citing the work of Joshua David Stone referred to him as our "Universal Logos", meaning that he represented the consciousness of our entire universe. I guessed that meant he was a bit like the president of the universe.

I had no idea what "Spiritual Alchemy" meant at that point, but it was abundantly clear that Melchizedek wanted me to further pursue my spiritual path – and so I did.

A Meeting with Archangel Michael

Years ago, I was home on a visit to Australia to see my family when we attended a church service in St. Mary's Cathedral in Sydney. Immediately upon entering the church, I felt that familiar tingling sensation and the rush of pure electrical love hit me once again. This time, the presence filled me with a beautiful, deep indigo-blue lightning, and I had a vision of the most amazing warrior-like Angel with blond flowing hair and deep blue and silver armour standing in front of all the priests on the high altar.

This time, however, my eyes were wide open, and I could see this huge Angel with my physical sight. The air was so still in the church, yet his hair was blowing in the breeze. He held aloft a huge sword made of light. He was magnificent, and I knew instantly that he was the mighty Archangel known as Michael, the protector of mankind.

Again, as I was seeing him, I was him. There was no separation between me and the Archangel. It was like he was merging with me or had somehow sprung up from within my own energy field. The surge of love and power was incredible, and I felt an overall sense of beauty, calm, and well-being.

Michael showed me his sword of light and swept a giant path of light with it in front of me that was lit up in gold. I had a vision of humanity lined up like horses at the start gate of a race, with the racetrack lit up in golden light. But the race track stretched off into the distance, and rising up over the horizon was a huge golden sun.

After my experiences of the Archangels merging their energy with mine, I began to look at ways to develop my abilities. For the next few years, I signed up for just about every spiritual and healing workshop in town and eventually, through the usual series of uncanny synchronicities, the universe guided me to a wonderful healing modality called Angelic Reiki.

In much the same way as I was already working with the Archangels, Angelic Reiki helped me to make sense of what was happening to me. It also gave me a good background and structure within which to frame the embodied angelic experiences I was already having. The teachings, which were channelled by Kevin and Christine Core, felt aligned with my own perception of the angelic kingdom, and I went on to teach the system for many years.

However, as part of my Angelic Reiki workshops, I would open and close each day with my own meditations, processes, and channelled messages from the Archangels. These processes all became part of my Archangel Alchemy body of work. I would often receive encouraging comments from my students and colleagues, who would tell me that the best part of the workshop had been when I opened to channel and shared of my own wisdom.

Channelling Archangelic Technology

In early 2012, Archangel Metatron and Lord Melchizedek, along with other Angels and Beings of Light, gifted me with a profound alchemical healing system using angelic technology in the form of symbols, sacred geometry, and the powerful golden angelic electricity I had experienced in the embodied visitations I had had. I now know this exquisite golden energy to be the universal ray of divine love. The name I was given for that particular healing system is Precious Wisdom Alchemy.

The full Precious Wisdom Alchemy attunement was gifted to me in October 2012 while I was staying at Healing Waters in Glastonbury, Somerset, in the UK. I woke up at 6 a.m. and, in a semi-trance state, I was taken through a sequence of symbols and *mudra* (hand gestures) as a similar golden electricity that was previously shown to me by Archangel Metatron and Lord Melchizedek coursed through my body. I knew this was the spiritual alchemy they had been teaching me over the years.

A few hours after I received the full Precious Wisdom Alchemy attunement, I had an experience of "enlightenment".

I was again overcome with a powerful vision accompanied by a profound physical rush of golden energy, which could only be described as the most intense feeling of pure love. My heart felt like it had burst open, and in my vision I could see tunnels of golden-honeycomb light stretching off in every direction. Dazzling gold hexagonal-shaped doorways between all the dimensions opened up, and I could see into what I felt to be every level of reality. It was as though I was looking into infinite geometric corridors of light, similar to when you hold up two mirrors opposite one another and can see into infinity. The vision kept unfolding and unfolding, like an endlessly blossoming and billowing kaleidoscope of light and geometry.

Then I began to see countless beings from other worlds and dimensions looking back at me. They were all sending love on beams of golden-white light straight into my heart. I was literally bathing in bliss. I decided I had better send love back to the beings, I had so much gratitude for them, and then, I had an instant epiphany: Each and every one of these beings in all the other dimensions I could see were actually other versions of me, all my other selves staring at me and offering me their love. I knew then that my heart had opened in its entirety, and I was being given a glimpse into my true infinite divine soul self.

With every fibre of my being I knew that the reason I was experiencing this had something to do with the Precious Wisdom Alchemy attunement I had channelled that morning. Tears began to roll down my cheeks. I was so overwhelmed with love. It was a feeling of coming home. And I was home.

I had come home to a profound truth—that through love we may know ourselves as divine.

I started to research the Precious Wisdom symbols and mudras I had channelled and was led on an incredible adventure, both within my own subconscious and around the globe. I knew my symbols were gateways to higher consciousness and the angels and my guides told me the system had been specifically gifted to humanity to help accelerate our Ascension.

During the same week I channelled the full Precious Wisdom Alchemy attunement, the culmination point of all the information I had channelled over the preceding nine months, I was attending a Golden Heart Merkabah workshop at the Chalice Well in Glastonbury run by Christine Core.

Christine had previously worked with Ascension teacher and author of *The Ancient Secrets of the Flower of Life* Drunvalo Melchizedek, and a big part of the workshop centred around sacred geometry. Again, the synchronicity was amazing, as Christine was able to teach me many of the mathematical principles behind the platonic solids and sacred geometric shapes, which also correlated with the ancient symbols I had been gifted with in my Precious Wisdom Alchemy attunement.

From that week on, I was geeking out on the mathematics of the golden mean, vortex maths and quantum physics, and anything else I could find on a scientific level that could prove the existence of life beyond the physical. I began to see the interconnectedness of all things in my everyday existence, just as I had done as a child.

Spontaneous past-life memories started to resurface in my mind, and extraordinary gifts and abilities began to be activated. Although I was never taught by anyone else how to do this, I soon found I could do remote viewing. My telepathic abilities became heightened, and I started to have dreams where I was visiting people in my sleep and the experiences would feel real. Many of my friends would confirm that we did indeed meet during the night, and we could each relay some of the shared experiences we had had in the dream state. Unbeknownst to me, my higher self would also perform healing on others during my sleep.

In my healing sessions with clients, I was able to see into their various timelines. I could see their childhood, past lives, parallel lifetimes, and even lives they had led in other worlds and dimensions. By accessing the information in these various aspects of the person, I was able to get to the root cause of any issue they were having and release the karmic or energetic programme from which the problem had arisen. It was like watching a 3D holographic film playing out in my consciousness. Often I found that the etheric body was holding onto memories of other lifetime traumas and injuries. Even if doctors had not been able to find the cause of a person's physical pain, I could see an injury from another lifetime had somehow scarred their energy. Once we healed the etheric body or the emotion or issue behind the trauma, the pain or discomfort would go away.

I then started to perform a kind of psychic surgery, where I can see into a person's body and pull out the trapped energies. I began to speak in a strange language, which could instantly raise the energy to a quantum level, whereby the holographic universe would open out before me, giving me instant access to the angelic and star realms. This frequency is what would allow me to do the psychic surgery. I use it a bit like sonar, and as I speak it, the energy speeds up, and I can then see into the energy field or body to do the clearing. I only find I need to use this technique when an issue or illness has proven extremely hard to clear by other means.

Many know the type of sound or frequency I use as Light Language. It is important to note that Light Language is not new to humanity. In the Bible, it is referred to as "praying in tongues", as in Acts 2, when Jesus and the disciples are filled with the Holy Spirit and are given the ability to speak in many other languages. Many mystics and healers have had this ability throughout history and many more are awakening to this ability now. (For a Light Language activation, head to chapter 18.)

Speaking in angelic tongues is also described as a spiritual gift in the Bible. In Corinthians 14:2, Paul says: "For anyone who speaks in a tongue does not speak to people but to God. Indeed, no one understands them; they utter mysteries by the Spirit." My mother also has this ability. For much of her life, she has been able to "speak in tongues" while praying for healing for another person or for the world.

I have since had Precious Wisdom Alchemy certified by the Complementary Medical Association and have been teaching it to light workers and healers for many years. Each student goes through a rapid transformation, and some of my students have even gone on to the channel their own unique healing systems after receiving their Precious Wisdom Alchemist and Master Alchemist qualifications.

Shortly after I channelled Precious Wisdom Alchemy, I was on a retreat to visit the ancient star temples of Egypt. The night before we visited the Great Pyramid on 21.12. 2012, I woke up in the middle of the night to see a large beach-ball-sized red orb hovering at the foot of my bed. It was pulsing as though it were alive and breathing. The room I was in had blackout blinds, and I could not figure out where this light could have emerged from. The orb began to communicate with me, and an angelic Group Consciousness spoke through it as one voice.

I received many messages about how the Angels are currently assisting humanity during this time of Great Awakening. Some of the Angels that spoke to me were intergalactic and interdimensional Angels, and referred to themselves as the collective of the Intergalactic and Interdimensional Elohim. They told me that there are now more Angels available to humanity than ever before—not because they didn't previously exist, but because we were previously operating at a lower level of awareness and not able to reach them, almost as though our radio antenna was out of their range.

The following morning, I looked for the source of the huge red orb. The only light I could find was a tiny red light on the TV, which was not noticeable from my bed on any other night before or after the event. The Angels tell me that they travel by light and can amplify any source of light readily available to them. They were able to use the tiny light from the TV, amplify it, and project their consciousness into it in order to get me to see it as a large, pulsing sphere of light so they could get my attention and communicate with me.

I write with more detail about my experience with the Intergalactic and Interdimensional Elohim in chapter 18 of this book, where you will also find a process to connect with their energies.

A Meeting with Archangel Adnachiel

The night after we visited the Great Pyramid on the 21st December 2012, we were having dinner outside on the terrace of our hotel by the Nile when I had another unexpected and fully embodied experience with an Archangel.

The being in question gave me his name as Adnachiel and showed me a beautiful vision. It was again as though I was him and he was me, and the power of love was rushing through my body like an electrical current. I was super-grounded, as though my feet were magnetized to the earth, and I felt myself grow taller as I merged with his presence. I became so tall that, in the vision that followed, I was able to see the horizon of not just our planet but our entire universe. His energy was a brilliant russet-red, like the red of the orb I had seen the night before, and the horizon in my vision was like looking at a brilliant golden-red sunrise. Adnachiel gave me the word "pioneer" and told me that I was accessing knowledge and information that was not previously accessible to humanity.

After taking my Precious Wisdom symbols to Egypt, I was told by the Angels that I was helping to reawaken the sacred temples and pyramids for humanity. In the years following that experience, leading all the way up to the COVID-19 pandemic and lockdowns of 2020 and 2021, I was called to various high energy places around the earth to help raise the frequency and reopen the multidimensional doorways of light. I was asked to perform my healing work on the grid lines and ley lines to heal the earth herself and to open portals of light to help bring her fully into the Diamond Frequency of Ascension.

I would often dream of the place I needed to go, or I would wake up with the name of the place going around in my head like an alarm clock. Even when I had no money in the bank, the Archangels and Councils of Light saw to it that I was able to get where I was going.

Between 2012 and 2020, I barely stopped moving. I visited the pyramids of Mexico and Guatemala. I went to Egypt and Machu Picchu in Peru twice. I explored the temples of Angkor Wat, India, Bali, and Sri Lanka. On Easter Island, I was stranded for eight days due to a flight strike. The strike miraculously lifted after I had completed my work and we were free to go.

Earth service is a huge part of the work of a true light worker and Earth Angel. We are here to embody this work, not only to teach it or write about it. If you are willing, the Angels will guide you to exactly where you need to be on your divine path. Sometimes, you need to have absolute trust in the process, as it can be challenging but, ultimately, so very rewarding.

Embodying the Angelic Presence

There have been a number of common factors in each of my fully embodied Archangel experiences and the many other angelic experiences I have had since. My visits from the Archangels have varied in intensity over the years, and I have chosen to share these few as examples of just how powerful and potent these beings can be.

These visitations have stayed with me as life-changing, profound, unforgettable, and almost unspeakable out-of-this-world events that happened spontaneously within my daily earthly life.

The common denominators in these huge, embodied angelic mergers I experienced were:

◊ Strong physical tingling sensations preceding a feeling of love in the form of fiery electricity or a kind of lightning rushing through my body.

◊ Seeing fiery, golden geometric shapes, symbols, and letters, and hearing tones, whooshing sounds, ringing, or roaring in the ears.

◊ A feeling of being overcome by the most heavenly bliss, almost like having a full-body, cosmic, multidimensional orgasm.

◊ Although incredibly expanded, simultaneously feeling powerfully grounded, as though my body and feet were planted to the spot and a strong pressure or heaviness around my neck, shoulders, and a sensation of the spine being lengthened or elongated.

◊ A feeling and sensation of being connected to everything in existence, and being gigantic, very tall and much, much bigger than myself, sometimes even bigger than the universe.

◊ The absolute knowing that another being or consciousness that was not human, but was formed of the very essence of love was inhabiting my body at the same time as my own consciousness.

◊ Hearing the Archangel's voice as though it was echoing out of the very heavens like a sonic boom.

I had no reference points for these experiences. No other Angel author seemed to write about such ground-shaking visitations. The closest examples I have found to date are referenced in the Bible, with accounts of Ezekiel witnessing the fiery angels of the divine chariot. In Isaiah 6:1:2, he speaks of God's heavenly court and describes the six-winged fiery Seraphim. Jacob also speaks of a divine ladder or stairway between heaven and earth, which is similar to the rainbow bridge I wrote about in my *Archangel Fire Oracle*. In Hebrews 1:7, there is reference to Angels, saying: "In speaking of the angels he says, 'He makes his angels spirits, and his servants flames of fire.'"

I have been on a mission to uncover why my angelic experiences have been so much more intense than those of so many other people. For a long time, I have wanted to seek out the science behind my experiences, but felt I didn't have the language or the scientific mind to know where to look or even to digest or relay such a wealth of information. The Archangels have shown me many times the secrets to life and the universe in the blink of an eye, but how could I begin to put such knowledge into words without sounding like a complete lunatic?

I do believe the Angels are aspects of our own innate divinity, and when they visit or connect with us, they are urging us to awaken and realize the interwoven nature of the entire universe and all of creation. They are like connectors between us and the God and Goddess Divine and, as such, they act as a bridge in our consciousness to higher states of awareness. The Archangels have shown me that by acknowledging and owning our own angelic qualities, we can strengthen our relationship with the divine, eventually allowing ourselves to accept and utilize our own divine gifts. Realizing our own divinity and acknowledging that God is alive and well within us is a powerful, transformative process that brings us closer and closer to Enlightenment and our Ascension.

The Science of Angelic Visions and Visitations

In the 1990s, Dr. Rick Strassman conducted research at the University of New Mexico in the US on the chemical known as N, N-dimethyltryptamine, or DMT. From his research, Dr. Strassman was able to conclude that DMT is connected to and produced by the pineal gland (otherwise known as the third eye) and facilitates higher states of awareness. Dr. Strassman believes that DMT assists in the soul's movement in and out of the body during birth and death experiences, and also during high states of meditation and transcendent sexual experiences.

> *I had always wondered why my visions were so powerful without ever needing the help of plant medicines or psychotropic drugs, and when I stumbled across Dr. Strassman's book* DMT: The Spirit Molecule, *it helped confirm for me that my traumatic death at birth had somehow opened a permanent doorway into the spirit worlds, allowing me to access and communicate with the angelic realms and other dimensions and beings for as long as I can remember. What I found most compelling and exciting was that, among the 60 volunteers under the influence of DMT in Dr. Strassman's study, many reported detailed mystical and profound encounters with extraterrestrials and other non-human intelligent beings.*[3]

CHAPTER 3

Angelic Prophecy – 2020 and Beyond

In 2018, after many years of working with and teaching Precious Wisdom Alchemy, the Angels asked me to start to gather all my Angel work together. They told me that I would soon be developing my Archangel Alchemy work into a dedicated healing system. I already had a large body of work, which I have now collated into the *Archangel Fire Oracle*, but something about this new system felt slightly different or somehow an extension of the work I had already done with the Archangels.

As part of the channellings for this new Archangel Alchemy system, I was shown how to place a large diamond or octahedron around my energy field and fill it with diamond light. This diamond became both a way to clear the energy field and also acted as a shield with the hardness of a diamond on the outside. All I had to do was visualize this diamond around my entire body and energy field.

The Angels told me that this diamond could be gifted to others, and I would be able to use it to attune people to the Diamond Flame of Ascension. I began to use it in my Archangel Alchemy classes as well as my Precious Wisdom, Crystal Consciousness, and Multidimensional Channelling workshops and my Order of The Goddess and Lightworker Healing Circles. People could feel its energy and said they felt an instant shift in their vibration as a result of the diamond attunement. The Angels told me that they wanted the "children of light" to feel safe to shine on Earth as brightly as we could.

Along with birds and other winged insects, the butterfly is another of the symbols you might see when Angels are around, and from 2018, I noticed more butterflies and images of butterflies around me than usual. That being said, I did spend a lot of time in tropical places, but the butterflies somehow seemed especially drawn to me.

On a visit to Cambodia in December 2017 and January 2018, I took many pictures of butterflies sitting on my shoulder or in my hands as I went about my daily business exploring the temples and jungles. I ran a workshop called "2018: The Year of Butterfly" on my return to London in early 2018.

In March 2019, I travelled to Bali for a friend's 40th birthday. After the week-long festivities, I decided to stay an extra week for a personal retreat near Ubud. I ended up booking a place a bit farther north, in Tegallalang, where I had a gorgeous wooden cabin overlooking virgin jungle.

Each day, huge bird-sized butterflies and giant iridescent black carpenter bees would swoop around my little wooden cabin overlooking the lush rainforest. I kept hearing the same message over and over while I was there, and especially when a giant butterfly or bee was near. The message repeating in my head was insistent: "The jungles of the planet are about to regenerate."

After I returned from Bali, large parts of Australia, Africa, and the Arctic went up in flames. I thought of the symbolism of the phoenix rising from the ashes in rebirth. In Australia, the eucalyptus trees regenerate via fire. I couldn't help but think that the Archangels were at work, and the flame symbolism was telling the world that we were being prepared for a rebirth. Afterwards, photographs of the speed at which the Australian bush regenerated following those fires were astounding. My older sister, Larissa, who is a talented photographer and photography teacher based in Sydney, took a beautiful image she called "Regen" of the new buds coming through the blackened bark.[4]

Throughout 2019, I could sense that something big was about to happen in the world. I was experiencing strong Ascension symptoms, such as electrical surges in the body and unexplained panic attacks and anxiety that would hit me out of the blue like a wave of overwhelm. I had to take a whole month off work in August of that year, and I was guided to take my whole business online. I still planned to work some of the time from my office in Victoria, but I wanted to offer more workshops to some of my international students. I set myself up on Zoom and began to plan a new website.

I had no idea what was about to happen, but the Angels kept reassuring me that it was all their doing, and that we were about to receive a big "wake-up call". In so many of my group channellings, the Angels would refer to a "great wave of change" coming to humanity.

In late summer 2019, I was travelling home from my office on the London Tube one day when four huge indigo Throne Angels suddenly and unexpectedly appeared around me. I was surrounded by the strongest energy of protection I had encountered in a long while. I could see my aura pulsing with indigo and electric-blue light that zipped through me as that now-familiar Archangelic electricity and fire. The force of these Angels and their vibration was so strong that, with no idea of what was yet to come, immediately after the experience I told friends—and even referred back to the experience in my

January 2020 online Archangel workshop—that it felt like I had been put in "lockdown".

As I sat on the Tube that day, my mind began to conjure up all kinds of potential threats. London had had its fair share of terror attacks, and I started to worry about why this protection might be needed, so I asked the angels why they had come. They told me not to worry and that they were putting this protection around everyone as it was about to be what they referred to as "the changing of the guard".

I asked for further information on what this meant and was told that anyone not acting with integrity would soon be called to account and those in their integrity were going to be lifted up and rewarded. They told me that for far too long on our planet, the innocent had suffered due to tyranny and greed and that was all about to change. But the changing of the guard was also happening within each of us on a personal level and we were going to be given the opportunity to go within and come into our own "truth".

Still with no idea what that all really meant for us in human terms, in December 2019, my husband and I travelled to Sri Lanka for the Christmas holiday. As part of the trip, we did an elephant safari.

On Christmas morning, I stepped out of our tent to come face to face with the biggest butterfly I have ever seen. It must have been as big as a bird and stayed with me for so long that I managed to take about 10 photos of it. I knew it was connected to the wakeup call the Angels told me was coming for humanity. The huge butterfly was white with black spots and had electric blue patterns streaking down its wings that looked like lightning bolts.

My mind immediately went to the huge Throne Angels I had met on the Tube months before. The first news of COVID-19 began to hit the airways while we were still away. After our return to London, as news of the pandemic spread all around the globe, I couldn't believe my ears when the governments began talking about putting us all into "lockdown".

Throughout the pandemic, so much fear and discord was brought to the surface for so many people all over the world, but the Angels kept reassuring me that the coronavirus was a halo, and that what we were experiencing was an angelic intervention on a global scale to prevent humanity heading even farther down the wrong path.

During the lockdowns, whenever I taught my Archangel workshops, similar messages would come through. Other Angel healer friends of mine were also receiving "halo" and "crown" symbolism in connection with Covid-19 (a coronavirus, so named for its spiky projections, which resemble the points of a crown, or *corona* in Latin). One of them said she was told the coronavirus was a "crown of thorns", and in many ways, it has been a bit like a symbolic crucifixion, in that so much suffering and death has arisen in the midst of this intervention. Wakeup calls can often come as a huge shock, but sometimes we need a proverbial slap in the face to make us wake up and get wise to the error of our ways.

The Angels also referred to the pandemic as a significant gateway of human evolution. While many souls had chosen to pass over, those who remained were having a spiritual growth spurt. Many of my spiritual friends spoke of their experience of the virus as being like an Ascension symptom, and they felt that they were undergoing rapid upgrades in consciousness as a result of contracting it.

The Science of Prophecy

In their book *The Premonition Code: The Science of Precognition, How Sensing the Future Can Change Your Life*, Theresa Cheung, a *Sunday Times* best-selling spiritual author, and Dr. Julia Mossbridge, a fellow at the Institute of Noetic Sciences (IONS) in California, present scientific evidence and share real-life case studies for the existence of precognition, which proves it as being far more than mere coincidence. The human capacity to foresee future events is supported using fascinating and accessible examples to demonstrate the remarkable possibilities of precognition, and how we can access these tools in our daily lives.[5]

The Birth of Archangel Alchemy

The name Archangel Alchemy was given to me directly by the Archangels to describe the unique way I work with their energies and spiritual technology. I started to publish my work as a column in *Prediction* magazine from 2010 until 2013, when the magazine closed. It never occurred to me at the time just how rapidly our world was about to change and how relevant and needed this work was going to become.

It was always my plan to develop the work into a book. From there, I began to write further chapters and channelled more information from the angelic kingdom. In 2019, I was introduced to my agent, and we decided to develop much of the work into an oracle deck, which has now been released as the *Archangel Fire Oracle*.

In summer 2018, I began to receive dedicated visitations from Archangel Gabriel, showing me that it was now time for me to develop the foundations of the Archangel Alchemy work into a beautiful and complete new healing system. During 2020, while in lockdown, as I was working on completing the

Archangel Fire Oracle deck, the final pieces of the work and the main attunements and healing techniques for Archangel Alchemy were gifted to me.

To me, this special Archangel healing technique was not so new as I had been working with various aspects of it for many years, but now all my work with the Archangels seemed to come together in one beautifully streamlined process and activation to allow anyone to access the pure diamond light of the angelic kingdom for themselves.

I share the simple processes and healing techniques with you here in this book, so you may perform Archangel Alchemy on yourself as a way to empower and align you to your own pure and true divine soul self and live out your highest purpose in this lifetime.

It is a big task to hold the angelic frequency, and for those who are truly on the path to Ascension, you may find yourself in the most unusual and challenging of circumstances. We are in uncharted territory here, and we are remembering that we are powerful co-creators of our own experience.

This work is a mighty energy to be asked to bring through, and at one point I faced a huge lesson in valuing myself as the channel and container for the angelic frequencies, as I almost lost the right to use the words Archangel Alchemy, the very words the Angels themselves had asked me to use to describe their healing energy and processes.

I speak more about the challenges and lessons I had to face and learn to birth this work a little farther into this book, but I want to reassure you that no matter how tough things get, when you stay the course and have absolute unshakeable faith, your higher self and the Angels will never steer you wrong. Some of the most rug-pulling moments I have experienced, where I felt as though my entire world was bottoming out, have proven to be the most enlightening, a time when I levelled up beyond my wildest imaginings and came to a deeper understanding of my own capabilities and merits.

The symbol of the diamond represents the true purity of the soul. As we come face to face with our pain and our suffering, our challenges and our growth, we are learning to lean in ever deeper to love. We are realizing that in surrendering to Source and allowing love to move through us and guide us every step of the way, we are making great leaps in evolution, purging huge swathes of programming that is no longer necessary for us to hold onto, and that is no longer serving us as individuals or as a greater community.

The more you allow yourself to be burnt up in the transmuting fires of the Archangels, the more you will align to your inner core diamond light—your angelic cosmic starfire—and the closer you come to embodying the divine presence and bringing Heaven to Earth in your daily waking life, for yourself and those around you.

What Is the Angelic Kingdom of Light?

The Angelic Kingdom of Light is a world like no other. It exists within all dimensions and realities simultaneously and yet is a realm all of its own. The doorway to access this realm is love. The word Angel is derived from the Greek word *angelos*, meaning "messenger", and Angels are here for everyone in unconditional love, no matter who you are or what your history.

Unconditional love is love without judgement, thus the door to the angelic kingdom is always open to all who seek it within their hearts.

Angels are effectively the consciousness of unconditional love both in the seen and unseen realities, so they are able to be present within both the world of form and non-form. They are the bridge between Heaven and Earth, the essence of light, truth, and the original thoughts that form the basis of all of creation.

Representing the individual thoughts of the divine itself, Angels are like the many rays of light scattered from the multifaceted diamond light of the One Mind of Creator/Source/God. Although the angelic kingdom works as a collective, it is made up of many individual Angels and Archangels, which have different roles and functions. As I wrote in my *Archangel Fire Oracle*:

> As the divine is infinite in nature, so too there are an infinite number of Angels—far too many to contain in a book. Essentially, the diamond-rainbow spectrum of the Archangels acts as a kind of bridge or pathway towards the enlightenment, reconnecting us to our own divinity and helping us realize that we are not separate from God; we *are* God. The key to "enlightenment" is in the word "light". The Angels' message is that by opening our hearts to deeper and vaster love, we are taking in more light and are then able to shed more light on who we are by accessing our own innate wisdom.

The Angelic Choirs

Though arranged in hierarchy, the Angelic Kingdom of Light has no linear hierarchical system like that of the Earth plane. Angels see all consciousness and all life and existence as equal. They do not ask to be put on a pedestal, and though they are here in service to humanity, they are not our servants. They help us to co-create and to recognize the pure consciousness of the Creator that lives within each of us and is accessible to all.

Most people have heard of the traditional angelic choirs, or hierarchies. They are depicted in the scriptures as:[6]

Elohim
Seraphim
Cherubim
Thrones
Dominions
Virtues
Powers
Principalities
Archangels
Angels

In my experience, there are many more varieties of Angels besides these, and as we humans expand our consciousness, we are beginning to know and work with many other levels within this vast kingdom of angelic light. The following meditation will help attune you to the angelic hierarchies, so you can get a feel for their overarching roles and functions.

Angelic Choirs Meditation and Attunement

Every time we go through a personal challenge, it heralds a time of rebirth and resurrection, so what better time to acknowledge the end—or death—of the idea of separation and allow ourselves to be reborn in the unity of God/Goddess/Source/Divine?

There is nothing more empowering than allowing yourself to really feel at one with the God/Goddess within. In this way, you discover that everything comes from within and everything exists within the space and existence we occupy presently, here in the "now".

When you discover this incredible knowledge, you come to realize that all things, even Angels and Ascended Masters, are actually part of you. They exist both inside and outside you, and it is, in fact, you who invokes their energy and creates the bridge in consciousness between Heaven and Earth.

This meditation shows you how to invoke the angelic hierarchy in order to bring healing to our planet on both a personal and universal level. For the very reason we exist in the physical world is to embody spirit in matter—in short, to live Heaven on Earth.

◊ Close your eyes, and take two deep, cleansing breaths. Let go of cares and worries, and feel yourself at peace.

◊ Imagine your entire body now filled with pure white light, and see yourself surrounded by angels. Feel your connection to your physical body, and maintain that connection throughout this meditation.

◊ Now start to expand your consciousness, like a bubble growing in size from the very core of you, and stretch it out in every direction to infinity.

◊ Feel your limitlessness and, as you expand, realize that you are travelling in consciousness out into the universe, past the planets and stars, yet you are still connected to your physical body but have grown in consciousness.

◊ Allow your energy to now travel farther up and out until you come to a glorious golden dimension of light. This is the Angelic Kingdom.

◊ As you connect to this space, you feel thousands of Angels around you, singing above you, and you are filled with pure love.

◊ The Angels tell you that you are to receive a special blessing from each of the angelic choirs on behalf of the whole of humanity.

◊ Firstly, your Guardian Angel steps forward and kisses you on both cheeks. They hand you a gift to symbolize your transformation into an Earth Angel. Take note of this gift, as you will see it in the physical world in a few days.

◊ Next, the Archangels surround you and give you a blessing to strengthen your own connection to God/Goddess and embody your own leadership qualities.

◊ The next group of Angels to surround you are the Principalities. They ask you to accept their blessing on behalf of any groups you belong to, such as your place of work, your city, or your country. They work to protect human rights and thus ask you to be a champion for this cause by standing up for your own rights.

◊ The Powers now bring forward a blessing of divine justice and protection for you and the whole world.

◊ The Virtues gift you with miracles, both on a personal level and to increase the awareness of magic for the whole population of Earth.

◊ Divine wisdom is gifted to you by the Dominions, and they remind you of the laws of cause and effect. "As above, so below" is their message.

◊ The Thrones govern all relationships, from human interaction right through to how the planets affect each other. They gift you with positive energy to become a global mediator for peace.

◊ The Cherubim are guardians of the light and the stars. They bless your light body, allowing you to connect more easily with the light and to help you embody the boundless love of the divine on Earth.

◊ The next highest order of God's Angels are known as the Seraphim. As these mighty Angels now surround you, their light is so bright you can barely see them. No negative energy can permeate their light, so they offer the ultimate in divine protection.

◊ Finally, the Elohim gift you a blessing for the divinity you represent and chant over you, "Holy, holy, holy is the Lord God of Hosts." The "hosts" they speak of are we mere humans. For we have no idea of our own true power. The "Lord God of Hosts" refers to divine spirit that exists within our physical matter. It is the marriage of above and below. And, as we come to realize that we are vessels of the divine, we take responsibility for our lives and embody Heaven on Earth.

◊ Spend a moment bathing in your Source light, and send pure love out across the cosmos. Then connect back to your physical body and open your eyes.

The Science of the Angelic Choirs –
Other Dimensions as Music and Sound

In an interview I did with renowned neurosurgeon Dr. Eben Alexander, near-death-experiencer and author of *Proof of Heaven*, he spoke in detail of his experience of the angelic and heavenly realms as being musical:

I was led by this brilliant orb up a pathway of light, leading into the ultra-real gateway valley. And that, of course, was a musical melody. To me, that's a crucial point to make, because of the music, sound, vibration, frequency—and, of course, in those realms, you're not hearing with the ears or seeing with the eyes, so our modes of knowing are far richer and more complete than they are here, where it's all very partial. But in that beautiful gateway valley, the best part was that I wasn't alone. There was a beautiful young woman on the butterfly wing.

He also spoke about his experiences with the Angels:

In my journey there were angelic choirs that were fuelling the incredible festival and mirth and joy that I witnessed in that "Earthworm-eye view"; I mean in that gateway valley. Those angelic choirs provided portals to higher and higher levels—all the way up to what I call "the core", that infinite inky blackness just filled to overflowing with the love of the divine.[7]

CHAPTER 4

Communicating with the Archangels

How Angels and Archangels Communicate

When the Angels are around, you may see repetitive signs in your physical reality, but there are many other ways in which the angelic kingdom, and especially the Archangels, can make their presence known. Some examples of how Angels and Archangels can connect with us are:

◊   Signs – such as feathers, coins, and so on

◊   Clairs – visions, feelings, hearing direct messages, and so on

◊   Symbols, geometries

◊   Light language

◊   Sounds, tones, ringing in the ears

◊   Orbs, seeing lights, colours, and auras

◊   Messages via TV and radio conversations

◊   Physical sensations, such as tingling in the body

◊   Direct downloads of information, where you just instantly know something you didn't previously know

◊   Healing energy flowing through the hands and body

◊ Evocation (when the Angels are invoked and show themselves as physical beings)

◊ Angelic walk-ins and physical messengers.

Angelic Messengers and Walk-Ins

Human Angels

Angelic walk-ins and angelic messengers can take the form of a random person who shows up in your life to deliver a message or support you in some way. Sometimes, these people are actual Angels that have materialized in a physical form for just a short time to deliver the message.

At other times, they are real people who have been led to you by the Angels to offer guidance or support. These people may not even know why they are speaking to you or even understand the words they are saying, but they will feel they are having a positive impact in some way.

One day around 2010, I received an email from a man wanting to submit some articles to the magazine I worked for. At the bottom of his email, he added an extra message: "By the way, I am an aura reader, and I would love to tell you about your aura—it's quite unusual. Can I give you a reading sometime?"

Rather intrigued, and thinking that an aura reading would be quite a cool thing to have in the magazine, I replied and offered to write him a review in exchange for the session.

We met over tea in a café in Angel for the reading, and I was taken aback by how clear his eyes were. They were like crystal pools, and I was struck by the otherworldly energy he had about him. He seemed to be surrounded in a subtle shimmering light. He told me that he had been seeing auras since the age of four, and that when he'd seen my picture on the front of the magazine he had been quite taken aback.

Gazing into the energy field around the side of my head, he said, "You have the most extraordinary silver aura."

He told me he could also see something coming into my aura on my left-hand side, and that, whatever this was, it was part of my soul purpose and was going to be very important both for my work and the planet.

I had no idea what this could be, but what he said next stayed with me long after this meeting. Giving me a serious look that almost bordered on stern, it felt as though he was looking right into my soul when he took my hand and said, "You do not have the measure of yourself, Alexandra."

I only had one or two brief exchanges with him again over email after that day and then I never saw or heard from him again. It seemed that he had only shown up to deliver that message. I have often wondered if this person was an angelic walk-in.

I am often myself called upon by the Angels to deliver messages or intervene for people when they need assistance. A year or two after the appearance of the mysterious aura reader, the Angels began to approach me in public places and urge me to walk up to random strangers to deliver a message.

Accepting the Role of Angelic Messenger

One night I went out to meet a group of friends, and as I walked into the bar, an Angel stepped into my energy field, and I found myself walking up a girl I had never met before to tell her that the Angels wanted her to know that they were with her and had heard her call for help.

The message was entirely channelled and, although my human brain was thinking, *What are you doing talking about Angels to a complete stranger?*, I knew everything was happening in the perfect way and that she would understand and receive the message.

When I finished speaking, she looked at me with the widest eyes and told me that just that morning she was talking to a friend and he had said that she should get in touch with her Angels. So, in her head, she had asked for a sign to know if Angels were real. That evening, I showed up as the sign she had asked for. She went on to learn Angelic Reiki with me and, to this day, we are very close friends.

My work as an angelic messenger and conduit continues to this day, and I am often called upon to assist people in their time of need. It is incredibly rewarding and beautiful work.

How to Be of Angelic Service

If you wish to be of service in this way, all you need to do is ask the Angels and Archangels—either aloud or in your own mind—to call upon you to help out whenever someone is in need. You will be strongly guided and will find that you intuitively know exactly what to do and say in the moment. Stay in trust, and allow their loving guidance and that of the divine to flow through you.

You can also be more specific about the kind of angelic service you wish to be involved in. For example, you might have an affinity with animals or children, or perhaps you prefer to work with nature and the plant kingdom. Follow what brings you the most joy in your day to day life, as that is usually where your skills are most suited and potentially the area where they are most needed.

World Angels, Planetary Lightworkers, and Grid Workers

Some angelic service workers are here to assist the whole planet and the entire human collective. You will have a strong knowing if you are one such planetary service worker. I call these people "World Angels". They are capable of healing and clearing the stuck energies of whole groups and areas of the planet by working on the sacred sites, ley lines, energy grids and especially their own emotions and healing whatever belief systems or programmes arise within themselves, and sharing that healing out to the collective.

Are You an Angelic Dream Walker?

Dreams are a doorway to the subconscious. They are also one of the ways Angels and Spirit can more easily communicate with us, because our mind is in a more relaxed and receptive state.

In January 2012, I had a powerful dream, in which I was a large man, standing chest-deep in the sea, helping to pull people from a huge ship that had run aground. I was aware that the language I was speaking was not English. There were other men helping. It was nighttime, and the sea was very choppy and dangerous. I felt afraid.

I looked towards a man on my right and recognized that he was actually the soul energy of my mother in my current life. I said to the man/my mother: "How is it possible that we are doing this?" And they replied: "We just go where we are needed and do what needs to be done."

The next day I saw on the news that a cruise ship had run aground in Italy and some of the locals had indeed been helping to pull the passengers from the boat. Some years later, an article about my experience of this dream appeared in *Chat – It's Fate* magazine.

Since that day, I have had many experiences of this kind of "dream walking", where I step into another person's life or consciousness to assist them in this way. I have often been called upon to "astral travel" so that I can assist other people in times of crisis or trauma. The experience is as though I have stepped into another person's life, and instead of them making decisions about where to go or what to do, I am making those decisions for them. It's like I'm acting as a kind of avatar, or walk-in, to help them through a situation they might not otherwise have the strength or ability to navigate themselves.

This is not currently something I can always control at will, but when I wake up from one of these dreams, the memory of the experience is as real as if I had been there in the flesh. Many different people have told me that I appeared in their dreams to offer them healing or help.

Sometimes, these experiences potentially save the life of the person involved. I have had glimpses into many present-day lives as a result of this, even experiencing the life of a famous celebrity in order to assist them when they were "going off the rails" in their life. Again, I wasn't at all trying to do this; it just happened. The next day, I saw this person on television, and they were driving the very same car I had seen in my dream and wearing the identical outfit I had on when I was experiencing being in their body.

Over the years I have become familiar with the nature of my dreamtime state. Often, when I wake up in the morning, I will spend a few moments recalling my dreams and analyzing them to see if there is any pressing guidance attached to the imagery. As a clairvoyant, I am naturally a vivid dreamer, but I often intuitively "just know" whether what I have experienced in the sleep state is merely a dream or a real journey through the astral realms.

Many times over the years, I have had people—including friends, clients, and even complete strangers—contact me to tell me that I have appeared to them as an angelic being in their dream in order to give them healing. My higher self is very busy and is often off doing service work, even when I am not aware of it, but I have come to learn that I am a kind of healing Angelic Dream Walker and, as in my waking life, I always ask to be of service in whatever way I am needed.

If what I have described here resonates with you, you may also be an Angelic Dream Walker who flies to those in need during your sleep state. Our dreams may not appear to make sense to us upon waking, but they can be a way for our subconscious to communicate with us. Learning to interpret your dreams is a handy tool for deciphering hidden messages that may unlock helpful guidance about our daily life and path ahead.

There are many different kinds of dreams. Some are symbolic, some recurring, some prophetic, some are past life memories and some aren't actually dreams at all, but out-of-body astral journeys through other dimensions and realities. "Lucid dreaming" is a skill you can train yourself to achieve, so that you can affect the outcome of your dreams, like a pick your own adventure.

Not all dreams need to be in service to others. You may also wish to travel to the Angelic Kingdom of Light within your dream state to receive healing for yourself.

Record Your Dreams and Astral Travel Experiences

Write down your dreams immediately upon waking. You may wish to consult a dream dictionary or look up the meaning of some of the imagery to see if there is any guidance you can glean from your dream. Over time, you may discover that some of your dreams are recurring.

This can be a hint or a clue as to where you need some healing or clearing work done to assist you in moving beyond whatever issue or blockage the dream is trying to alert you to. The more you study your dreams, the easier it will be to read them and you may even begin to develop a natural ability to dream lucidly or astral travel at will.

Try setting an intention to receive answers from your dreams before going to sleep.

Questions to Ask Yourself

◊ What are my dreams telling me?

◊ Do I have any recurring or prophetic dreams?

◊ Have I ever had a lucid dream?

◊ Have I ever had an out-of-body experience?

◊ If I could go anywhere in my dreams, where would I go?

The Science of Sleep, Dreams, and Lucid Dreaming for Healing

Sleep and the dream state have long been a subject of scientific study, and there are far too many explorations to recount here. According to experts at the National Institute of Neurological Disorders and Stroke at Harvard, sleep occurs in cycles, with the two main sleep states being REM (Rapid Eye Movement) and non-REM sleep. Most of our dreaming tends to occur in the REM stage of sleep, which usually occurs within the first 90 minutes of sleep, while our body does most of its healing in the non-REM stages.[8,9]

Insomnia, sleep disturbances and lack of sleep can all contribute to poor physical and mental health, according to Mental Health charity Mind, so a good night's sleep has been scientifically proven to improve our overall well-being.[10]

Exciting new research has recently proven that two-way communication is possible between lucid dreamers and the waking world. Kristoffer Appel, a sleep and dream researcher at Osnabrück University and the Institute of Sleep and Dream Technologies in Hamburg and co-author of the study, said that six lucid dreamers correctly answered 29 questions, including simple maths problems and questions with a yes/no answer, using previously agreed-upon eye signals.[11]

Further research is currently being conducted by Garret Yount at the Institute of Noetic Sciences (IONS) on whether a lucid dream state could be beneficial for healing. The Healing Lucid Dreaming Pilot Study will explore whether physical health can improve as a result of internally generated intentions in a lucid dream state.[12]

In an interview for The Alexandra Wenman Show on YouTube, Karen Newell, co-founder of Sacred Acoustics, told me of numerous case studies where people had had out-of-body experiences as a result of listening to healing brainwave entrainment sound recordings.[13]

CHAPTER 5

Opening to Channel

One of the most direct ways to communicate with the Archangels is through channelling. Although I channelled poetry as a child, I didn't know there was a specific term for what I was doing.

My first experience of channelling in public was at an Angel workshop I attended in 2008. I was covering the workshop for a magazine article, and half-way through the day, the teacher called me to the front of the room and invited me to sit in her chair. She then announced that I would be channelling a message for the group.

There were about 25 people in the room, so it was quite daunting, but I felt the support of the Angels around me, and when I opened my mouth to speak, the most beautiful and loving words tumbled out. I knew they were not coming from me, but through me, and I could feel the most loving vibrations and sensations moving through my body and up my spine as I spoke.

Anyone can learn to channel and, in my experience, there is nothing more empowering than learning to read, adjust, and communicate with the energies around you. We live in a vast multiverse that reaches well beyond what we can tangibly see and feel with our 3D physical awareness. Our ever-increasing sensitivity means that we are becoming more and more affected by the energies around us.

The following process will help you tune into the various realms, dimensions and states of consciousness that are always available to us and into the beautiful and loving angels and beings of light who reside there. In this way, you can receive healing and guidance and set firm boundaries as to which energies you wish to access for your own benefit and which ones you wish to dissolve, transmute, and send out of your space, so that you can choose the way you wish to feel in any given moment. When you dispel any fears you may have of accessing your divine gifts, you realize that the unknown is really a vast and beautiful landscape to explore, rather than something that should be feared. Learning to channel is so much more than just communing with spirits and other beings. There are many other aspects of channelling, including channelled healing, writing, speaking, and above all, connecting with your own divine higher mind to align to your highest purpose and your best possible timeline.

Why Channel?

Channelling is not just a party trick. When you can learn to discern where your thoughts are coming from, you can choose which thoughts you wish to receive and which ones you would rather not be influenced by. Learning to channel means you can also tune in to your own body and ask what it needs to help it heal and be nourished.

Channelling is incredibly powerful as once you learn how to channel effectively, it is difficult for anyone to be able to lie to you. In this way, channelling is a bit like having access to an angelic truth serum. Once you know your own truth, and can discern it from the opinions and agendas of others, you can then know and understand your true innermost desires.

We are influenced every minute of the day by advertising, the news, media, and other people's beliefs, viewpoints, and even by absorbing others' emotions. When you know how to tell the difference between your feelings and beliefs and those of another person, you can also clear and release other uninvited energies from your sphere of influence and align to your authentic wants, needs, and desires. The TV might tell you that you need that pair of new shoes, but you might actually just need to go for a nice nature walk and listen to the birds to connect with the real joy of being alive.

Channelling will connect you with your own depth and wisdom, and it is in that space that you become more easily able to access your inner genius. Many artists and scientists throughout history knew about the sacred art of channelling to reach higher states of awareness. Leonardo Da Vinci was one such person, and he created many works of art that have encoded sacred geometry and symbolism within them. In the book *The Templar Revelation* by Lynne Picknett and Clive Prince, you can learn about the wealth of hidden symbolism and coded truth behind Da Vinci's work and that of other artists. It's important to note that the term "channelling" can cover a vast array of techniques. The form of channelling I am referring to is not the same as trance mediumship or physical mediumship, and it does not mean that a disincarnate spirit will be allowed to take over your body.

The form of channelling I teach and use only connects you with loving light guides and angelic beings that work on a level of consciousness operating at the vibration of unconditional love or above. These loving Angels and light guides exist at a vibration above the fifth-dimensional frequency (turn to chapter 8 for more information on the dimensions), so they transcend duality and are able to offer wisdom above and beyond the kind of knowledge to which a spirit guide or loved one who has previously had a human incarnation would have access.

In this book, I will show you specifically how to channel the Archangels and share with you my own channelled and tried-and-tested techniques to help you channel safely and in a way that is fun and enjoyable.

Activating Your Psychic Senses and Developing the "Clairs"

As we raise our vibration, our consciousness expands and we begin to tap into our higher mind and awaken to our innate gifts. This means that our own natural psychic and healing abilities begin to switch on. This is our birthright. I believe that every human being is naturally psychic and we all have a natural-born gift for intuition. As we shift into a more fifth-dimensional mindset, this subtle gift of extrasensory perception is now deepening far beyond the way we have been used to using it.

Most people tend to dismiss their intuition, or gut feeling, but if you learn to tune into it and develop it, it can guide you towards the right decisions and situations for your highest good and for your soul's growth. This is all part of our awakening and accessing our super-consciousness, or divine mind.

Some of the natural gifts people are beginning to access are what we call the Sixth Sense, or psychic senses; I like to refer to them as the "clairs". All of these senses require you to be able to use your imagination and trust your intuition, so it's best not to expect them to fit into the realm of logic.

Most people have one or two of these natural intuitive gifts that are stronger than the others, but as you develop them, you begin to strengthen all of your clairs until you are using them all at once. When you receive messages or information from beyond the third dimension, it becomes a more holographic or multidimensional experience, in which you can feel, see, hear, taste, smell, and know everything about what you are experiencing in the other dimensions, or levels of awareness, with which you are interfacing.

Awakening the clairs naturally expands your consciousness into other realms and experiences. The more you practise, the easier it becomes to tap into and use your extrasensory abilities. Eventually, it starts to become second nature.

The Main Clairs

Clairvoyance, or "clear seeing"

This includes having visions or receiving psychic messages in the form of pictures both inside your mind or, as you develop this gift, even with your physical sight. Many famous clairvoyants can see spirits and Angels with their eyes open. This happened to me as a child and returned in 2011 on a retreat in Ibiza, where I started to open up to my gift of mediumship. I could see faces coming out of the walls, as though I was watching a CGI motion picture.

Clairaudience, or "clear listening"

When I first began to open up psychically, I really wanted to hear. I always imagined that it would sound like someone speaking loudly in my ear. Sometimes, people do experience clairaudience in this way, but it can often be much more subtle than this. I discovered my own gift for clairaudience while skimming through the workshop manual of a psychic development course I had booked many years ago.

I was sitting in a cafe across the street from the course venue, waiting for class to start, when I decided to take a peek at what we would be covering that day. I opened the manual at the page for clairaudience, and it said, "Sometimes, clairaudience sounds like your own thoughts, although it is usually much more loving and gentle." I had experienced this many times; I just hadn't recognized it as clairaudience. I thought to myself, "Oh, I can hear," and, as clear as a bell, a voice inside my head said, "Yes, you can".

Claircognizance, or "clear knowing"

This is perhaps the most amazing psychic gift to have. It's when you just know things. You don't know how you know it, but you know it with every fibre of your being. This is often how I experience channelling. I tend to just know which Angel or guide is speaking through me, and I don't even have to see them in my vision. This use of claircognizance is often accompanied by clairsentience.

Clairsentience, or "clear feeling"

Most people are already using this sense without realizing it. Have you ever disliked a person immediately upon meeting them without ever having met them before? Or walked into a room and known you didn't like the energy just by having a "feeling" about it? Our feeling awareness is the first port of call when accessing our intuitive gifts. We begin with sensing or feeling energy and then the rest of our senses interpret what we are feeling.

Clairolfactory, or "clear smelling"

This one pops up a lot when I am doing mediumship. If someone was a smoker when they were alive, I can often smell strong cigarette smoke in the room.

Clairgustance, or "clear tasting"

Likewise, clear tasting allows you to taste psychically. Sometimes, during deep meditation, I get a taste in my mouth that is distinctly like a combination of sand and stone. I believe this taste is a memory of some of my lifetimes spent in the desert and temples of Ancient Egypt. For most of my life, I couldn't place what this strange subtle taste in my mouth was, until I actually went to Egypt in 2012 and experienced that same flavour of dry sand and stone as I breathed in the air inside the temples. It was especially evident inside the King's Chamber of the Great Pyramid. I can taste it now as I write these words.

Exercises to Strengthen the Clairs

A way to strengthen your clairs is to strengthen your connection to your physical senses. Most people who are clairvoyant are naturally more visual. They notice things visually, and their memory recall is better when they have seen something rather than having it described to them. Likewise, those more tuned into clairaudience will recall things with more clarity once they have heard them spoken. An example of this is learning a new language. Some need to see the word written down to be able to remember it, and others will prefer to hear it spoken. The combination of hearing and seeing it makes it even more likely to recall the information.

Always open your space with the channelling checklist in chapter 7 of this book before beginning any spiritual work.

Strengthen Your Clairvoyance:
Learn to Visualize

Choose an object, and gaze at it in detail for as long as you think it will take you to remember all of the detail in that object. It's best to start with something simple, such as a vase.

When you think you have retained all of the details of the object, close your eyes, and try to recall exactly what that object looked like with your eyes open.

◊   Open your eyes, and see how good your memory recall was.

◊   Practise building a rainbow in your mind, colour by colour.

◊   Then make the rainbow dance and move.

◊   See if you can imagine it turning into a giant Angel, and ask it for a positive sign or a message in the form of a symbol.

◊   What does this mean to you?

Practise, practise, practise, and you will begin to build up your visual memory.

Strengthen Your Clairaudience:
Learn to Listen

Having done some work with Australian aborigines, I learnt that our voice was mainly created for devotional song and prayer and that humans are designed to communicate telepathically. There is some truth in the saying "Silence is golden." How often do we speak without actually thinking about what we are going to say? In conversation, how often do we wait for the other person to finish speaking, all the while thinking about what we are going to say next and not really hearing what they've said?

Listening consciously, or active listening, is a great skill. It not only allows the other person to be really heard and feel accepted, thereby strengthening our human relationships, but can also help us develop our own abilities for memory recall through sound.

Take a moment to sit quietly and listen to the sounds around you. It's best to do this exercise outside, if possible, and with the TV and radio switched off, as birdsong or ocean waves work much better. Having said that, if you live in a busy city, there could be plenty of noise pollution around, but even that can be useful for this exercise.

◊   Close your eyes and listen, really listen, to all the sounds you can pick up around you. Listen as long as it takes to feel that you have taken them all in.

◊   Open your eyes, and write down all the sounds you heard.

◊   If you like, you can take it one step farther, and write down how each sound made you feel or what it reminded you of. This way, you are beginning to combine your clairaudience with clairvoyance and clairsentience.

Sounds can set the atmosphere of a place or situation, and they often do affect our emotions. Think about how the music in a sad film can make you feel tearful, or how a horror film can use sound to build up the feeling of fear and the anticipation of impending doom.

As you become more attuned to listening, you will soon begin to distinguish between the loud and often judgemental voice of your ego mind and the gentle, more subtle loving voice of your higher mind, and even your guides and Angels.

Strengthen Your Clairsentience: Learn to Feel

◊ Centre your consciousness in your stomach area and take a deep breath.

◊ Ask yourself, How do I feel? Consciously notice whatever emotions come up, and become the observer.

◊ Sit quietly, and breathe in and out gently. Focus on your breath and how you are feeling.

◊ Try not to judge any emotions that arise, and don't stuff back down any uncomfortable feelings or try to block them out. Allow yourself to feel whatever comes up, and honour whatever feeling or emotion does arise by sending it love through your intention.

Our feelings are a valuable tool for both developing intuition and healing. You cannot heal something while it remains hidden. When we avoid our feelings or block them, it can also lead to physical illness, so it's much healthier to acknowledge that all of our feelings are valid. And the more you allow yourself to feel, the more you will develop your intuitive feeling radar.

Strengthen Your Claircognizance: Learn to Trust Yourself

Many people discount their intuition, but how many times have you had a gut feeling about something, ignored it, and then later said to yourself, *I should have trusted my intuition in the first place?*

Learning to trust yourself is a big part of the spiritual path. It can be challenging at first, but the more you get into the habit of trusting your gut and acting on that trust, the more it pays off. No one else can do this for you. We live in a world where everyone is giving everyone else advice and rules are made that treat us as though we should all be the same. But we are all different and unique. What is right for one person may not suit another. You are the best judge of what is right for you in any given moment, and learning to trust your inner wisdom and intuition—whether it comes as a feeling, a message, a knowing, or some other form—will always lead you in the right direction. This will begin to develop your gift for claircognizance, as your clear channel to your own divine mind opens up.

Develop Clairolfactory and Clairgustance: Savour Scents and Flavours

For clairolfactory and clairgustance, develop your sense of smell and taste by smelling and tasting mindfully. When you eat a meal, really savour all the flavours and smells of the dishes. Exotic curries and stews are particularly good for this.

Another way to practise this is to choose a time when you aren't cooking or eating, then sit quietly and see if you can recall the flavours and aromas of your favourite meal. Or think of a childhood treat that you used to love to eat or drink, and recall all the flavours and/or smells connected to it.

Think about how smells can transport you back to a place in your memory banks. YSL Paris perfume always reminds me of my childhood, as my mum wore it. Ribena is a comfort drink I had as a child.

◊   Which smells and tastes bring you joy?

◊   What do certain smells remind you of?

◊   What's your favourite smell?

◊   What's your favourite flavour?

CHAPTER 6

Grounding and Preparation

The Angelic Consciousness within the Human Body

Every single human being exists as both physical matter and spirit. Our physical bodies are made up of all the key elements and building blocks of creation that hold together our world. The key elements of our physical reality include: earth, air, fire, and water. The physical body is the vessel within which our spirit resides.

The Archangels and my guides have shown me that we each have multiple bodies that exist on multiple levels of reality, and these bodies are layered and intertwined to make up the whole human being. For example, as well as our physical body, we have an energetic blueprint, or etheric body; an emotional/desire body; another body that houses our mental processes and thoughts; an intuitive body that governs our psychic and healing abilities; a celestial body that understands the workings of the cosmos, and so on, all the way up to the purest aspect of our soul, the divine body.

If we were to look at this model in a linear fashion, it might look like a ladder or a flow chart. I have seen other models such as this used in various religions and mystery schools. Some examples include the Kabbalistic, Norse and Celtic traditions of a Tree of Life, the Yogic teachings of the chakras and the subtle bodies, and the Egyptian Hermetic model of the Mer-Kah-Bah, or light body vehicle.

Our physical bodies are alive and, as living beings in their own right, they do have an innate intelligence of their own. I like to call this physical intelligence the "Body Angel".

Communicating with the Body Angel

All physical blockages and dis-ease begins with energy and emotional blockage. The good news is that it is absolutely possible to clear stuck or negative energy—which often comes in the form of limiting thoughts, feelings, emotions, beliefs, and contracts, as well as foreign energies—as long as you know how to do this.

As our bodies are incredibly intelligent beings in their own right, they are in total alignment with our higher mind, or divine consciousness. The body always knows what the higher self wants and needs; it's only our human, egoic mind that is out of sync. So we can ask yes and no questions of the body that relate to what is for our highest good, and the body will reveal what the higher mind thinks is best.

The pure energy that animates the body is the same pure energy that permeates all life in the universe. It's like a supercomputer containing the infinite wisdom of the divine. It is pure consciousness, and we can access it through our feelings and emotions. When we learn to listen to the body and our feelings, we can learn a lot more about ourselves than we realize. Dowsing is just one way to tune into the wisdom of the body to find answers to the questions we need to know in order to take right or appropriate action to ensure our personal growth and development.

Connect with Your Body Angel
via Your Sensory Awareness

Step 1: Bring Your Conscious Awareness into Your Physical Body
Picture a yellow flower. Take your time, and close your eyes to do this. Allow the image to form in your mind, then ask yourself if you are now visualizing that flower outside yourself; that is, do you see it hovering in front of you? Ideally, you want your awareness, or consciousness, to reside inside your physical body, not outside you. Your consciousness is part of you, so it should be connected to you.

Picture the flower once again, but this time, allow the image to form in the centre of your brain or within your heart centre. You can even imagine that the flower is within your elbow, if you like. As long as it is within your physical body, the experience will be grounded and perfect.

Step 2: Ground Yourself within Your Physical Body
Using your awareness, connect to each part of the physical body, starting with the toes and working upwards. Tune in to the emotions that each part of the body is bringing up, and bathe that part of the body in love, then bathe your whole body in love.

Fully connect with your physical body in this way as you do the exercises in this book and you will experience them on a much deeper level and they will have a more positive effect on your daily life. This is how we are able to bring Heaven to Earth.

Receiving Guidance through Dowsing and Muscle Testing

What Is Dowsing?

Dowsing and muscle testing are kinesiology techniques that read the electro-magnetic field of a person or place in order to test for a positive or negative reaction to a question, situation, substance, decision, and so on. You can use dowsing to give you a positive or negative response to any question you wish to ask to ascertain the highest and best result or outcome for you.

The art of dowsing has been used for centuries by psychics, healers, mystics, and even, once upon a time, doctors and physicians. Essentially a technique for reading energy in order to search out or find objects, energies, and information otherwise hidden from view, it has also been widely used by shamans, geologists, archaeologists, and scientists to locate ground water, ley lines, oil, and even treasure or artefacts.

Dowsing is not meant to be a crutch or to take precedence over your inner guidance and intuition; instead, think of it as a helpful tool to validate and confirm that what you are feeling or sensing intuitively is correct and that you are on the right track with your investigations. This is especially helpful in any spiritual investigations in the world of healing and the clearing of foreign or unwanted energies from the energy field.

I share below some of my own experiences and methods with dowsing and muscle testing. However, although I have done some professional training in these techniques, I want to stress that I am not a Kinesiologist and this is by no means the most extensive guide to this topic. This chapter will give you a good grounding in communicating with your Body Angel through simple dowsing and kinesiology techniques. To go further, I suggest signing up to a dedicated course or purchasing a more comprehensive book on this subject.

Methods of Dowsing

Dowsing is traditionally performed using hand-held tools over an object in order to test for a positive and negative response; for example, using angle rods to search for water beneath the ground. But you can also work with parts of your own body, such as your thumb and forefinger or your elbow or outstretched arm to test for a positive or negative charge in response to a question, substance, or situation.

Muscle Testing, or Kinesiology

Muscle testing, or kinesiology, is traditionally used as a form of diagnosis. It works by asking yes and no questions and reacting to the positive or negative charge within the electromagnetic field, or energy grid network, of the body. Pure energy runs through the muscles of the body, so if anything happens to interrupt the flow of this energy the muscles will automatically weaken in response; therefore, it is possible to ask questions of the muscles to find out what is good for the body and what is perhaps not having a positive impact energetically and physiologically.

For muscle testing to be effective, the person must be well hydrated and just the right amount of pressure needs to be applied.

Muscle-Testing Exercises

Exercise 1: Pull Thumb and Forefinger Apart

Press the tip of the thumb and forefinger together, and hold firmly. With your other hand, try to pull the thumb and forefinger apart. An easy way to do this is to place the thumb and forefinger of the opposite hand inside the ring formed by the thumb and forefinger you have pressed together, then gently try to open the circle. If you are unable to separate the thumb and forefinger, it indicates a positive response; if they come apart, it indicates a negative response.

Exercise 2: Ring-in-Ring Test

Make two interlocking rings using your thumbs and forefingers. Ask your question and then gently pull the rings apart, attempting to separate them. Resistance (the rings staying together) indicates an answer is positive, or a yes response, while a lack of resistance (the rings come apart) indicates an answer is negative, or a no response to the question or query.

Exercise 3: Rub Tip of Thumb and Forefinger Together

Rub the tip of your thumb and forefinger together, and feel the texture of your thumb and fingerprint. For a yes, or positive, response, the skin will feel smoother or more slippery, and for a no, or negative, response, the skin will feel rougher or more sticky, creating more friction as you rub.

Exercise 4: Arm or Elbow Test

This exercise is easier to do on another person, and is best used when you are working with a partner or client. The client or subject holds one arm outstretched in front of them, parallel to the floor. The tester then places two fingers on the subject's wrist and asks a question, placing a small amount of pressure on the wrist. If the subject's arm resists, indicating strength in the muscle, it equates to a yes, or affirmative, answer. If the arm is weaker or gives way under the pressure, it equals a negative, or no, response. Another option is to have the client or subject bend their elbow and hold the bent elbow out parallel to the floor. The tester then tests the resistance by pressing firmly down on the tip of the elbow.

Exercise 5: Standing

Stand up straight but relaxed, with knees slightly bent. With your eyes closed, ask your body to show you a yes response by gently allowing yourself to start to fall. You will automatically begin to rock in a certain direction. The key is to relax just enough in order to let yourself begin to fall, without actually allowing yourself to fall over. The direction in which your body naturally falls will indicate the yes response. For example, you may sway forward, and this will indicate a yes. Catch yourself the minute you are aware of the direction in which your body is moving, so as not to fall over.

Repeat the process by asking your body to show you a no response, then begin to let yourself fall in order to ascertain the direction the body wants to move in for a no response. Whenever I do this exercise, I fall forward for a yes and backward for a no, but it can differ for different people so it's best to test your own responses first.

This is a handy exercise to do in the supermarket when you want to know if your body agrees with your tastebuds when deciding what you want to buy for dinner.

Dowsing with Rods

Perhaps the best-known form of dowsing is water divining with metal rods. I remember being intrigued as a child when my father hired a farmer to come to our property in Australia to dowse for bore water. We were not connected to the town water mains and had been relying solely on a rainwater tank for a large family of seven. Low and behold, it was discovered, through the use of the farmer's divining rods, that we had water beneath our property. I must have been about seven years old, but I remember thinking that the farmer was a magician. I was amazed when he demonstrated to me how the L-shaped rods would vibrate and swing in towards each other, crossing when there was water present in the earth. Other tools, such as twigs and wands can also be used in a similar way.

Dowsing with a Pendulum

A pendulum is a weighted non-magnetic object hung from a single length of cord or chain. Pendulums are often made from metal, wood, or crystals specifically intended for the purpose of dowsing, but you can also use a bead hung from a piece of thread, a pendant necklace, or even a key on a chain, and it will still do the trick.

As previously stated, dowsing can be used to find lost objects, uncover trapped energies, reveal information, diagnose an allergy, or even discover the correct method of healing a person may need in response to a symptom. As well as being a dowsing tool, pendulums can also be used to dispel negative or unwanted energies in a room or a person's energy field. Essentially, the pendulum acts as a transmitter of higher wisdom or information from the higher mind via the body's energy field to the person asking the questions.

Internal or Emotional Dowsing

This form of dowsing is something I taught myself to do long before I even knew there was such a thing as dowsing as a concept. I was sitting my Life in The UK test to get my British citizenship back in 2006. Although I had studied for it, the test was multiple choice and some of the answers were deceptively similar, give or take a few minor details.

I decided to test my intuition. I sat back in my chair and closed my eyes. I asked my body to please show the feeling for a positive response. Immediately, I felt a welling up of positive energy in my body. My heart felt like it was expanding and a rush of positive emotion, akin to excitement, ran through me like a current. Then I ask my higher mind to show me a negative response, and I immediately felt my energy contract and a sort of dulling down of emotion.

I answered all of the questions on the test in this way and then went back over the whole test to check if each response looked right in relation to the information I had studied in preparation. Even though I had been given 45 minutes to complete the whole exam, I was done in under 20 minutes. I double- and triple-checked my answers both energetically and logically. When I handed in my test, I discovered I had passed with flying colours and became a British citizen.

How to Dowse Internally with Your Body Angel

◊ Close your eyes, and centre your awareness in your heart. Imagine you are surrounded by a bubble of pure white light.

◊ Ask you higher mind and Body Angel to show you a clear yes response through the sensations in your body.

◊ Relax and feel into what is going on in your physical and emotional body.

◊ Come back to neutral in your heart space.

◊ Next, ask your higher self and Body Angel to show you a clear no response within the sensations of your physical and emotional body.

◊ Pay attention to how your body and emotions react.

◊ Come back to your heart space and begin to ask any questions you would like guidance on.

◊ Practice makes perfect with this exercise, and it works better the more you relax into it and learn to trust your higher mind. Do not try to control your response. Allow your body to show you, rather than preempting what the response should feel like. I have only included my experience as an example. Your responses may be totally different to mine.

Choosing Your Preferred Dowsing Method or Pendulum

When deciding which dowsing tool to use, it's best to go with your intuition. When I first started working with a pendulum, I wasn't even looking for one. I had been working with clients for many years and using thumb and forefinger muscle testing in my sessions; however, constantly pulling people's fingers apart was getting tiring, and hurting my arm and neck muscles.

I had started to explore the different methods of muscle testing when I decided to attend the Mind Body Soul Exhibition in London. Wandering among the stalls, I was guided over to a crystal stand and felt immediately drawn to a beautiful rose quartz pendulum. Having never used one before, I was surprised at how easily I took to it and it to me.

"Please show me a clear yes," I commanded, and the pendulum began to swing back and forth immediately—and I almost swear, excitedly.

"Thank you," I said, grinning. "Now, please show me a clear no." The pendulum changed direction in an instant and began to swing round and round in circles.

Then, already knowing the answer, I asked the pendulum if it wanted to work with me. I could almost hear it squealing with glee as it swung wildly back and forth, back and forth. It was like being reunited with an old friend. Even though I have worked with many pendulums over the years, I still have my old faithful rose quartz. I can't seem to part with it, and I think at some point I will come full circle and begin to work with it again.

What If My Pendulum Won't Play Ball?

If your pendulum isn't cooperating, or won't give you straight answers, ask yourself if you have become too reliant on it. Never give your power away to anyone or anything outside of yourself and your own divine mind. If you have been asking the same question over and over in the hopes of getting the answer you want, rather than what your higher mind is guiding you to do, your higher self and, therefore, your pendulum, will stop cooperating until you learn to listen to your own intuition.

When a pendulum stops working, something is usually out of alignment. Sometimes, this can also mean that there is external interference involved. Perhaps, like every magical tool, your pendulum may need cleansing, or you may not have opened and prepared your space properly before beginning your spiritual work.

Check to see if there is any interference by asking: "Am I receiving 100 percent pure divine love and light guidance from my higher self through my pendulum?"

Ask this question three times consecutively and see what the response is. If the pendulum does not give you a direct yes answer three times, you can be sure something untoward is afoot. Immediately stop using your pendulum, and do an energy clearance on the pendulum, yourself, and your space. Once you are sure the space is clean and clear, you may resume your questions.

The Science of the Body Angel and Our Gut Instinct

While doing research at the University of Michigan, neuroscientist Dr. Sarah Garfinkel discovered that our bodies have more influence over our minds than we expect.

> In a study of traumatized war veterans, she discovered that their fears were as much physical as they were mental, and that being in a safe environment didn't improve their experience. Dr. Garfinkel concluded that the body is a key part of consciousness and helps generate our sense of self. She learned that our perceptions of the world can be influenced by electrical signals coming from the organs, particularly the heart, and that internal signals arising from the body actually help shape the way we think and can influence our feelings, perceptions, and behaviours.[14]

As with my unexplained panic attacks prior to the pandemic, in 2019, it seems the body is able to communicate directly with us to influence our decisions and perhaps warn us of impending danger. I believe the internal signals in our bodies, which mystics refer to as clairsentience, can be extremely informative and often aid in making the most productive choices. When we think of our gut instinct, the logical mind rarely comes into the equation. Dr. Garfinkel's research supports this. Listening to your heart and body can have a positive influence on your mind, reduce stress, and aid healing.

> Researchers at HeartMath Institute in California have discovered that the heart has an electromagnetic field bigger than the human brain, and that the body is constantly sending signals to the brain, and vice versa. Rollin McCraty, Ph.D., Director of Research at the HeartMath Institute, has found that the heart has a sophisticated intelligence of its own with an intricate circuitry than means it can make decisions independent of the brain, acting as an overall coordinator of the body's functions.[15]

CHAPTER 7

How to Align with the Angelic Vibration

This process will adjust your vibration to the angelic dimension by allowing you to receive your own Angel wings.

Something very special the Angels have shown me is how to activate and work with our very own pair of glittering and magnificent angelic wings. The following meditation will help you activate your own powerful wings of light and accept your role as an Earth Angel.

Once you receive your unique pair of Angel wings, you can activate them at any time to bring comfort, healing, and protection to yourself or anyone around you, or, in fact, the entire planet.

You will soon find you can easily extend your wings as far as you need to—even sending them out to people in other countries, but you'll probably find that there is no limit to how far you can stretch your wings because you are, in fact, limitless yourself. As a being of unconditional love and light, you are without beginning or end. This might sound a little overwhelming or difficult to grasp as first, but intention is everything, and so, if you can imagine it, then it can become so. Spread your wings and fly into your own magnificence for the good of all.

Meditation: Discover Your Angel Wings

This simple but empowering exercise allows you to understand your angelic nature as someone who can do so much good for this planet.

Do you often feel drawn to helping others? There is a very good reason why you may feel that you are one of the more open-hearted, kind, and compassionate people on Earth, and why friends and loved ones often seek you out for help and guidance.

If you have been guided to this book, then it is highly likely you have a special connection to the angelic realms and you have come to this planet at this time to live out a very special mission. If you are reading this, take it as absolute confirmation that your soul has brought you here at this time to be a living example of love and compassion for humanity. You are, therefore, what I like to call a "Human Angel", "Earth Angel", or "World Angel".

Getting Your Wings

◊ Find a quiet place, where you may sit comfortably and relax.

◊ Close your eyes, and start to take a couple of deep, cleansing, and relaxing breaths.

◊ Imagine a tube of golden-white light going right through your body, connecting you to the very core of Mother Earth below you, and then, from your heart centre, reaching all the way up into the pure diamond light of Creator or Source above you.

◊ As you breathe in, breathe this light into your heart. Breathe in pure love.

◊ As you breathe out, breathe out pure love, and send it out to all the corners of the universe and to all living beings. Your intention alone is enough for this to occur.

◊ Feel your loving connection to everything in existence, all at once.

◊ Now you find yourself travelling upwards through the golden-diamond tube of light. You travel out of the top of your head and continue up past the planets and stars to the very edge of the universe.

◊ Before you is a huge golden-white doorway flooded with light.

◊ You step through this doorway and find that you have entered the Temple of the Angelic Kingdom of Light.

◊ There are millions of angels surrounding you, and you feel utterly bathed in love.

◊ A huge golden angel, Archangel Metatron, representing the highest attainment of our divinity, steps forward to greet you.

◊ You kneel before him, and he lightly taps you in the very centre of your upper back just below your neck, in between your shoulder blades.

◊ You begin to feel a tingling sensation and, suddenly, your own magnificent pair of ethereal angel wings unfurl in all their splendour.

◊ Your wings are huge and glittering. Take a moment to explore the sensation of spreading your own angel wings and getting to know them. What colour are they? Are they feathered or of a gossamer quality like those of the fairies?

◊ Imagine wrapping your wings protectively around all the people you love.

◊ Now wrap them around anyone you know who needs a little extra help or healing.

◊ Now try visualizing yourself wrapping your wings around a whole place, such as your city, and then try doing this visualization for your entire country.

◊ When you have explored your wings, expand them as far as they will go—you may find there is no limit to how far you can stretch them.

◊ When you feel ready, wrap your wings around our entire planet, and visualize yourself pouring love, healing, and protection onto Earth via the light of your sparkling angel wings.

◊ Now travel back down into your body, and centre your awareness back in your heart.

◊ Ground and protect yourself by imagining that your wings have now turned a dazzling, sparkling white and then wrap them right around yourself like a cocoon of pure white light. Seal your cocoon in protective gold and indigo light.

◊ Sink your weight into your body. Bring your awareness all the way back into the now moment within this time, space, and dimension, and open your eyes.

◊ Keep an eye out for images of wings or white feathers as you go about your day. These physical signs are a confirmation of your experience from the angels.

Everywhere I go, I find huge pictures of wings and wing murals. This is the kind of sign it is hard to miss!

How to Channel an Archangel

The following channelling checklist will give you a step-by-step framework within which to safely channel an Archangel. You may call on an Archangel of your choice by setting a clear intention to work with whichever Archangel you feel would be of most help to you now.

Similarly, you may also use this same checklist and process to call upon any other loving light guide or being that is available to assist you at this time. You may even find that a whole healing team shows up.

I have used this process for years and, as well as the Angels, I have connected with beautiful star councils, the fairy realms, Ascended Masters and high-level wisdom guides, and even healing and psychic surgery teams.

Channelling Checklist

◊ **Grounding:** Ensure that you are present and in your body. Be acutely aware of your physical sensations, and anchor your consciousness by imagining it as a ball of light and centring it in your heart.

◊ **Intention:** Set a clear intention to only connect with the most loving angelic beings that have your highest and best interests in mind.

◊ **Open the space:** Visualize a pillar or column of diamond-white light cascading down from infinite Source above you, surrounding you, and flowing all the way into the core of the earth. Visualize it plugging into a huge diamond in the very centre of the earth.

◊ **Shield and protect your space:** Next, see a spark of light at your heart centre. With every in-breath, allow the light to expand into an orb and then into a huge sphere of light around you and your whole space. Seal this orb in golden light to protect your space. Intend that only the highest energies and beings of love may enter your space, and all else is to be transmuted into divine love or sent to the highest point of its own divine evolution available.

◊ **Raise your vibration:** Breath in the energy of pure love through the white light, and invite love to enter every facet of your being. Imagine you feel tingles all over your body, and you may begin to see sparkles of light around the room and feel tingles in your feet and the palms of your hands. Sometimes, I get the sense that the air in the room has become thicker or more tangible, as though I can reach out and grab the energy.

◊ **Invocation and connection:** Call on the Angel, Archangel, spirit guide, or deity you wish to connect with. You can do this silently in your own mind or aloud.

◊ **Communication:** Using all your psychic senses, or clairs, ask to connect with and receive messages from your Angel or guide. Ask questions, and receive the messages your Angel wishes to impart. These may come in the form of words or pictures inside your mind, colours, symbols or shapes, or you may just get a clear knowing.

◊ **Evidence:** Ask for a sign or a symbol that you will see in your waking life as evidence and validation to your ego mind that this experience has definitely happened. If doing mediumship or channelling a spirit that previously had a human incarnation, you can also ask for a piece of evidence that you or whoever you are reading for will know them by.

◊ **Gratitude:** Once you have finished your communication, say thank you to the beings/Angels for their guidance and for showing up. This also lets them know you would like to work with them again in future.

◊ **Close down and seal your space:** This is a process I call Shrink, Sink, and Shield. Shrink your energy field and consciousness down so it becomes body-shaped and contained within your body. Sink your weight into your body and the chair, and ground yourself by placing your attention in the lower belly or your feet. Shield yourself by wrapping the sphere of golden light around you like a cloak and then wrap an indigo blue wizard's cloak over the top of it to seal your energy. Finally, visualize a huge diamond octahedron around you, and fill it with white light, allowing you to shine as brightly as you can while remaining protected.

The Science of Channelling

Dr. Helané Wahbeh at the Institute of Noetic Sciences (IONS) in California has been conducting research into channelling through the IONS Channeling Research Program and has published some of her findings in a book entitled *The Science of Channeling: Why You Should Trust Your Intuition and Embrace the Force That Connects Us All.*[16]

Much of the research conducted at IONS involves uncovering evidence that human consciousness transcends the physical body and brain. As director of research at IONS, Dr. Wahbeh has been conducting experiments to prove that channels are able to receive information that is later found to be legitimate and verifiable.[17]

Dr. Wahbeh uses the term "channelling" as an umbrella term to include anything from gut hunches to trance mediumship. Her work draws on famous case studies, such as that of trance channel Edgar Cayce. For decades, Cayce worked with the US Government-funded parapsychology research centre StarGate, which investigated psychic abilities and their attributes and verified many of his predictions and diagnoses.

The IONS Channeling Research Program has been able to demonstrate that channelling is a common phenomenon, does not reflect any mental health pathology, and has definable characteristics, including a positive impact on the channel's life. The programme has been able to verify that the information the channels received in this research study could not have been discovered through any other source.[18]

PART TWO

Guardians of the Non-physical Worlds

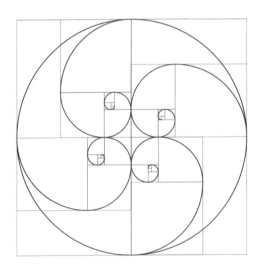

CHAPTER 8

The Main Archangels, Ancestors, and Guides Overlighting This System

Archangel Gabriel

Archangel Gabriel is the keeper of the white ray of purity and holds the keys to the gateway of crystalline communication with our divine presence. This Angel is the one to call on to enhance your channelling abilities, so you align to the highest guidance and wisdom for you at all times.

Gabriel's message is one of hope and realigning with our soul's calling and mission during this time of the great revealing of truth. Humanity is emerging from a long period of collective shadow, where much has been hidden from us. You could say we have been in hiding from ourselves.

The Archangels tell me that this long period of darkness was necessary. Like a slingshot or an arrow, the farther you draw back the bow, the more momentum you build towards what you wish to achieve or how far you wish your arrow to fly in order to hit its mark.

Our trajectory is a powerful one indeed for, from here on in, the only way is up. Humanity is moving into a collective phase of enlightenment, and I am told by my Angels and guides that because of our dedication to the evolution of our love consciousness, we will not experience another fall from grace again. We are on the path home to oneness with our creator. And we are beginning to understand that, although we are unique individuals, we are all part of a larger field of consciousness. This group consciousness includes all other human beings, but it is also vaster than that. Many ancestors, ancient ones, star nations, and tribes of light are all eagerly awaiting our return to the unity collective of love.

The Angels and ancestors tell me that there was a time on Earth—long before our history books would have us believe humans were even in existence on this planet—when people walked as giants and knew themselves divine. They understood they were part of the earth herself and part of the cosmos.

They were physical in form yet angelic in nature. They knew that all things, all life, are part of a vast network of supreme love consciousness connected by the living light that makes up the very fabric of our universe. This light could be referred to as the light of Source or Creator or God, depending on which school of thought you ascribe to. But it is both within us and all around us. When you consciously breathe in this pure energy, filling yourself up with its wellspring of love, compassion, grace, and positivity, you instantly connect with the collective consciousness of the brothers and sisters of light.

The Diamond as the Gateway to Infinite Consciousness

The diamond symbol I was gifted by Gabriel and the Archangels is perfect in its symmetry and simplicity, but despite its simplicity, this symbol represents the key to all life and existence. As such, it acts as an instant gateway or doorway to the multi-universal levels of all consciousness, and allows us to interact with the many loving guides, Angels, Masters, and beings that inhabit the myriad dimensions beyond this physical world.

When I was in Egypt in 2012, I visited the Osirion at the temple of Abydos, where an intriguing symbol appears to have been mysteriously laser-cut into one of the stone pillars. The symbol is known as the Flower of Life. I write about the mathematical significance of this symbol in more depth in a later chapter, but in simple terms, this shape represents the multidimensional nature of creation and how creation, and our awareness of it, is constantly unfolding and expanding like a blossoming flower.

The Flower of Life depicts 13 overlapping circles, or spheres, and can also be seen to represent the 13 dimensions of consciousness. These 13 dimensions repeat into infinity and can also be understood in terms of music. When looking at an octave on a piano keyboard, you find eight notes, but the eighth note is also the first note of the next octave. These eight notes are known as the Diatonic Scale.

However, if we include the black notes, we have 13 keys in total, which is known as the Chromatic Scale, and the 13th note becomes the first note of the next level of 13, and so on. Interestingly, in Greek, the word chroma translates to "colour", so forms yet another link to the rainbow-diamond frequency of the multiverse.[19]

According to John 1:1 in the Bible, sound and vibration were the first thing to take form within our universe: "In the beginning was the word, and the word was with God, and the Word was God." Like music, with higher and lower notes on the scale, the universe, and indeed the multiverse, acts in the same way—with higher and lower frequencies creating higher/lighter and lower/denser dimensions of reality.

The Science of the Creative Force of Sound

NASA Scientists have discovered that acoustic sound waves helped to influence the nature and distribution of the galaxies in our universe.[20] *New Scientist Magazine* has reported that these sound waves, called Baryon Acoustic Oscillations (BAOs), rippled out across the cosmos when it was formed from a sea of charged plasma particles in the first half-million years of our universe. The energy was too hot for the particles to stick together so they bounced off one another, creating waves or vibrations that spread out the plasma, and as the universe cooled, it formed into clusters of stars.[21]

The Seed of Creation within the Flower of Life

If we look at the Flower of Life model and zoom in on the place where each sphere, or circle, overlaps, we find the almond-shaped symbol of the *vesica piscis*, or "bladder of the fish".

We can find this symbol throughout nature; for example, our eyes and mouths all correlate with this shape, including the female vagina, our very first entry point into the physical world, the doorway to the womb/the void where we ourselves are miraculously created, moving from the non-physical into physical form.

We can also see this shape in the leaves on the trees and another potent symbol of creation, the tiny seeds that spring forth life in the form of huge and majestic trees. This is why the humble apple is known as the fruit of the tree of knowledge, as it contains within it the symbolism of creation in the form of the Vesica Piscis, and also the five-pointed star of the pentagram, which represents all the elements that make up life in our world: earth, air, fire, water and spirit/ether.

Likewise, the humble acorn is in the shape of the Vesica Piscis and holds within it all the information required for it to grow into a mighty oak. In terms of our sovereignty and the human capacity to evolve into something far greater than we believe ourselves to be, this is a wonderful metaphor. So, too, is the glorious sunflower, whose seeds grow in the pattern of the Fibonacci sequence.

The Vesica Piscis symbol of two merging spheres also represents the marriage of opposites and in this the middle path of unconditional love or non-judgemental love. When we awaken and harmonize the opposing forces within ourselves—our male and female aspects, our light and our darkness, and so forth—we awaken what the Gnostics called the "holy child within", and open a new energy field in perfect alignment with our true state of innocence and purity. From this space, we can open to absolute trust that all things will unfold in perfection with our divine destiny.

When we work with the unified field, we must not only ask for what we need but also surrender any desire for specific outcomes. The divine will never lead us astray, and everything will play out in alignment with the holy plan for our lives.

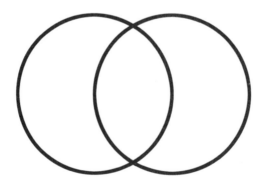

Within the feminine curves of the Vesica Piscis shape, if we then draw straight lines that meet at each edge, we reveal a diamond, which can, in turn, be halved into two equilateral triangles.[22]

If we were to view this diamond in 3D, we would arrive at the geometrical shape of the Octahedron Platonic Solid. This symbol is commonly used to depict the physical structure of the mineral diamonds of the earth because natural diamonds generally grow in an octahedronal form.

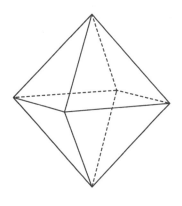

The Science of the Diamond

The diamond is the toughest and hardest stone on Earth. It was previously believed that these precious stones were formed when coal was placed under immense pressure; however, it is now understood that diamonds are far older.[23]

They have been formed over millions, sometimes billions, of years by the extreme heat of the earth's mantle, at a depth of around 150–200 km below the surface of the earth, then carried to the earth's surface via a natural event, such as a volcanic eruption. These much-sought-after stones are quite literally forged in fire, under immense pressure and almost unbearable conditions. This makes them the perfect symbol and metaphor for the journey of spiritual awakening.[24]

As a symbol for the enlightened soul, the diamond is like the phoenix: Rather than being destroyed by the extreme forces it is up against, it becomes stronger and forms into the most beautiful version of itself before surfacing and revealing itself as a gift to the world. Is it any wonder that the diamond has become a symbol for love and the sacred union of the feminine and the masculine the world over? As above, so below—the diamond frequency, ray, or flame can be accessed via the crystalline diamond consciousness that resides deep within the earth.

Archangel Alchemy and Harnessing Unconditional Love

The nature of unconditional love is neutrality, or perfect harmony and balance. In healing circles, this is often referred to as the "zero point". In simple terms, the zero point is the vacuum.

We can access this zero point frequency by bringing our conscious awareness into our centre, letting go of judgements, and resting in perfect stillness within. The nature of the energy of the divine itself is perfect unconditional love, and this perfect space of harmony that is the nature of the divine also exists deep within the Earth. By connecting regularly with Mother Nature and grounding ourselves, we can feel safe and secure. This allows us to raise our vibration and open our hearts and minds more easily to the infinite realms of love operating at a higher frequency.

These other dimensions are not separate from us, and they do not exist in another place. They are around us all the time. When we refer to a higher plane or dimension, it simply means that the energy of that dimension and the beings that inhabit that plane are vibrating at a higher, faster rate. On the earth plane, our human energy moves more slowly, so we appear to be physical and can see all that exists within our frequency with the naked eye.

As I explained previously, higher-level beings may sometimes show up in our physical vision as orbs or flashes of light, but to the majority of us they are invisible, for the simple reason that they are moving too fast for us to settle on their image. When we learn to raise our vibration, open our energy field, and awaken our inner sight, we are able to use our imagination and our innate extrasensory gifts to sense, feel, and know when these beings are around, so we can communicate with them.

Learning to channel also allows you to invoke these loving beings at will, so you can converse with them regularly and receive guidance. As they inhabit a higher realm, they also have a higher perspective on things—a bird's-eye view, if you will. And when viewing any problem or issue from above, it usually seems much more insignificant in comparison with being caught up in the little details when you are in the middle of it.

The Science of the Holographic Universe

While studying the afterglow of the Big Bang, researchers from the University of Southampton (UK), University of Waterloo (Canada), Perimeter Institute (Canada), INFN, Lecce (Italy) and the University of Salento (Italy) have found there is substantial evidence supporting a holographic explanation of the universe.[25]

The scientists believe that by investigating irregularities in the cosmic microwave background, they now have enough information to support the idea that everything in our 3D reality emanates from a flat 2D field, like the hologram on a credit card or a 3D film playing on a 2D movie screen. Recent advances in equipment and telescopes have also allowed scientists to detect data and activity beyond the 3D world, hidden amidst white noise and microwaves. [26]

The Nature of the Multiverse and Living Consciousness

We exist in a living universe, and when you engage with the universe from this unlimited perspective, you come to realize that everything in existence has a consciousness—animals, insects, plants, even rocks. Your own house has a consciousness of its own.

From my perspective, the entire universe is alive, and we are all like the cells, molecules, and atoms that make up that universe. As such, we are all connected and all part of the whole. The underlying energy, or essence, of this whole is pure, unconditional love. We are built on love. Our bodies are made up of the very same stuff as the stars.

Because of my ability to see, feel, hear, and experience existence beyond this 3D reality, I have discovered that I have the ability to communicate with any being, guide, or group consciousness, such as Angels, Ascended Masters, spirit guides, and celestial beings of light. But I can also speak to tree spirits, the stone people, animals, interdimensional beings that exist independently of any planet or physical dimension, and even body parts, organs, and objects.

When I first discovered that I could speak to galactic beings from other star systems, I nearly fell off my chair. In fact, it began many years ago, with me having random memories of other lifetimes I had lived in some of those other star systems. Far from being frightening, it was one of the most beautiful and humbling experiences I had ever had. I met with members of my various star families, and they taught me directly how to channel their healing energy, technology, and wisdom.

Although I have been attuned to various healing systems over the years, I never set out to be a channel and never realized I was already doing it regularly. I hadn't read any books on the subject or studied it. It awakened within me very naturally, and I began to develop it and teach it with the direct help of my Angels, guides, and celestial friends.

When I found myself being put on the spot in that Angel workshop all those years ago, I was not prepared at all, yet the words flowed out of me with such ease. I had an overwhelming feeling of being so very at home and aligned.

The Guardians of Diamond Earth

Along with the Archangels, there are many other loving beings and groups of beings overseeing our Ascension process. These groups inhabit various dimensional levels and frequencies above the level of unconditional love consciousness. They include Ascended Masters, a group of enlightened souls that achieved a state of transcendence during their earthly lifetimes, such as Jesus, Mary Magdalene, Buddha, Kwan Yin, and many others.

Other guardians of our evolutionary process include the Higher Galactic Councils of Light; the Galactic Federations of Light, including our families from Arcturus, Andromeda, the Pleiades, Orion, Sirius, Alpha Centauri, Aldabaran, Auriga, Venus, Lyra, Cygnus, Cassiopeia, and multiple star systems; the interdimensional and intergalactic Elohim; the Lemurian High Councils and Inner Earth guides; animal guides; the elemental and devic kingdoms; and all manner of magical beings, such as dragons, unicorns, and many more.

As we remember our place in the multiverse, we are rejoining a vast family and network of light through the unified field of our reawakened love.

The Guardians of the 13 Dimensions

The Flower of Life as a Model for the 13 Dimensions of Creation

There are many varying models of the 13 dimensions of creation, and one thing to note is that, like time, linear existence only occurs at our current human level of awareness. All dimensions coexist and, therefore, our idea of a linear hierarchy and of one state of being as being superior or better than another does not wash here.

All dimensions are equal yet different and merely inhabit a different vibrational or spatial state. To tune in to any one of these dimensions, you just have to alter your vibration and level of consciousness. It is a little like turning the dial to listen to a different radio station.

During my explorations over the years with channelling beings from various dimensions of existence, I explored different models of the multiverse and the various ways of depicting them in a linear fashion. Then, on my trip to Egypt in 2012, while standing in the Valley of the Kings, I had a vision and was shown a vivid image of creation as a 3D version of the Flower of Life symbol, with 13 spheres all overlapping and interweaving. The image showed me that the multiverse is not linear at all, but non-linear and holographic in nature.

Again, the universe brought me confirmation of my visions, when I attended a New Shamballa Healing Workshop in Glastonbury in 2014 and was attuned to channel the healing vibrations of each of the 13 dimensions.

A Potential Linear Model of the 13 Dimensions

If we were to flatten out these dimensions into their various levels in a linear fashion, it might look something like the following:

1st Dimension: Mother Earth, rocks, minerals, crystals, gravity

2nd Dimension: Plants, fairies, elementals

3rd Dimension: Humanity, animals, insects, everyday magic, geometry

4th Dimension: Emotions, desires, manifesting, law of attraction, spirit guides, deceased loved ones

5th Dimension: Ascended Masters and inner plane masters: Lemurians, Atlanteans

6th Dimension and Above: Laws of the universe and the celestial realms. Star beings. Discovering your stellar origins.

7th Dimension: Angelic realm, and the unicorns, music of the spheres

8th Dimension: Light and sound, light language

9th Dimension: Portal to the divine bliss

10th Dimension: Divine masculine and feminine: Hieros Gamos – sacred union within yourself and the whole planet

11th Dimension: Awareness of and feeling connected to all

12th Dimension: Achieving oneness with all and God

13th Dimension: The Void. Awareness of the infinite multiverse. Start of the next level of consciousness.

The Science That Supports the Living Consciousness of the Universe

Scientists have discovered that the cosmic web of the universe acts like a giant brain, with nodal networks acting in a very similar way to the neurons of the human brain. The findings were recorded in a report entitled "The Quantitative Comparison between the Neuronal Network and the Cosmic Web" published in *Frontiers of Physics* in November 2020.

Astrophysicist Franco Vazza at Bologna University, who worked on the study with Verona University neurosurgeon Alberto Felitti, said in the *Independent* newspaper:

> We calculated the spectral density of both systems. This is a technique often employed in cosmology for studying the spatial distribution of galaxies.[27] Our analysis showed that the distribution of the fluctuation within the cerebellum neuronal network on a scale from 1 micrometer to 0.1 millimeters follows the same progression of the distribution of matter in the cosmic web but, of course, on a larger scale that goes from 5 million to 500 million light-years.[28]

Thus you could indeed have the entire universe inside your head.

CHAPTER 9

The Archangels as the Bridge to Unity Consciousness

The Archangels are here among us always, and their function is to reunite us with our true soul selves, so that we may know the God/Goddess within. There are more Angels in existence than we could ever hope to imagine.

Likewise, there are more beings and tribes of light within our multiverse than we could ever count. They are infinite in number and, to our human minds, that may seem inconceivable, but to our greater awareness, our heavenly mind, anything is possible.

There are no limits in the field of infinite consciousness, for the universe is ever expanding and giving birth to new dimensions and universes all the time. It never ends. Just as we, ourselves, never end. The soul goes on and on.

Even after physical death, we leave behind the vessel, or "vehicle", of our body and return to the dimensions of spirit. Where we go after death is entirely dependent on what we know or have learnt in life. There are multiple levels and layers to the realms of spirit, but the soul is multidimensional and can be split into various aspects, all inhabiting different timelines or lifetimes simultaneously. From the perspective of the soul, time does not exist, so all things and all timelines are occurring at the same time within the eternal now moment. Our souls are holographic.

When we look at the nature of the soul from this perspective, we are already home; on some level, we have already returned to oneness with the divine, so you might say that we are already divinely perfect and there is actually nothing we need to learn. Yet, there is always paradox when it comes to the spiritual path. The truth is, there is no path; however, here on Earth, we inhabit a third-dimensional reality that is denser than the ethereal realms beyond, and time does exist in our dimension, so we must work with it and move through it.

Here, everything moves at a much slower pace. In the faster-moving planes of the spirit, our thoughts are like quicksilver, and we are able to manifest thought into form in the blink of an eye. But here, our desires can take much longer to come to fruition for us to experience them as tangible, real, physical experiences. There can be many layers of built-up energy, trauma, belief systems, self-sabotage, outdated contracts, trapped emotions, fears, doubts, misconceptions, and social conditioning to work through and transform before we are able to access the clear channel to the higher soul's knowing.

There are many systems of healing currently available to help us move through these layers—to do our spiritual work and progress along the path—and more new healing systems are being developed and channelled every day. There has been a bit of a trend for people to create their own techniques, and this is one way we can measure how rapidly human consciousness is developing. Many channels are also tuning in to the same, or similar, frequencies and bringing through similar information, as our minds begin to link up to higher sources of knowledge, wisdom, and remembrance.

As with all things, there is a shadow side to this, and the ego self is more present than ever within a spiritual environment. You may have seen a level of competition arising among healers and spiritual teachers, and even examples of copycat behaviour. On the spiritual path, one must master the lesson of discernment to know how to find the best teacher or guide for them and how to lovingly say no to those whose views and practices do not resonate.

There is also a common misconception within our human condition that says in order to be a good and kind person, you must always be gentle, or even weak. It takes immense courage to stay in the vibration of love when you are being wronged or even abused. But to stay in a loving vibration does not mean you must allow yourself to be taken advantage of.

Many sensitive people go through this realization in their lives. If you are naturally empathic and giving, it can be difficult to come to terms with situations in which you find yourself giving out more love, time, and support than you are getting from others. But all of our relationships and interactions offer a mirror to help us heal the wounded parts of ourselves submerged within our subconscious mind. When conflict or difficulty arises, try not to take it personally; use it as a tool to journey even deeper into your psyche and find the unhealed parts that are yearning for your attention.

As we become more willing to see into these hidden parts—dubbed our "shadow self" by psychologist Carl Jung—we begin to heal and integrate our multiple timelines and the fragmented aspects of our unified soul self.[29] In short, we are calling the lost and wounded parts of ourselves home and integrating them.

Again, if you could view your own soul as a multifaceted crystal, the unhealed parts might look like cracks or blemishes on the surface of the crystal, or there may even appear to be whole chunks missing. As we heal and integrate our painful memories and experiences, we are repairing and polishing the crystal of our whole being. And as all humans and all beings are connected through the vast web of living divine unity consciousness, as we heal ourselves, we are also helping to heal each other.

A Story about Integrity and the Mirror

In 2020–2021, while the world was in the throes of the COVID-19 pandemic, I found myself involved in a legal dispute, where I was left with no choice but to defend myself. Another woman had trademarked the words "Archangel Alchemy" and contacted me to ask me to stop using the name I had been using to describe my Archangel healing work for 11 years.

After much deliberation and painful soul searching I sought legal advice, and it was recommended that I try to have her trademark invalidated, and she then took me to high court. It was one of the most difficult experiences I have ever had to face.

As an angelic channel, a Libran, and an empath, I never liked to get angry, and the last thing I would ever want to do is hurt somebody, but that had often meant potentially allowing myself to be hurt, instead.

I knew I was being given a big test—I was being forced by the Universe to learn to stand in my power.

I realized fairly early on that the other person had been sent to me as an exquisite gift. We were each holding up a mirror to the other, as I felt that neither of us had been fully valuing ourselves. I searched my heart often and could find no anger towards her. Instead, throughout the entire 21-month-long process, I sent her love, forgiveness, gratitude, and many blessings daily. But I also knew, on a human level, that I had to honour myself and my own needs first.

As a multidimensional channel and alchemist and, as part of my soul purpose, I do a lot of service and grid work behind the scenes and in my own time for the planet and humanity as a whole. As I have mentioned, the Angels had been warning me for a few years that we were entering a time they referred to as The Changing of the Guard, when humanity as a whole is being urged to move into integrity. But this changing of the guard is also happening within each of us, and I realized that if I didn't stand my ground and speak my truth, I would not be acting in true integrity. Finding the balance between love, wisdom, and power is essential on the awakened path.

I felt that this personal challenge had a bigger, more far-reaching impact than I could possibly imagine. I received many messages during meditation that I was being put in the position I was in by the Angels. No matter what I did to try to avoid going to court, all attempts to find a solution failed, and I had to stand up to this person with a counter claim. It was clear the Universe was not going to let me get out of it. Like it or lump it, this was an initiation I was being made to walk through. My pacifist human self was terrified, but my soul self knew that if I surrendered and trusted and got out of my own way, all would be well.

A very big realization dawned on me that I had actually been the enabler of all the people who had hurt me throughout my life. In some way, by not previously standing up for myself or voicing my true needs, I had been complicit in my own lack of success and had thus kept myself trapped in the role of the victim.

Far from being light and fluffy, angelic energy is a big energy to hold. I work with all Angels, but I had been channelling the Holy Fire Archangels, the Seraphim, the Cherubim, the Hayyoth, the Thrones, and the Elohim for some time, and theirs is a power beyond any rational argument. If you are involved in anything that is not serving your highest good, these Angels will send their heavenly fire like a dragon's hot breath to purge it swiftly from your life. The old programme of keeping myself small and on the back foot in life had to go.

I was about to publish my *Archangel Fire Oracle* card deck when the legal situation appeared as the final initiation. After 11 years of walking the path of alchemical fire, I was about to get a big lesson in how to master it.

At the time of writing the *Archangel Fire Oracle* card deck, I had not received a verdict on that court case and had to remain in my centre with it. I trusted that the Universe would not bring me anything I could not handle, and I made a commitment to open myself up to the divine and allow it to work through me. In my devotion to the cause, I asked to be put where I was needed and had to be willing to go either up or down in flames.

Although I moved through many emotions in the lead-up to giving my evidence in court, far from bringing me down, the situation taught me to value myself and my gifts and to be unafraid to step up to my leadership role and capabilities. The biggest blessing I received was to learn to wholeheartedly say yes to myself, to be unapologetic for who I am, and to stand up for my truth with absolute faith, dignity, and integrity. These are vital keys to hold as the world goes through many shifts in awakening and more truths are finding their way into the light of our awareness.

Anger is a valid human emotion, and when used with love and for the right reasons, clean anger can help you harness your inner sacred power and become an unstoppable force for good. It is symbolized by Archangel

Michael's flaming sword of truth. Sometimes, we find ourselves with no choice but to use our anger to say no to the situations and the people who are doing the wrong thing by us or causing us harm.

Now that I have finally learnt to say yes to what sets my soul on fire, I want to gift all my potential to the world to inspire others to do the same.

The time for truth is now. If each and every human being spoke their truth from a place of love, without fear, there would be no need for conflict to arise in the first place. This situation occurred because I was initially afraid to speak up for myself. It has taught me that suppressing our truth, even to keep the peace, can often do a lot more harm than good.

On the day the sun entered the sign of Libra (the scales of justice) on the 22nd September, 2021 (a date that adds up to the magical number 9), I won the court case. All the details of the case are in the public domain and can be found online.[30] But the real win for me was having the opportunity to heal so many hidden wounded aspects of myself, discover my own inner power, restore my faith in divine justice, access the voice of my own authority, deep-dive into levels of forgiveness and love I never knew I had and, most of all, to learn the real value and might of standing in my divine truth.

Sometimes standing in the light of your own truth may not make sense to the people around you, but when you truly know how to trust and follow the guidance of your heart, it will never steer you wrong.

As humans, we do so much of our learning and growing through relationship. Some of those relationships can be difficult or challenging in order to stretch us, like the one I described above, but others can be intensely loving and supportive and move us forward in ways we could never hope to imagine. I believe some of these relationships exist on an angelic and divine level and are entirely guided by our soul as we learn to integrate the ego on this human journey and return to love.

Love the people who challenge you, as they may just turn out to be your greatest teacher.

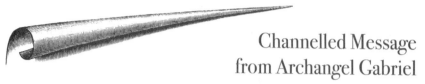

Channelled Message from Archangel Gabriel

The Power of Uncovering Our Truth

Beloveds,

We urge you to come back into your centre and breathe. Every time the weight of life and its challenges threatens to pull you out of balance, slow down, breathe, re-centre, find your faith, and then proceed.

When your experiences bring you out of focus and away from a place of trust, hope, and optimism, remember the power of your perspective.

Your feelings and emotions are not your enemy. They are the key to finding your way back to your divinity. We gift you an emotional alchemy process to assist you at this time of growing intensity for each of you. Your emotions may at times feel like an insurmountable mountain, and yet that mountain will melt, as ice turns to slush, when you open your heart to deeper faith and trust.

Rather than turning from your feelings, let them arise within you. Allow them to be felt, and love yourselves in the feeling, for your compassion is born of feeling and of understanding what it is to feel deeply.

Where is your sorrow located within you? Where do you feel the core of your innermost pain? Where is the tension and resistance? You may feel it like a tightness, or even at times like a foreign energy with a consciousness all of its own. Why do you continue to fight it and resist it? Give it light, give it air, give it space, give it breath, and let it reveal both its secrets and its gifts to you.

There are hidden messages and truths tucked away inside you, hidden behind the invisible walls of your emotions and beliefs. What a relief to turn and face your grief. You have no need to fear yourselves, dear ones. You have no need to fear your feelings.

Take back the power of your emotional intelligence, and let your feelings guide you deeper and deeper within yourself, to the place of purity that rests like a sleeping pearl within the vessel of the sanctuary of the soul. Do not look for your answers outside yourself, for all truth is to be found within.

The incorruptible source of infinite soul's light cannot be harmed. It cannot be destroyed, and it cannot be changed, for it contains your original divine blueprint and is the very essence of who you are at your core. And what that core is can only be described as exquisite, unshakeable, and unchangeable love.

It goes on and on, creating and expanding, growing and illuminating, but never in its purest form can it be diminished, diluted, or destroyed. This is the invincible soul self that lies at the heart of the innocent within every human being.

You are all conceived without sin. There is no "original sin". There are only a multitude of pathways back to the one true knowing. The pathway you choose is up to you, and everything comes down to a choice in every moment, every second and millisecond. It is the human part of you, with its limited viewpoint, that judges and tells you it is even possible to take a wrong turn or venture down a wrong path.

The middle path is the way. Release your judgements, and see everything as playing out perfectly in exactly the right way, and the true way will open before you.

Sometimes the best path to take remains concealed until you can understand that the right way to proceed is not found in the workings of the human mind alone, nor is it only to be found in the heart, but these two combined, when you sit back and invite the divine to guide you.

When you are willing to release your fear and judgement and surrender to the almighty within you, allowing it to lead, then your feelings will clearly show you the right way to proceed.

Master your feelings, beloveds. This does not mean that you must control them. It means, let them out to play, and follow the feeling to your inner sanctum of sovereignty, where the truth unfolds like a bud in bloom.

The "right" way is not born of a need to hide or run or escape, or to fight one's way through. The right way is often born when you accept that, in your humanness, you do not know what to do and so you offer it up to a higher source and wait and trust until the light breaks through. Then as you soften and open to more love, the way opens before you as a miraculous path.

What if there was no right or wrong way to proceed? What if you simply had implicit trust and faith that the best solution was always making its way to you and through you? Could you then relax and let yourself enjoy your life?

For every blessed moment that arrives is a surprise, a gift. It is beautiful in its simplicity, and every single time you come back to this place of truth and knowing, know you will succeed—perhaps not in the way you thought you would, but you will always get exactly what you need and learn precisely what you should in that moment. Your feelings and emotions are like the wrapping paper you need to unravel to find the present. And in the present, where you breathe and centre and open, is where you find the prize.

From the angelic perspective, there is no right or wrong; there is only perspective. Two differing perspectives are possible and allowed. Can you relinquish your control and let people live according to how they best see fit for themselves?

Can you live in harmony with differing opinions and views?

What, then, if harm is being done to another, you ask? Again, the way forward is to be found within the inner recesses of the heart, for to avoid conflict, one must learn the art of standing in one's truth to begin with and then imbalances can be avoided later. When entire groups or communities are complicit in a lie and invested in believing it to be a truth, then larger, more intense, and more obvious experiences and lessons may need to play out to bring things back into divine order and balance. In human terms, this may take many years or even lifetimes. It is all relative.

Untruths usually occur where one misses the mark. Untruths can often appear to some to be true, and they can hide within the mind like wolves in sheep's clothing ready to pounce. Therefore, know your own mind also, and be aware of how you lie to yourselves and others or allow yourselves to believe in others' lies in order to avoid discomfort. Anything that is suppressed for long enough will rise to the surface and be revealed eventually. The deeper the lie and the longer it is denied, the bigger the shock wave when the revelation comes.

Therefore, know yourselves, beloveds. Know yourselves well, and be deeply honest.

Know your own truth, and be willing to look deep into the belly of your worst fears and darkest imaginings. Lies are born of a misguided necessity to survive, but if you knew without a doubt that your needs would always be met by the divine, you would never have a need to suppress or block your truth or your true thoughts and feelings again. What is your truth? What is your lie? Are you willing to shine a light on both at the same time?

I am Gabriel. I am known as the Archangel of Communication. Only you can know your innermost truth at any given time, but it takes courage to seek it, and even more courage to share it. When you communicate your truth from a place of love and trust that it will be well received, it shall surely be. Misunderstandings are often born when one or another party is not being entirely honest with the other or themselves.

Seek the truth at every turn. Find it within your own being, and make every decision from your purest truth. This is the straight path to your divine perfection. Truth is a long, straight road. Deviate from it, and you may take a more scenic route, with obstacles, delays, and lessons to help you get yourself back on track.

When trouble and strife come calling in your outer experience, use it as a mirror to seek out what has arisen inside you to be resolved, and align yourself to your deepest truth once more to steer yourself back onto the best path.

Some of you know this well and have studied for many lifetimes to achieve alignment within your mind, body, and soul. Many of you reading this have come to be examples of truth for others. Some of you have also volunteered to resolve untruths in the collective to help steer humanity as a whole onto a higher timeline.

You may feel at times like a cat among the pigeons, and it may appear to you that speaking your truth is stirring up more trouble than it is worth. Even still, do not deviate from your inner knowing. There are many levels of consciousness and many hidden layers in the psyche, where your fears may try to trip you up and make you doubt yourself. To question and go on questioning is good. And do not be afraid to admit when you have been hoodwinked and need to re-centre and realign once more.

Likewise, do not be afraid to change your mind when it is required of you to align to the highest path available to you, even in the face of criticism and disbelief from those closest to you. For what was once right for you, may yet change as you grow and learn—always expanding in your wisdom and spiralling higher and higher into Source, as you travel deeper and deeper within.

To some, as you follow your own soul's path, you may appear to have "gone off the rails". They will soon realize that you are merely dancing to your own tune and following the inner wise soul that is guiding you on the best, most beautiful journey of life you could ever wish to dream.

Then, unrestrained, you rise into the realms of co-creation, and the dreams you once thought were merely dreams start to become part of your earthly reality. For many older souls, the dream of the kind of world you wish to inhabit is much more than a mere dream, for you hold the blueprints of the highest vision of Earth within your ancient memory, in the Akashic Libraries in the master cells of your DNA.

This world was always meant to be a playground. In many ways, it is a sort of a game. The only way to leave the game is to know thyself. All the world is a mirror. Use your outer life to view yourself from within. And once you know yourself within, you can begin to create your outer world in the image of your most exquisite imaginings.

This is the pleasure garden. If you do not like something in your world, endeavour to change it by transmuting any emotions that arise within, and continue to move forward by following your bliss.

I have left you much to ponder. We Angels gift you these tools of Archangel Alchemy to help bring balance and restore your equilibrium. Unconditional love is the pure frequency of creation that allows all life to unfold and thrive on this planet.

When the outer world as the mirror has shown you the power you hold within, the outer world can then become the magnifying glass of your highest and most desirable inner visions, for as without, so within, and as within, so without.

Know this, and you shall know the secret to experiencing Heaven upon Earth.

I am Gabriel, and it is written.

The One Flame –
Reuniting of the Councils of Light on Earth

Over my many years of working with the Angels and Archangels, they have guided me to connect with certain individuals, who I refer to as "soul family". I recognize these people instantly, even though we have never met before, as there is a deep feeling of unconditional love that flows between us.

These connections run much deeper than any other earthly relationship I have had, including family and blood relations, and they also differ greatly from other spiritual connections, such as past life relationships or purely karmic bonds.

Soon after I have met one of these souls, what follows is a rapid acceleration in consciousness, spontaneous kundalini awakening, and unified chakra experience, where all my centres are open, aligned, and streaming white light.

There are other key signs I know to look out for and incredible synchronicities that play out between us. Often we have a telepathic bond and turn up in each other's dreams and share joint missions to help heal the earth and the collective.

In late summer 2021, as I neared the completion of this book, I met another such soul, and the Angels began speaking to me about the concept of "the one flame". They used this term specifically in reference to these intense soul-bond relationships.

I was, of course, already familiar with the expression "twin flame", a term used by Elizabeth Clare Prophet, and had helped many clients and friends to navigate that journey. But I knew that this "one flame" concept was something different. The idea of having just one other soul counterpart never fully sat with me, as I had met a number of people with whom I shared an inexplicable and almost supernatural link.

If the soul is infinite and part of the divine, then it also stands to reason that on some level we are all connected through one main greater soul, and it is from that one soul or consciousness that life separates itself in order to become individualized, like the branches of a tree.

From the oneness of God/the divine, many times over the years, in various visions and meditations, I was shown by my Angels and guides how the soul splits itself again and again and how a group of humans at a higher level can form the one soul of a much higher dimensional, or higher frequency individual being.

I could see how it worked through my channelling abilities. Whenever I would channel or work with the Angels or the councils of light, they would often speak as one united voice. Sometimes individuals would come forward with particular messages, but mostly they would work as a collective and speak in unison.

I began to understand how the more we open our hearts and minds to our true gifts and abilities and expand our knowing, the more we connect to the vaster network of the one field of the unified soul, and humanity unifies. We are also unifying with a multidimensional family or network of light. We are becoming part of the councils of light, and are able to connect and communicate with them for healing and to access higher wisdom and support.

Androgynous Angels and Our Original Blueprint

Angels have no gender. They are perfectly balanced in the masculine and feminine, and as they are the very essence of unconditional love, they are neutral. As such, they help show us our true non-dualistic nature and lead us to the balancing of our own inner masculine and feminine halves.

When we meet a soul counterpart or flame—commonly known as a "twin flame" in new age language, although this is not strictly the true definition—it accelerates the process of our integration via an internal alchemy within the self. The purpose of these relationships is to highlight where we are still feeling incomplete or unhealed within ourselves.

There has been a lot of distortion around human sexuality, gender roles, and also our relationship to sexual energy, which, in its purest form, is one of the highest healing energies available to us. Sexual energy, when harnessed in a healthy and balanced way, is one of the most beautiful and devotional ways to reach ecstatic bliss of sacred union with the divine.

In 2017, while visiting my family in Australia, I met a new guide. As I was dozing on the sofa with jetlag at my brother's house in northern Queensland, a group of very tall and fair, almost albino-looking humans appeared. They called themselves The Ancient Ones and told me they were from among the original human root races on Earth. They pointed to an area on the globe somewhere north of Iceland, but I had the sense that the map looked very different during the time they inhabited the planet. They showed me that there had been others like them, some darker-skinned and of differing physical appearance, in other parts of the world.

One guide, who calls himself Erithea, has been with me ever since that day. Erithea is a male, but he is totally balanced in his masculine and feminine aspects. He tells me that there were human beings inhabiting Earth long before our current history books would tell us there was any human life here. Not only that, he tells me that there were great civilizations on this planet long before any that are on record today.

There are numerous stories about Atlantis and Lemuria, and we know of one story of our origins through the book of Genesis in the Bible. But Erithea says that he comes from a time that preceded even the story of Adam and Eve. Due to his size and stature—he stands around 12 feet tall, so is technically a giant—I have often wondered if some of the ancient megalithic structures and temples around the world are potentially far older than our current science has the capacity to date.

Through messages and visions, Erithea has shown me that during his time on Earth, humans were both physical and angelic nature. They were connected to each other and all dimensions through pure consciousness, and they were aware that everything was part of the one energy of the divine god/goddess source. As such, they were of a level of super-intelligence that we could scarcely fathom in our limited state of separation.

Erithea says that, at some point, there arose within the unified group a desire to know oneself as separate or individual from the collective. I have not been privy to the finer details of this, but what occurred as a result was what he and the Ancient Ones refer to as the Great Schism. As I understand it, this was the beginning of our proverbial "fall from grace" or "fall from Heaven". When we see it from this perspective, I think we must have some kind of collective core belief programme running that we are somehow "fallen Angels", and perhaps on some level have decided we are not worthy of Heaven. Since the Great Schism, or separation in consciousness, humanity has been on a quest to reunify with our true divine nature and know ourselves as part of everything again.

I believe that the new human we are evolving into—whether female, male, asexual/neutral, or female or male identifying in physical form—is the completely healed divine child, who has integrated their inner masculine and feminine, their inner light and dark, and all their other opposing aspects, to become a fully embodied and united being of light experiencing the pleasure

115

of being alive in this heavenly garden while residing within a luminous physical vessel.

The Archangels tell me that our light body will become permanently activated as we reach this stage of evolution, and we will no longer need to pursue active forms of meditation, as we will live naturally from this state of bliss in our everyday life. Our relationships will be healthy, loving, and balanced as a result, and men and women and all tribes of the earth will once again live in harmony.

As we work with the Archangel Alchemy processes, we are gradually integrating our masculine and feminine, transmuting our lower or limited idea of the self and rejoining the one unified soul.

The idea of the "one flame"—of individuals starting to experience deeper soul connections, meeting and joining on the astral plane, as well as having telepathic experiences—starts to make perfect sense to me in light of this information. It signals the beginning of our return to the unified divine state of love we were part of before that Great Schism, or separation, occurred.

I decided to put the question about what the "one flame" represents to the Archangels and received the following answer:

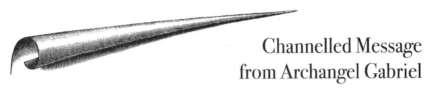

Channelled Message
from Archangel Gabriel

What Is the One Flame?

The "one flame" is the soul in its pure primal state. As the human realizes their own divinity, a higher gateway of light opens, and it pours forth like a truth.

When two such souls meet, they become magnetic to one another, creating a powerful vortex of universal love energy that even the deepest programming cannot withstand. Together, they begin to purge themselves and each other of any untruths and impurities.

Unlike "twin flames", these individuals may be from different soul groups, but have reached a high level of unity love consciousness with the divine.

If these souls also happen to be gridworkers, they have the capacity to purge and transmute irregularities and impurities from the collective and the earth herself much more quickly. This type of meeting will result in rapid transformation for the parties involved.

Sometimes bigger groups are formed of three or more of these souls and they are able to effect huge positive change for the many in a very short amount of time.

The dedication and devotion to knowing oneself is the catalyst that brings about such a powerful alchemy that the individual may feel as though they are losing themselves and being swept up in the momentum.

If they can hold their centre and rest within the eye of the vortex, they will learn to control it, then they will have the power to control the elements and perform miraculous healings at will.

If you have come to this place, beloveds, it has begun. Do not fear each other or the power you have come to wield. This is the time. The force you are encountering is love at its most potent, and this is the day of the reckoning.

You are the shining ones who have come to burn.

More of you will meet in the coming months following the reading of this message. You are the councils of light made manifest upon the earth, and holy are you among humans.

I am the Archangel Gabriel, keeper of the flame of one.

You are ready. It has begun.

The Science of the "One Flame" – Quantum Entanglement

Some scientists believe that when humans fall in love or form a strong bond, microscopic subatomic particles in our energy fields are able to interact with one another due to a phenomenon called Quantum Entanglement, in which two objects are able to react and relate to each other, even though they are spatially or physically separated. A change induced in one can affect the other, even if they are billions of light-years away from one another.[31]

In a wonderful nod to the diamond flame, in 2019, the University of Glasgow was the first to offer visual evidence of quantum entanglement using small crystals or diamonds in a Bell entanglement experiment, in which photons in entangled pairs measured the phase of the particles.[32] In his books Entangled Minds, The Conscious Universe, Supernormal, *and* Real Magic, *Dr. Dean Radin, chief scientist at the Institute of Noetic Sciences (IONS), also explores the nature of consciousness as being interconnected.[33]* Entangled Minds, *in particular, explores how human minds appear to be interconnected in the same way and how this entanglement of our reality is the key to psychic phenomena.[34]*

CHAPTER 10

Archangels as Bodyguards and Protectors

One of the primary functions of the Archangels, alongside our Guardian Angels, is to keep us safe and offer protection. You can call on any single one of your personal Angels to walk beside you daily and keep you safe, but the Archangels offer an extra-strong layer of protection, especially in potentially life-threatening situations.

In this chapter, I share some examples of how the Archangels have spectacularly come to my aid over the years, as well as some of the other ways they can offer you protection on your spiritual journey.

A Very Near Miss – Archangel Michael

On my way out for a jog one autumn morning in 2015, I was crossing the road at a pedestrian crossing to my local park. An oncoming silver car was going very fast and showed no signs of slowing down, but I simply assumed that once I stepped on to the crossing they would stop. I completely misjudged the speed of the oncoming car and the distance between us, however, and as I started to cross—already jogging—I could see the car coming full pelt towards me. I instantly leapt into a faster run and then everything went into slow motion.

There was no time for me to go to back, and I knew I couldn't move fast enough to get out of the way in time. The car was going to hit me.

Just one thought flashed into my head: *Angels! Help!*

In the millisecond of that thought I was suddenly pushed hard from behind. I literally felt invisible hands at my back, shoving me rapidly forward and out of the way of the oncoming car. It was like I had been lifted on the crest of a wave as I was taken off my feet and rushed forward in mid-air. To the onlooker, it might have appeared that I had jumped the last few feet, but I had zero control over my body at the time.

As the car whizzed by me, it so narrowly missed me that I heard a swish and felt it gently swipe the back of my padded body warmer. The driver was going so fast that there was no time to get a number plate, either. By the time I turned back around, the car was disappearing around a bend. I half-wondered if the driver would have stopped even if they had hit me. I stood on the footpath, panting, feeling badly winded. The whole thing happened in mere seconds. It was terrifying, but, miraculously, I was alive and completely unscathed.

When I regained my composure, as I turned to continue on my way to the park, a tiny white feather floated diagonally down in front of my face. *Thank you, Angels*, I said silently in my mind.

One word entered my head in response: *Michael.*

Surviving a Bus Crash – Archangels Michael and Raphael

In February 2010, I was late for work as I had an early-morning doctor's appointment. I jumped on the first bus towards London Bridge station. From there, I would then need to get the train to my office, where I then worked as the editor of *Prediction* magazine.

I headed upstairs on the no. 141 double-decker bus and noticed that it was fairly empty. I remember that I was glad of the opportunity to get a seat and relax for the journey.

As I sat down and the bus pulled away from my bus stop, however, I was suddenly overcome with a strange and unexplainable feeling of dread. It set me immediately on edge. I had the overwhelming sense that something bad was about to happen, but I did not know what it could be. I immediately called upon Archangel Michael and his legions of light to surround the bus and protect everyone on board. This seemed to help shift that feeling, and I was able to relax for most of the remainder of the journey. I even had two seats to myself, so was very pleased at not having to travel during the usually busy rush-hour period.

It was a typical wet day in London, and as we approached London Bridge, about to turn right at the big intersection by Monument station, I was turning sideways in my seat, absent-mindedly rummaging through my bag for my phone. As we turned the wide corner onto the bridge at around 10.15 a.m., the driver suddenly lost control of the bus, and I was slammed sideways into the seat in front of me. My knees—especially the left one—smashed into the hard back of the seat, and my neck was bent sideways over the horizontal hand railings on top of the seat.

I was pinned in that position by the force of gravity as the bus careered sideways across the wet intersection and mounted the pavement on King William Street. I heard a loud high-pitched scream from the female bus driver as a woman crossing the street just managed to throw herself out of the path of the oncoming juggernaut. We slammed violently into the railings at Monument station, and the out-of-control bus finally came juddering to a stop, hovering precariously over the stairwell into the underground.

As soon as we were stationary, I panicked that I might have badly injured my neck, but although I was in pain, I was able to move and made my way very carefully down the stairs. The driver had opened the doors, but it was a sheer drop into the stairwell and the other passengers and I realized we were trapped.

Again, I called on the Angels to help, and suddenly, seemingly from out of nowhere, some men who were working on the roadworks nearby appeared on the scene. They acted quickly and managed to pull us through the emergency exit. I barely remember how I got off the bus or into the ambulance, but the next thing I knew I was in hospital being checked over by a doctor.

Miraculously, there were only 11 people taken to hospital, and we all had only minor injuries, such as whiplash and bruising. Thanks to the intervention of Archangel Michael and the Angels, no one was seriously hurt.

Shortly after the accident, I went to have some physiotherapy on my knees to help with the slight bruising and swelling I had sustained in the crash. As I was lying on the therapy table, I asked Archangel Raphael to send me healing and was astonished when I looked down at my knees only to see them surrounded by a physical halo of emerald-green light, the colour of Raphael's healing ray.

The Angelic Policeman – Archangel Michael

In the summer of 2008, I went on a night out with a close female friend who was visiting from Australia. We went to a music gig in Hoxton, but it finished quite late, and we wanted to continue our night out and go dancing. We decided we would head to a late-night club in Kings Cross and waited in the taxi queue for a cab.

This was in the days before Uber, so our options were to get a black cab (which were scarce) or a mini cab. As it was common in those days for most mini cab companies to use unmarked private vehicles, there was no way of knowing if a taxi was licensed or just a random person in their own car trying to make some extra money. In any case, I was with my friend, so we weren't too concerned about the issue of safety as we jumped in the first cab that pulled up to collect us.

On our way to the club, we asked the driver to pull into a petrol station near Old Street station, so we could use the cashpoint. He said it was no trouble and pulled into the left side of the driveway in front of the cashpoint at the Shell garage.

I was the first to jump out, while my friend waited in the car. It seemed the right thing to do, for one of us to remain in the vehicle while the other made their withdrawal, so the cabbie wouldn't worry we might do a runner. In the glare of the headlights, I tottered over to the ATM in my brand new red suede high-heeled shoes and little black dress.

Once I had my money, I went to the right side of the car and got into the passenger seat, while my friend proceeded to make her way to the cash machine. I was sitting sideways inside the car, with the door open and my feet on the pavement, when the driver suddenly shouted at me: "Shut the door!" His voice sounded urgent, but I couldn't figure out why he was so concerned about me leaving my door open. The forecourt was quite wide, and there was plenty of space for other cars to pull up to the petrol pumps to our right.

To try to calm him down, I pulled the door in a little closer, but didn't close it fully, leaving one of my legs still outside the car.

"Shut your door, shut your door!" He yelled again, this time more urgent. I went to shut the door in response to his complaints, but something instinctively made me stop.

"Why?" I asked, for some reason, deciding to challenge his request.

"I'm blocking the drive. I need to move the car. Shut the door. Shut the door!" he repeated with more urgency, and this time, I noted, a slightly menacing tone to his voice.

Something was up. My friend was still concentrating intently on the cashpoint (what was taking her so long?). At that point, I looked up to see the driver's face reflected in the rearview mirror. The look in his eyes sent a feeling of cold dread right through me. I don't know how I knew it, but I knew with every fibre of my being that as soon as I shut that door, he intended to drive off with me inside the car and leave my friend behind.

I was in danger, and I knew it. Time slowed to a standstill. A million thoughts raced through my mind. Do I jump from the car? Do I call out to my friend? Instead, I was frozen to the spot. My heart leapt into my throat, and somewhere in the back of my mind came a distant reminder to ask for protection from Archangel Michael.

It wasn't a conscious thought exactly. More like another very subtle voice was coming into my mind and telling me to have the thought. I didn't even have time to ask. The moment I had the intention to ask him, Michael was there. I felt an immediate loving presence envelope me and then, out of nowhere, a loud male voice said: "Step out of the car, please, sir."

I turned to see that a policeman had appeared—more like materialized—right beside me and was peering into the car. As I registered him, I noticed a large police van had stealthily pulled up directly behind us. The policeman had popped his head around the corner at the exact moment I had had the intention to have the thought to call for help from Archangel Michael.

I shudder to this day to think what that cab driver's intentions might have been. He was a very large man, and I would not have stood a chance against him. I am still utterly flabbergasted by the speed at which my angelic support showed up—literally in the nick of time.

As nothing had actually happened, the police couldn't charge the driver with anything, but they did fine him for driving an illegal taxi and sent him on his way.

They then offered us a lift home in the police van and, to add even more synchronicity, it turned out the policeman who had come to my rescue was originally from my home country of Australia.

Spread Your Wings – Archangel Ariel

In 2006, I was on holiday in Turkey with an old friend I grew up with in Australia, and we decided to try out parasailing. Being in a country with no safety laws didn't faze us as we were in that carefree, devil-may-care, holiday mode and, as far as we were concerned, we were invincible.

We soon realized our folly. To get to the top of the mountain in Oludeniz, where our parasails, and therefore, our bodies, would be launched into mid-air, we had to travel in an open-backed truck with no seat belts. This truck was fishtailing and swerving dangerously around hairpin bends on a dirt road along the sheer clifftops strewn with huge rocks.

Did I mention that there were also no roadside barriers and the driver was a total maniac? And all this, while holding our parachutes!

I thought we were going to die, so I started praying to the Angels to protect us, and I specifically felt the urge to pray to an Archangel named Ariel, who is meant to bring you courage. I looked up, and on the back window of the driver's cab was a bumper sticker with a pair of shiny outstretched wings, with the slogan "Spread your wings!" I instantly knew we would be safe, but the following events were a big test of my faith.

Suddenly, the spare tyre, which was stored on the roof above the driver's cab, came loose when the bar holding it in place swung open and almost hit me in the head. The tyre started to fly out of its place towards me. If it had hit me, I would have been propelled out of the truck and over the side of the cliff edge to certain doom. But my friend was as quick as lightning. In the split second before the tyre actually left its cage, he leapt to his feet and with all his might pushed the tyre back into place. For the remaining 20 minutes of the journey up the mountain, he stood there, holding the tyre in place with one hand and clinging desperately to the railing with the other, trying to balance and hold on as the truck swerved wildly all over the road. And, all the while, he still managed to keep hold of his parachute, which was wrapped by one strap around his left foot.

By the time we arrived at the top, my legs had turned to jelly and I went immediately to the nearby toilet block to throw up. But any ideas I had of chickening out of the jump were put to the back of my mind. I truly believed, by this stage, that jumping willingly off a cliff would be a doddle compared to getting back into that hazardous truck.

There was nothing for it. I put my faith in the Angels and allowed myself to be strapped into the chute. Strapped in behind me was the pilot of my tandem parasail, who spoke not a word of English.

As the sail started to fill with air, dragging us backwards, another man came up to give me just one sentence of instructions: "Do not sit down! When I say run, you run!"

And then he shouted: "Run!"

I felt like I was running to my death. My heart leapt into my throat and my legs were moving, but I was so weak from being sick and the parasail was so full of air that I was immediately swept backwards off my feet and into a sitting position in the harness. The other man ran up to me, dragged me back up to my feet and, pointing at the edge of the cliff, shouted again: "Run!"

I was absolutely freaking out, but I ran with all my might, thinking I was just going to plop over the edge. But, to my surprise, the parasail was swept into the air and, as it caught the wind, I was lifted so gently off my feet I felt as though I were taking flight.

As soon as we were airborne, my pilot grunted: "Sit down now." I sat back in my harness and finally began to relax as we soared over the breathtaking turquoise ocean beside Oludeniz Beach. It was like touching heaven. I felt so safe and calm that the terror of the moments before now seemed hilarious, and I began to laugh. I felt euphoric. The adrenalin coursing through my veins must have been on overload.

When we swooped down over the beach to land, three men ran out to grab us, and the landing was almost as smooth as the takeoff. I wanted to kiss the ground.

Thank God and the Angels, I am alive, I cried out in my head. What a rush!

Our parasail was quickly bundled away, and I was unstrapped from my harness, as we moved to the side of the landing area to watch my friend and his pilot come in to land. The usually cool-as-a-cucumber guy looked overwrought. As he stepped from his harness, I noticed how badly he was shaking, and he had tears in his eyes.

"Are you okay?" I asked. I was sure he would have really enjoyed his sail—he was way more brave than me and seemed much more together after the previous horror of the truck ride from hell.

"No, Al, I am not okay. We could've been killed!"

He pulled me away from the men to tell me that his parachute had not been done up properly. One of the carabiners connecting his harness to the parachute was missed when they strapped him in, and it had been left undone. It wasn't until they were in mid-air that Steve noticed his life was literally hanging by a thread. If the strap of his chute, which was merely hooked over the open carabiner, had come loose, one side of his chute would've slipped out, dragging the whole parasail sideways, and they would have gone hurtling to the ground, and surely death.

I was speechless. This was the second time today that one of us had cheated death. There was no more doubt in my mind that I was receiving help outside of the realms of humanity. My Angels had heeded my call.

The week after we arrived home, I decided to walk to work one morning and popped into a little spiritual shop near Smithfield Market on my way. I had set off early, as I had noticed the shop the week before we left for our trip, and I wanted to check it out.

I wandered in and, straight away, I spied a new pack of Angel oracle cards by Doreen Virtue called *Archangel Oracle Cards*. I bought the pack and excitedly unwrapped them that night when I got home. Upon opening the pack of cards and starting to shuffle them, one card came flying out of the pack and all but hit me on the forehead.

The words written on that card made my heart almost stop. Right there in black and white were the words "Archangel Ariel", with the message "Spread Your Wings!"

How to Ask the Angels for Help and Protection

Asking for help from the angelic kingdom is the easiest thing in the world. Whether silently or aloud, just say your request, and trust that any assistance you need will arrive at the right moment.

CHAPTER 11

Getting to Know the Angel and Devil Within

We attract and reflect what is within us. If you are attracting angelic energies, that is the frequency you are giving off. If you are attracting dark energies, you must look to your own darkness, your own shadow and lower self.

This is brave work for it means facing the parts of yourself you are ashamed of and would rather hide or deny. Sometimes, though, the only way back to light is through your own darkness.

We are in a time when humanity is being forced to face the darkness in our collective subconscious. For years, the Angels and my guides spoke to me about a "great upsurge" coming to the planet; they also referred to it as a "great wave of change". There is so much that we do not know, and we are conditioned to see the unknown as frightening. But what if we could flip our perspective and see the unknown as miraculous and exciting?

We are on a great adventure, and we are learning more about our true nature as we go. As more light is shed on the hidden and unseen parts of ourselves, we must be willing to love, forgive, and embrace all those parts to become whole.

False Light and Discernment

Discernment is key when learning to channel or connect with Angels and guides in the spiritual dimensions. As well as being a place inhabited by beautiful loving beings, the astral plane is a playground for lower-frequency energies, and many tricksters may be afoot.

It is wise to know yourself well when embarking on any form of inner work, including healing, channelling, spiritual development, and other practices involving awakening your psychic gifts. By that, I don't mean to instil fear in you, but to help you get comfortable with the truth of your own dual nature.

It is worth understanding that any so-called negative experiences, either in our external reality or coming from a spiritual source, are an opportunity for deeper self-enquiry and growth. Sometimes these experiences can feel terrifying at their most extreme or, at the very least, quite challenging, especially if you encounter something as frightening as a "psychic attack". Psychic attack occurs when negative energies are being sent to you from another person or group of people. These lower energies are usually thought forms, but in some extreme cases they can include hexes, curses, other forms of black magic, and even entities.

While experiences such as a psychic attack can feel incredibly uncomfortable, they are always an opportunity to level up and usually lead to a period of accelerated spiritual growth.

The Archangels are always on hand to offer protection and guidance, should you happen upon any such experience, but I am including a little more information here in the hopes that it may help you better understand and navigate the extreme duality that can be encountered within the astral dimensions.

False Light Teachers and Beings Masquerading as Angels

Contrary to some of the new age information out there, the spiritual world is not all light. Energy inhabits a myriad of spectrums, and the multiverse, along with our own consciousness, inhabits every one of those vast and intricate dimensions.

The point of discovering, acknowledging, and working with our inner darkness is not to let it take over, but neither is it healthy to suppress it or avoid it. We need to know what is under the surface of our awareness in order to integrate it and bring it back into loving balance and wholeness.

When any person, especially a spiritual teacher or someone on an awakened path, avoids acknowledging the parts of themselves that make them uncomfortable, those parts can often subconsciously run the show. The ego is very clever and can create all sorts of programmes to help us avoid looking at our unhealed aspects, such as our pain, shame, and hurts. What we aren't looking at within ourselves can then become a hidden playground for other forces to piggyback on.

False light entities are trickster spirits that are very good at feeding the ego and making a person feel special in order to get them to play out and live their own agendas. Know that no true Angel or loving guide will ever try to dominate you, take you over, tell you what to do, or take away your rights or choices. If you have any doubt whatsoever as to the integrity of the being you are communicating with, you are well within your rights to send it away, put up protection, clear your energy field, close down, and shield yourself. Always remember: You are divine, and you are in charge.

An example of this might be a spiritual teacher who claims to be all love and light and wants to help others, but behind the scenes what they are really craving is the love and attention they perhaps didn't receive as a child.

Many healers become healers so that they can heal themselves, and this is indeed a valid part of the path; however, when a healer is avoiding healing themselves, they can project their hurts and grievances onto their students and clients, and this makes for very tricky terrain.

As the saying goes, "Hurt people hurt people." So even if we aren't aware that our suppressed emotions are creating unhealthy behaviours in ourselves, we may be unconsciously harming another and ourselves at the same time. It is up to each of us to take full responsibility for our own energy and for keeping our energy fields as clean and balanced as possible. We must ensure we help, heal, and take care of ourselves and our own needs first to ensure we are optimal when working with others.

Psychic Attack – Protection and Self-Defence

I felt it was important to include this section in the book. Firstly, because I know from personal experience that psychic attack is real, and when you are under this kind of attack it can be extremely frightening, not to mention sometimes even dangerous if left unchecked. And, secondly, as I have mentioned, there is a lot of shadow rising on the planet, and it is useful to know how to keep yourself safe in a time of so much chaos with so many different energies flying about.

In 2016, I found myself under severe psychic attack from several people at different times. Some of the attack was being sent consciously, and some was being sent unconsciously. It is helpful to know the difference between an unconscious and a conscious psychic attack so that you can get to the bottom of why it is being sent and, hopefully, put a stop to it permanently.

As always, the key to dealing with this kind of energy is to stay in the vibration of love and joy as much as possible. Try to stay out of fear, and don't take anything personally. If you remain as matter of fact as you can, you will keep your head, even when the most bizarre or frightening experiences are occurring around you.

Trust that your higher self will never let you go through anything that isn't ultimately for your highest good. If you are experiencing psychic attack, you are most likely undergoing a rapid expansion of consciousness and an upsurge of old karma. Know that everything being shown to you is a reflection of something that needs resolving and transmuting within you, and greater levels of self-love and self-care will be necessary as you move through your personal shadow karma.

Take anything like this as an acknowledgement that you are preparing to move to another level in your lightwork. Coming up against any kind of darkness is often a big test of faith and a huge test of will. Stay true to love and to your purpose, and know that you are divine and that there is absolutely nothing you cannot handle. You have access to all the infinite wisdom of the multiverse, which is held in an etheric library of all the information of all time and existence, known as the Akasha.

Sometimes, when you are experiencing an attack of this kind, your guides may step back to allow you to call on your own inner strength and resolve to move through it. It is often like an initiation. As with the experience of a Dark Night of The Soul, you may feel as though the light has abandoned you. Do not give in to that feeling. Continue to call on the light of your soul, and trust that your guides will step in and intervene, if necessary.[35]

It is important to note that we never send back negative energy. The only way to resolve anything of a lower vibration is through love. No matter how severe the attack or how much fear and anger it evokes within you, always hold forgiveness in your heart, and surround yourself and the other person with divine light. If you must send anything, or if you are worried that you might slip up and project a negative thought their way, ask your higher self to transform any lower energies coming towards you or from you back into love. Remember, at a soul level, you will have signed up for this experience. Trust that what you are going through is a necessary part of your journey for you to resolve and heal your own inner darkness and reveal more of your true self, which is a pure state of unconditional love. From your higher self's perspective, there is no dark and light; there is only love. When you learn to transcend the idea of "good" and "bad", "right and wrong", and see the blessing in every experience, person, and situation in your life, then you become aligned with your divinity, and that is what we call en-"light"-enment.

Subconscious or Unconscious Psychic Attack

An unconscious psychic attack happens when the person sending the negative energy doesn't realize they are sending it. They may be having feelings towards you, such as jealousy or anger, which they are not addressing. When repressed emotions are left unchecked, they can fester and end up being expressed in an unhealthy way.

When these emotions are felt in response to another person and not acknowledged, expressed, and resolved, they can end up being sent into the other person's energy field. Sending negative thoughts to someone else is a little bit like throwing poison darts at them. This is what can happen when a person does not accept and integrate their own shadow side.

Conscious Psychic Attack

A conscious psychic attack is when a person knows they are sending you negative energy, because they have deliberately set out to do so. Usually, these kinds of attacks are played out by people who are deliberately on a path of darkness or working with black magic (yes, this still happens). If you cross the path of anyone sending you this kind of attack, you may need to seek the help of a trained professional or trusted healer who can help you get to the bottom of why the attack has occurred and help you clear it.

How Can You Tell If You Are under Psychic Attack?

The symptoms of psychic attack can vary widely, depending on the level of intensity of the attack. Usually, you will feel very low in mood and energy, and you may notice little things starting to go wrong. You might realize you are misplacing items or things around you are breaking. If two or more little mishaps occur in a row, then you are most likely experiencing some kind of negative interference from a source outside yourself.

Personally, I have experienced some pretty extreme attacks, where symptoms have ranged from dizziness and severe nausea to my hair falling out. Once, I discovered I was under psychic attack when I went out for a jog and had a fall while running. I knew it was an attack, as I had literally felt someone push me over, but there was nobody physically anywhere near me. I knew I had been pushed to the ground by an unseen entity.

A psychic attack can present itself in many different ways. I have witnessed remote viewing and tracking, where I have seen the person's face appear as an apparition floating above me, as though they are watching me. I have even been pulled out of my body in my sleep and taken to other dimensions where not very pleasant beings have been awaiting me. If you are not especially clairvoyant, you may not have any visions, but your feelings will always tell you the truth. You may just experience a strange feeling that you are being watched.

It is also possible for a person to siphon or drain your energy or power, and even to project their astral body into your space so that their energetic self is effectively harassing or "haunting" you. This can certainly happen without their knowledge, if they have had other lifetimes where they were trained in magic; they don't necessarily need to know how to do it consciously in this life. Subconscious astral projection usually happens at night, when they would be asleep. It's a bit like astral sleepwalking.

Sometimes, the unresolved karma triggered may reveal other lifetimes where black magic was employed, and so the psychic attack may reveal an old curse, spell, or hex that needs clearing and resolving.

In severe cases of psychic attack, the level of negativity being sent can conjure entities in the form of trapped souls or lower astral spirits. Again, for particularly severe cases, you may need to seek the help of a professional to assist you in resolving the issue.

Symptoms of Psychic Attack

There are various symptoms of psychic attack and they may vary in intensity:

◊ Exhaustion

◊ Excessive worry and self-doubt

◊ A run of bad luck or a series of things not going your way, i.e., disruptions to transport, computers, plans going awry, and so forth

◊ Unexplained pains in the body

◊ Bad dreams, night terrors, or sleep paralysis

◊ Low mood – feeling angry, sad, overwhelmed, insecure, frightened, and so on

◊ Helpless or, in some cases, even suicidal thoughts

◊ Feeling as though you are being watched

◊ Questioning your sanity

◊ Physical weakness

◊ Skin issues or hair loss

◊   Clumsiness, falling over

◊   Ongoing mishaps or accidents

◊   Feeling as though you are in a trance

◊   Feeling ungrounded, dizzy

◊   Constant unexplained thoughts or dreams about another person

◊   Feeling like you can't control your thoughts

◊   Heaviness in the body

◊   Dramatic temperature changes.

What Causes a Psychic Attack?

The first time I ever realized I was experiencing psychic attack was on a healing retreat a number of years ago. Every time I tried to ask the teacher a question or engage, I would experience a sharp stabbing pain in my shoulder and, as the days went on, I began to feel very low and extremely tearful and vulnerable. As it was an event being run by a fellow healer, I wasn't at all expecting anything untoward and initially thought all my "stuff" was just coming up to be looked at, as is often the case when healing work is involved.

However, I soon started to notice that the usually pleasant teacher was going out of her way to avoid me, and I even caught her rolling her eyes during more than one of our conversations. Finally, when none of the healing was helping and I continued to feel more and more depressed, I called a good friend of mine, who is also a therapist, for her insight. She dowsed on it with her pendulum and confirmed that I was under psychic attack from the teacher, and what had provoked it was good old-fashioned jealousy.

This was a classic case of an unconscious psychic attack, where the teacher clearly believed that in order to be a good healer she had to be all "love and light". On the surface, she came across as sweet as pie, but she had been unwilling to look at her own shadow, so underneath, she was seething with repressed emotions. As she didn't want to take ownership of those lower emotions, she was looking for someone else to blame for them. Unfortunately for me, I happened to somehow trigger her, and so I became the target.

As a healer, I believe this can be very dangerous, especially if you are assisting in other people's healing journeys. One of my favourite phrases is "Healer heal thyself." It is very important to keep a clean energy field when engaging in any healing or spiritual work; this is both for your own benefit, as well as others. After all, if you are not willing to look at your own garbage, how can you clean it up?

The Role of Karma in Psychic Attack

It is my firm belief that there is always a blessing in every situation. There is always a lesson that we, as individual souls, have signed up to learn. Any interaction with another person in your life rarely comes without some kind of karma attached to it.

Karma, however, is not punishment. It is simply the universal law of cause and effect. As with all things in this universe, there has to be a balance. When something goes wrong in your life, or if someone is mistreating you, it is the universe's way of holding up a mirror so that you can see the kind of vibes you are sending out into the world. We are like magnets. We only attract what we are putting out; whether we are putting it out consciously or unconsciously, there is always a consequence to every thought, word, and action.

The blessing in the previously mentioned situation for me was that it made me sit down and take a really good, hard look at my own shadow. As I delved into my "dark" side to heal the karma between that teacher and myself, I uncovered a past life during the Inquisition where I had been the inquisitor who sentenced her to be burnt at the stake for heresy.

That psychic attack opened a very big door, which propelled me into a long journey of walking through my own personal underworld to heal my shadow. I was, of course, doing shadow work before that point, but now I was determined to face my own personal demons, once and for all. Little did I know that I was heading straight into the thick of my own wilderness. That journey doesn't really end, but you can learn to navigate it and find your balance within this experience of duality.

That first incident was the beginning of a sequence of psychic attacks that followed in quick succession. A bit like a baptism of fire, each one was slightly worse than the last. These energy attacks usually came out of the blue, and from spiritual people I trusted. But the positive outcome of each of these brushes with my karma is that they forced me to go within and explore the depths of my own subconscious to heal any repressed emotions, thoughts, or feelings I might have been harbouring. It ended up being a thorough spiritual deep-clean.

As a result, past-life memories began to surface like ordinary everyday memory. In some of these lifetimes I was the victim, and in some I was the offender. It can be quite confronting to be faced with your own darkness, or to think you may have wronged somebody in some way, especially when you are firmly on the path of light.

We are all mirrors of each other and, in my experience, no one is ever just the victim or the perpetrator. The soul is whole, and in that wholeness we all have light and shadow. The farther you go into the light, the more shadow you will reveal.

How to Deal with Psychic Attack

The first thing to do if you realize you are under psychic attack is to immediately cease all spiritual work and close down your energy fields. Ground and shield yourself, and be in the 3D as much as you can.

◊ **Close down and shield your energy fields.** For instructions on how to close down, ground, and shield your energy fields, see the Channelling Checklist in chapter 7.

◊ **Return to joy.** Joy and laughter are the best remedy for anything. Watch a comedy, have a good belly laugh with friends, and raise your vibration as much as you can. Be determined not to be dragged into negative thoughts about yourself or get caught in a downward spiral of self-doubt.

◊ **Ascertain where the attack is coming from.** Ask yourself who would have a motive to send you negative thought forms? The giveaway is usually if you have had a recent run-in or argument with someone, but quite often psychic attack can come out of the blue from a person you think you have a good relationship with. If you are sensitive, you might notice that you are thinking about a certain person more than usual, or they just pop into your head. Or your gut feeling just tells you something is off in your relationship with someone, even if they are insisting everything's fine and not being transparent about their true feelings. It is also a good idea to ascertain whether the attack is coming from more than one person. You can use a pendulum to dowse for confirmation to check if the person you suspect is indeed the culprit. See the chapter on Dowsing and Kinesiology to learn how to get confirmation from your higher self on any question.

◊ **Resolve your karma, and clear to the point of origin.** You may need to seek the help of a professional healer to help you ascertain where the attack is coming from. Someone who is trained in this kind of clearing can help you look at and resolve whatever karma has attracted it in the first place.

Psychic Protection Tips

◊   Know you are divine and your power comes from you. Nothing is separate from you.

◊   Offer self-forgiveness and compassion to yourself before anyone else.

◊   Know thyself! Know as much about your life and past lives and clear as much karma as you can.

◊   Get comfortable with all your flaws. When you love your shadow, you are less vulnerable to attack.

◊   Stay healthy and strong physically and mentally. Begin by feeling safe from the inside, as happiness and confidence are key.

◊   Your joy is what makes you invincible to lower forces and energies, as it raises your vibration above the levels of energy and consciousness they can reach.

◊   Forgiveness is a powerful force. Be willing to forgive yourself and others for all their transgressions, and be open to whatever lesson is being revealed to you in the other person.

When Psychic Attack Is a Blessing

As with everything in our world, there are two sides to every coin, and when looking back on any experience of psychic attack, it is well worth acknowledging any blessings that arose as a result and taking full responsibility for your part in the experience.

More than a few times early on in my journey, I found myself being moved away from certain teachers and healers, merely because I had outgrown them and was meant to move forward on my path. An experience of the symptoms of psychic attack arose simply because I was not ready to let go of my comfort zone, so the universe had to create a scenario that would force me to move on.

CHAPTER 12

Archangelic Protection Rituals and Prayers

Prayer for Clearing and Protection

In preparation for this prayer, ground yourself fully and open, cleanse and protect your space in accordance with the Channelling Checklist. Ensure you feel safe, centred, and calm before reciting the following aloud. When you first begin working with this prayer, I recommend saying it each day for 33 days as a powerful clearing, protection, and energetic upgrade, but you can say it whenever you feel you need an extra boost of protection.

I [insert your name], lovingly command the Archangels, my angelic divine self/higher self/celestial soul/sovereign being, and primary guide:

To surround me and shield me with an invincible diamond forcefield of pure divine white light. And to infuse this dazzling white light with the indigo-blue light of the will of the divine and protective energies of Archangel Michael, the Angelic Kingdom, the Legions of Light, the Higher Galactic Councils of Light, the Ascended Masters, The Elohim, and any other guides or Angels that need to be present for my highest good.

To cleanse, clear, and delete from me all foreign, unwelcome, unwanted, negative, and imbalanced thought forms, emotions, soul fragments, projections and transference, hooks, cords, psychic attacks, curses, spells, hexes, dark seed thought forms, black magic of any kind, rituals, ceremonies, offerings, ideas and energies that are not in my highest and best interest or in the interest of the divine. And to send them into the pure light of the divine, to be transmuted back into love and divine light and returned as love to where they originated.

To release any entities, spirit attachments, waywards, fallens, disincarnate spirits, lost or trapped souls, demons, dark forces, elementals, extraterrestrials, aliens, false light beings, intergalactic entities, artificial intelligence, and any other low-frequency beings and send them to the highest point of their own divine evolution or into the pure source light of the divine to be immediately transmuted back into love and divine light.

To remove, deactivate, and transmute all implants, chips, grids, control grids, pins, devices, spyware, frequencies, false light matrix and projections, portals, vortexes, wormholes, augmented realities, dead light zones, transmitters, coils, crystals, tracking devices, sublimininal programming, brainwashing, imprinting, memory screening or deleting, codes, contraptions, blocks, locks, bindings, etheric interference, internal or external interference of any kind. To be immediately transmuted back into love and divine light.

To cancel, clear, delete, revoke, and complete any and all beliefs, thoughts, feelings, contracts, oaths, vows, promises, decrees, confessions, treaties, sentences, agreements, and so forth that I have made in any time frame, dimension, reality, body or personality with any being, entity, belief system, religion, organization, school, church, teacher, healer, guide, spirit, guru, master, priest, parent, guardian, or leader, and so on, that is or was not aligned with pure divine love, truth and integrity, or acting in my highest and best interests.

To cancel, clear, heal, revoke, destroy, and delete all instances where I may have misused my power and my healing and psychic abilities, and I command that my gifts and abilities now be used only for the highest good of myself, the divine, and all who come into contact with me.

To deactivate and eliminate all blocks to me accessing and using my true multidimensional, divine consciousness, my own innate psychic and healing abilities, and to acknowledge my true birthright as a divine human being.

To open, cleanse, and balance all of my chakras and meridians, and align my energy with God, the Angels, and the consciousness of the planetary and cosmic spiritual hierarchy on all levels.

To activate my DNA and original divine blueprint to the highest level possible for my highest good at this present time in my earthly, human reality.

To reinstate and activate my master soul aspect at the highest level possible for my highest good at this present time in my earthly, human reality.

To also do all of the above for all levels of my being, in all dimensions, realities, and for my home, garden, car, modes of transport, place/s of business, places of recreation, and every place that I frequent in future as an automatic clearing and protection as I go about my day-to-day activities.

And only with the permission of their higher self, and where necessary for their highest good, to perform all of the above cleansings and protections for my family, friends, and loved ones and anyone else whose soul requires it for their highest good.

To remove, cancel, clear, delete, revoke, and transmute anything else I haven't mentioned, but which my higher self knows needs to leave this space at this time for my highest and best good.

To invoke anything of the highest and purest divine love and light vibration that I may not have mentioned, but that my higher self deems necessary to be in this space at this time for my highest and best good.

When you have completed your prayer, close down and seal your space in accordance with the "Shrink, Sink, and Shield" practice in the Channelling Checklist.

Purification with the Angels of Water

Here in the UK, where I currently live, we get a lot of rain, which is perfect for cleansing and renewal. Rain itself can be very healing, not just because everything on our planet needs water to survive but because it also fills the atmosphere with positive ions, which oxygenate the air around us, helping us to breathe better while also reducing pollution.

I like to see the rain as an energetic doorway or gateway between the dark of winter and the light-filled days of summer; as being like walking under a waterfall of pure light that washes away any stagnant energies and leaves you feeling refreshed and renewed, ready to allow your new projects to literally "spring" to life. Crossing or bathing in clean water is also symbolic of energetic cleansing and is also known to transmute lower-vibration energies.

You can do the following exercise outdoors in the rain, inside in the bath, or swimming in a pool, river, stream, or even the sea, if you so choose. However you connect to the spirit or spirits of the water is perfect.

Personal Cleansing Ritual

Before you begin, sit somewhere quietly, and call to mind all of the things you want to release from your life, whether it be a job, a relationship, or a situation; it can even be something to release on behalf of the whole planet, such as pollution or violence. Whatever it is, just call it to mind now, and hold it in your consciousness, ready to release. When you are ready, immerse yourself in a warm bath, or go outside in the rain, ready to cleanse away all of these issues you would like to resolve.

Invoking the Angels of Water

Now close your eyes and call upon the Angels and spirits of the water. I like to connect with Archangel Ariel, the nature Angel; Archangel Gabriel, who governs the cardinal direction of the West and water; Archangel Phuel and Tahariel, the Angels of purification; and Archangel Asariel, the Angel of the sea. You may also like to invite in the energy and support of the dolphins, whales, mermaids, and undines. Just breathe deeply, and allow these energies to surround you now. Make sure you send them a pulse of gratitude for assisting you in creating your own personal Angel showers to heal yourself and the entire planet.

Ready to Release

Imagine you are standing underneath a beautiful waterfall of brilliant white light. As the light cascades around you, it washes away any negative energy or energy that doesn't belong to you. Imagine you are now offering all of the issues you first called to mind to this pure white light, to be dissolved and transmuted back into pure love. Visualize a whirlpool of light in front of you now and imagine you are being drawn into this whirlpool. As the light and the energy of the water holds you, spinning you around and around, imagine you are being carried down through a magical tunnel, almost like a water slide or ride. This tunnel is carrying you to the core of Mother Earth and, as you reach her centre, you see a brilliant diamond. This diamond is emanating a beautiful silvery-blue light, the light of the divine feminine. This light is warm and comforting, and it now floods upwards through your whole body. As it does so, you feel yourself now being propelled upwards, back up through the tunnel of pure white light.

Cleansing for the Earth

You emerge from the tunnel above a vast ocean and a huge spout of white and silvery-blue light emerges with you, like the water spout of a gigantic whale. Light is radiating from you and pouring over all the oceans of the world, blessing all the waterways, seas, rivers, and streams, even the puddles, and being collected in the rains to be transported to wherever the planet needs this healing light the most.

Gently bring yourself back to the here and now in your own bathtub, garden, or wherever you started this meditation. Become aware again of your surroundings and your physical body.

As you open your eyes and release the bath or shower water, or dry off from your outdoor shower, imagine that the water going down the plughole or into the earth is also sending this healing and cleansing light into the earth as a gift to be distributed to wherever it's needed. Thank all of the energies involved. Visualize a golden dome of protection around you, and ground yourself in your usual way.

The Pillar of Light and Inner Sun Process

Clear and Shield Your Energy

Find a safe and calm space where you will not be disturbed.

◊ Come into a space of harmony, neutrality, and unconditional love, and close your eyes.

◊ Visualize your conscious awareness as a sphere of white light, and bring it into your body. Then anchor it into your centre, behind your navel.

◊ Call up diamond-white light from the core of Mother Earth, and connect it to your centre. Then allow it to rise and activate and open your heart.

◊ Call down golden-white light from the divine through the sun and into your heart. Then bring it into your centre and anchor it there.

◊ Imagine, see, intend, or feel your consciousness sphere as though it is an inner sun. Let it blaze with divine fire, and expand it out through your energy field to clear and transmute, or lower, any negative, limiting, or unwelcome energies.

◊ Expand it out as far as you wish around you, and set your safe perimeter. Seal it with protective golden light.

◊ Centre, and ground yourself. Open your eyes.

Create Safe Sanctuary
with the Pearlescent Cocoon

This process takes the Inner Sun to another level, adding in softness and serenity. Find a safe and calm space where you will not be disturbed. The best time to do this practice is first thing in the morning, before getting out of bed, or last thing at night, after getting into bed and before going to sleep. You may fall asleep while doing the practice, and that is okay. If you do the practice in the morning, perhaps try doing it sitting up in bed, or set a backup alarm in case you fall back to sleep.

You may wish to voice-record this meditation, and play it back to yourself, or you may wish to read through the whole thing first and do the steps from memory.

◊ Close your eyes, and centre your awareness in your heart.

◊ Breathe in, and imagine there is a small spark of pearlescent-white light appearing in the centre of your chest.

◊ Breathe out, and imagine that you are releasing all your stress and tension and any lower emotions that may be surfacing.

◊ Breathe in, and imagine you are drawing light in the form of pure divine love into the spark of light at the centre of your chest.

◊ The more you breathe in, the stronger and more powerful this spark of light becomes, until it holds all the power of the fiery sun.

◊ The spark of light also grows bigger. It becomes a sphere around your whole heart, like a blazing, white, inner sun.

◊ You feel more and more relaxed with every breath in, and you release more and more tension with every breath out.

◊ The sphere of light continues to expand to fill your whole energy field, so you are inside a large pearl of radiating, white, iridescent light. This light has formed a loving shield, or cocoon, around you.

◊ Imagine that this cocoon is now filling with hundreds of white feathers made of pure angelic light.

◊ As your sphere fills with these soft feathers, you feel yourself softening and relaxing deeper into safety and trust.

◊ The feathers now transform into hundreds and hundreds of loving Angels surrounding you and embracing you in their white wings of love.

◊ You feel so safe, warm, and protected. Imagine what it would feel like to feel this safe, warm, and cocooned everywhere you go.

◊ Carry this feeling with you throughout your day, and keep an eye out for any white feathers that may cross your path, as this is a sign of confirmation from your Angels that they are indeed with you.

◊ Imagine the outer circumference of your sphere is now turning a brilliant silver like a shiny silver coin.

◊ This silver light, like the lining of a storm cloud, seals your energy field so that only goodness and love may enter your personal sacred space.

◊ Keep an eye out for any shiny silver coins in your path as these "pennies from heaven" are another sign from your Angels that you are safe and secure.

◊ Trust the feelings of security and safety. The more you imagine you feel safe and practise this, the more the positive feelings will build day by day.

◊ When you are ready, imagine you can wrap your cocoon or sphere around your body like a silver cloak or security blanket.

◊ Centre yourself in your heart once more, take a deep breath, and open your eyes.

Try this process for 21 or even 33 days, and see what happens. You may even experience an angelic visitation or receive the name of your personal Guardian Angel during or after the experience.

Keep an open heart and mind, and let your imagination out to play, as that is what allows the Angels to connect with you more easily.

Stand in Your Power with the Tree of Light

Find a space where you will not be disturbed. You may wish to voice-record this meditation and play it back to yourself, or you may wish to read through the whole thing first and do the steps from memory.

Do not worry if you find it hard to visualize. Simply intending to follow each step is enough; your Angels will take care of the rest. The most important thing is to imagine you can feel all the positive feelings the Angels are gifting you with.

◊　Close your eyes, and centre your awareness in your heart.

◊　Breathe in, and imagine that there is a small spark of diamond-white light appearing in the centre of your chest.

◊　Breathe out, and imagine that you are releasing all your stress and tension and any lower emotions that may be surfacing.

◊　Breathe in, and imagine that you are drawing light in the form of pure divine love into the spark of light at the centre of your chest.

◊　The more you breathe in, the stronger and more powerful this spark of light becomes, until it holds all the power of the sun.

◊　The spark of light also grows bigger. It becomes a sphere around your whole heart, like a blazing, white, inner sun.

◊　You feel more and more relaxed with every breath in, and you release more and more tension with every breath out.

◊ The sphere of light continues to expand, until it fills your whole energy field.

◊ Imagine sealing the sphere in golden light, and then bring your attention to your stomach area. Find another spark of light within your navel—this time a brilliant spark of golden light.

◊ Imagine that from this spark of golden light, a shimmering and sparkling golden rope is forming and starting to stretch and grow upwards.

◊ The golden rope grows like a vine, spiralling and reaching from your centre all the way up through the mighty sun into the light of creation, where you plug into the source of All That Is.

◊ Feel the love of the divine cascading down through the golden rope and into your body through your crown and spine, filling your inner sun with the celestial solar power of the divine.

◊ Next, see or imagine the golden vine extending downwards from your core and into the earth. It spirals into the centre of the planet where, like the roots of a glorious tree, it winds around the crystal-diamond heart of Mother Gaia.

◊ Feel the love of Mother Earth travelling back up through your golden cord, illuminating your spine and anchoring into your centre.

◊ Breathe into your centre, and imagine this cord expanding around you until it forms a huge golden tree of light with branches reaching into all the stars of the cosmos and roots reaching down through all the kingdoms of the earth—the crystals, rocks, and minerals; the plant and elemental kingdoms; and the Inner Earth caverns of light.

◊ Breathe into your centre once more, and feel held, loved, and stabilized by the infinite golden solar love of Source and Mother Earth, of both God and Goddess.

◊ Feel, see, or sense one of the Archangels now appearing behind you. Imagine your personal Archangel enveloping you in their wings of light and sending an extra boost of love straight from their heart into yours.

◊ Next, imagine them sending you an extra boost of power from their solar plexus into your centre.

◊ Finally, imagine your Archangel sending you their divine wisdom direct from the crown of their head into your crown.

◊ Allow yourself to feel centred and grounded in your own infinite soul consciousness. Open your eyes when you feel ready.

When you are in extra need of centring, do this practice for nine days in a row. Nine is a powerful number and opens a portal or doorway directly to the divine. Your process will strengthen day by day.

On the ninth day, place your wishes and intentions into the vine, and send it up into Source and down into the earth, and share it with your Guardian Angel, with a request for your desire to come to fruition if it be for your highest good.

The Lesser Banishing Ritual of the Pentagram

The Lesser Banishing Ritual of the Pentagram is one of the chief rituals of Western Magick. It has been with us at least since the era of the Golden Dawn of the 19th century, and has made its way into various spiritual groups, schools, and practices since.

This is a powerful ritual to cleanse and protect your space before and after any healing or spiritual work, and is particularly handy if you are experiencing any form of energetic interference. Much of the symbolism and meaning is derived from the Hebrew Kabbalah, a Jewish mystical tradition that has strong links to the study and practice of alchemy. As part of the ritual, an equal-armed cross is invoked through the centre of the body. Known as the Kabbalistic Cross, this symbol has come to represent the awareness of ourselves as divine and the centre of our own universe. The practice also uses sacred geometry in the form of four illuminated pentagrams. Far from being a satanic or negative symbol, the pentagram is actually the perfect symbol for the divine human, as it represents nature and the coming together of the five elements: earth, air, fire, water, and ether/spirit.

The pentagram is used here as it is well known in many magical circles and mystical traditions the world over that any symbol you can draw without lifting the pen from the page in an unbroken line, such as the circle, the pentagram, and the unicursal hexagram, offers powerful protection. The pentagram is also aligned to the Golden Mean ratio of unconditional love and so it is a neutral symbol until we place our intention on it.

I first encountered this ritual during my Angelic Reiki training many years ago, and while learning about the Angels and higher consciousness, and I still use it as part of my regular spiritual practice. I have also included this process in my Precious Wisdom Alchemy Healing System as part of the opening of the space. I have added a few extra elements here to reflect my own take on the practice—notably, calling in Archangels Metatron from above and Sandalphon from below. In my own practice, I also call in the mighty Elohim Angels to stand in each corner to raise the energy to its highest potential.

If you wish, you can take the symbolism even farther, and imagine beautiful landscapes to represent each of the elements. For example, you might picture a tornado for air, a volcano for fire, the ocean for water, and a desert, lush jungle, or a mountain for earth.

You can also call in any animal spirit guides or magical elemental beings for each cardinal direction. For example: the sylphs and the birds for air; the dragons and salamanders for fire; the mermaids, undines, dolphins, and whales for water; and the gnomes, stone people, earthworms, ground-dwelling critters, and also the large animals of the jungle, such as elephants, gorillas, and lions, for earth. The stronger your visualization, the more powerful the magic.

Interpretation of the Kabbalistic Cross

For reference, here are the meanings of the words used in the Kabbalistic Cross that follows:

Ateh. This Hebrew word means "Thou art" and acknowledges the being of God.

Malkuth. This Hebrew word means "The Kingdom", and the sphere at your feet symbolizes the here and now in which you find yourself, now perceived as filled with the holy light of the divine.

ve Geburah. These Hebrew words mean "The Power". It symbolizes your power and vitality, your ability to define boundaries and defend them, and your strength to resist harmful negative influences.

ve Gedulah. These Hebrew words mean "The Glory". The blue sphere symbolizes your ability to be giving, loving, compassionate, and forgiving.

le olam. These Hebrew words are variously translated as "unto all the ages" or "forever".

Amen. This expresses your conscious decision to elevate and shift your consciousness to a centre of perfect spiritual balance.

Ritual of the Kabbalistic Cross:
Morning – Invoking

As you invoke the Kabbalistic Cross, picture yourself growing very, very tall, so that you transform into a huge angel surrounded by white light. Let the light fill your whole body, and imagine you have vast sparkling white wings. Feel yourself growing immensely powerful as you fill with pure divine love. You are now a gigantic angelic being towering over the world below:

Touching the crown of the head, say "*Ateh*" ("unto Thee").

Touching the lower abdomen, say "*Malkuth*" ("The Kingdom").

Touching the right shoulder, say "*ve-Geburah*" ("and The Power").

Touching the left shoulder, say "*ve-Gedulah*" ("and The Glory").

Clasping the hands upon the breast, say "*le-olam, Amen*" ("to the Ages, Amen").

Pentagrams of the Cardinal Directions: Morning – Invoking

To draw each of the morning pentagrams, start from the top, and draw an imaginary line down to your bottom left-hand-side by your left hip, then draw a diagonal line up and across to the middle of your right shoulder, across to the middle of your left shoulder, then take the line down to your bottom right hip, and join it back up in the centre, at the top, above your head:

Turning to the East, make a pentagram (that of Air in yellow) with wand or index finger. Say (sing/vibrate) "YHVH" (Yod-Heh-Vav-Heh). Visualize Archangel Raphael stepping through the pentagram, wearing emerald green robes and carrying a golden caduceus (a healing staff with two snakes entwined and wings at the top) in his hands. Behind Raphael, visualize a very tall and ethereal, pale-blue-white Elohim Angel.

Turning to the South (that of Fire in orange). Say "ADNI" (Adonai). Visualize Archangel Michael, wearing indigo blue robes and carrying a flaming blue sword and a gold shield, stepping through the pentagram. Behind Michael, visualize another tall Elohim Angel.

Turning to the West (that of Water in violet). Say "AHIH" (Eheieh). Visualize Archangel Gabriel stepping through the violet pentagram towards you, carrying a copper-gold trumpet and wearing white robes. Behind Gabriel, visualize a third tall Elohim Angel.

Turning to the North (that of Earth in olive, russet, citrine, and black). Say "AGLA" (Agla). Visualize Archangel Uriel, wearing ruby-red robes and carrying in his hands a red candle with a red-gold flame, stepping through the pentagram. Behind Uriel, visualize the fourth tall Elohim lit up in pale blue and white light.

From above your head, imagine a portal of brilliant golden-white light opening and showering over you, like a spotlight overlighting you from above. See a gold crown descending over the top of your head. This crown represents Archangel Metatron and the Heavenly Kingdom.

From below your feet, imagine another portal of light opening and radiating up through your energy field, as though you are lit by a spotlight from below. See golden sandals being placed upon your feet. These sandals represent Archangel Sandalphon and the Earthly Kingdom.

Visualize the light of Metatron and Sandalphon meeting to form a six-pointed 3D star of golden-white light around you.

Say:

> Before me, Raphael and Elohim;
> Behind me, Gabriel and Elohim;
> On my right hand, Michael and Elohim;
> On my left hand, Uriel and Elohim;
> From above, Metatron;
> From below, Sandalphon;
> Around me blaze the mighty Pentagrams,
> Within me shines the six-rayed Star.

At this point you invoke whatever you need for the day ahead, such as light, love, power, Angels, Ascended Masters, and so on.

Place your right index finger against your lips in a *shhhh* gesture to seal the space. Repeat the Kabbalistic Cross invoking ritual above.

Kabbalistic Cross:
Evening – Banishing

As you invoke the Kabbalistic Cross, picture yourself growing very, very tall, so that you transform into a huge Angel surrounded by white light. Let the light fill your whole body, and imagine that you have vast sparkling white wings. Feel yourself growing immensely powerful as you fill with pure divine love. You are now a gigantic angelic being towering over the world below:

Touching the crown of the head, say "*Ateh*" ("unto Thee").

Touching the lower abdomen, say "*Malkuth*" ("The Kingdom").

Touching the right shoulder, say "*ve-Geburah*" ("and The Power").

Touching the left shoulder, say "*ve-Gedulah*" ("and The Glory").

Clasping the hands upon the breast, say "*le-olam, Amen*" ("to the Ages, Amen").

Pentagrams of the Cardinal Directions:
Evening – Banishing

To draw each of the evening pentagrams, reverse the direction from the morning.

Start by drawing an imaginary line from the top down. Start in the centre, above your head, going down to your bottom right-hand-side at your right hip, then diagonally up and across to the middle left at your left shoulder, across to the middle right shoulder, then down to your bottom left at your left hip, and back up to join it at the centre, at the top above your head:

Turning to the West, make a pentagram (that of Water in violet) with wand or index finger. Say (i.e. vibrate) "AHIH" (Eheieh). Visualize Archangel Gabriel stepping through the violet pentagram towards you, carrying a copper-gold trumpet and wearing white robes. Behind Gabriel, visualize a very tall, pale-blue-and-white Elohim Angel.

Turning to the North, make a pentagram (that of Earth in olive, russet, citrine, and black). Say "AGLA" (Agla). Visualize Archangel Uriel, wearing ruby-red robes and carrying in his hands a red candle with a red-gold flame, stepping through the pentagram. Behind Uriel, visualize another tall Elohim lit up in pale-blue-and-white light.

Turning to the East, make a pentagram (that of Air in yellow) with wand or index finger. Say (i.e. vibrate) "YHVH" (Yod-Heh-Vav-Heh). Visualize Archangel Raphael stepping through the pentagram, wearing emerald-green robes and carrying a golden caduceus (a healing staff with two snakes entwined and wings at the top) in his hands. Behind Raphael, visualize a third Elohim Angel.

Turning to the South, make a pentagram (that of Fire in orange). Say "ADNI" (Adonai). Visualize Archangel Michael, wearing indigo-blue robes and carrying a flaming sword, stepping through the pentagram. Behind Michael, visualize a fourth tall Elohim Angel.

From above your head, imagine a portal of brilliant golden-white light opening and showering over you, like a spotlight overlighting you from above. See a gold crown descending over the top of your head. This crown represents Archangel Metatron and the Heavenly Kingdom.

From below your feet, imagine another portal of light opening and radiating up through your energy field, as though you are lit by a spotlight from below. See golden sandals being placed upon your feet. These sandals represent Archangel Sandalphon and the Earthly Kingdom.

Visualize the light of Metatron and Sandalphon meeting to form a six-pointed 3D star of golden-white light around you.

Say:

> Before me, Gabriel and Elohim;
> Behind me, Raphael and Elohim;
> On my right hand, Uriel and Elohim;
> On my left hand, Michael and Elohim;
> From above, Metatron;
> From below, Sandalphon;
> Around me blaze the mighty Pentagrams,
> Within me shines the six-rayed Star.

At this point you banish anything that doesn't need to be in your space, such as anyone else's energy, thought forms, entities, and so forth.

Place your right index finger against your lips in a *shhhh* gesture to seal the space. Repeat the Kabbalistic Cross banishing ritual from above.

PART THREE

Archangels and Our Ascension

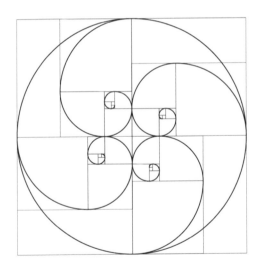

CHAPTER 13

How to Navigate Personal Awakening

The path of awakening is different for everyone, and the truth is that there is no set path, as each and every one of us is unique. In the same way, no two people will require the same level of help or support to navigate their way towards sacred union with the divine within.

When I began to awaken, I had no reference points for what was happening to me, and there were many times when I felt totally alone and unsupported. This often led to me feeling completely out of balance and off-kilter, which would then lead to a spiral of depression and sometimes panic attacks and severe anxiety. It didn't help that I was all alone in a strange, new, big city when it really began to switch on. At times, I thought I was having a nervous breakdown or losing my mind.

I know first hand what it is like to feel utterly alone in these strange times, so I would like to share some of the bizarre, zany, and sometimes quite frightening experiences I have had in the hope that it will help normalize the experience of awakening symptoms a little more for you.

Symptoms of Enlightenment

In no particular order, here is my list of just some of the physical, emotional, and spiritual symptoms I encountered:

◊ Seeing repeated "signs" in the form of physical images in your daily reality, especially in response to questions inside your own mind

◊ Sudden interest in symbolism, sacred geometry, and numbers, such as seeing double numbers, 11.11, and so forth

◊   Insomnia

◊   Extreme fatigue

◊   Extreme spikes of energy and joy

◊   Changes in appetite

◊   Random food intolerances

◊   Eyesight and hearing changes, such as ringing in the ears, blurred vision

◊   Heart palpitations

◊   Developing new phobias

◊   Irrational and extreme fears arising

◊   Experience of psychic attack

◊   Vivid or lucid dreams

◊   Enhanced creativity

◊   Desire to try new things and learn new skills

◊   Intolerance for harsh and aggressive people and environments

◊   Intolerance for cruelty

◊   Unexplained loneliness

◊   Unexplained self-hatred alongside new heights of self-love

◊   Extreme experience of duality

◊   Urge to travel to random places or just knowing I have to be somewhere and do something without a logical reason why

◊   Spontaneous past-life memories resurfacing

◊ Visitations from Angels and light beings

◊ Feeling super-connected to nature and all life

◊ Sudden changes in friendships and relationships

◊ Meeting new people who feel like soul family

◊ Nonlinear thought processes, understanding the nature of the universe, and receiving instant downloads of knowledge that it's hard to articulate to others

◊ Spontaneous outbursts of light language

◊ Spontaneous urge to move the body or dance

◊ Strong urge to leave the planet and go "home"

◊ Buzzing and a spinning sensation in the chakras and energy centres

◊ Seeing auras, orbs, and other light phenomena

◊ Seeing faces in rocks, nature, and even physical clairvoyance, clairaudience, such as spirit audibly shouting in your ear

◊ Heightened gut feeling, claircognizance, clear knowing, such as a strong feeling not to get on a train or bus and later discovering the train or bus was in an accident, and so on.

On top of all this, with my Sun in Libra and my Moon in dreamy Pisces, staying in my centre is already a challenge; however, in the midst of this heightened energetic training ground, my Archangels and guides taught me a handy centring and grounding process that I will share with you below. I call it the Seed of Light Process.

The Seed of Light Process

How to Ground, Rebalance, and Centre Yourself in Your Own Energy

◊ Close your eyes, and centre your awareness in your belly, just behind your navel.

◊ Imagine a seed of pure diamond light shaped like a tiny Vesica Piscis (upright almond shape) located there.

◊ With your imagination and intention, begin to pull all of your energy and awareness into the seed of light.

◊ Shrink yourself down so that you become a tiny speck of light within the seed.

◊ Keep shrinking and pulling all your energy inward and, as you do so, consciously let go and release yourself from the outer world and universe.

◊ See any cords or grids of energy being released, and feel them leave you as you become so small they can no longer attach.

◊ See, feel, and imagine that no one else's energy, feelings, thoughts, agendas, or intentions can touch you or influence you any more.

◊ Set the intention that you are completely disengaging from the matrix of this dimension now and returning to your pure, sovereign, innocent state within.

◊ Imagine you are entirely within that tiny seed of light, and see it spinning around you like an atom of pure source energy.

◊ Now, in one breath, pull yourself backward and into the void, the darkness of pre-creation.

◊ Find yourself within a velvety-black, inky void, like a safe womb space.

◊ Rest for a moment here, and let yourself breathe absolute stillness in this secure sanctuary.

◊ When you feel ready, set the intention for how you want to feel in your world—safe, grounded, protected, joyful, and so on. Whatever emotions and feelings would help you survive in the outer world, you create here in the unmanifest.

◊ Next, in one flash of light, feel these positive emotions filling you up and exploding from the void, expanding with your awareness through your body and out into the wider world and the whole universe.

◊ Like a "big bang" explosion of positive emotion, you now reclaim your world as a powerful creatrix of your own outer experience by choosing the emotions and sensations you wish to feel within your daily life.

◊ Claim your world, and feel centred and powerful.

◊ Return your awareness to your navel, and let the energies settle around you like a diamond cloak of protection.

◊ See this cloak forming into a silver-diamond lining around your whole body, sealing your energy fields in a powerful protection, so that only love and positive energy may enter.

◊ Place your right index finger to your lips as though in a *shhhh* gesture to seal your space.

◊ Open your eyes.

CHAPTER 14

Archangel Alchemy and the Angels of the Ascension Flames

This chapter introduces you to the 40 Ascension Archangels overlighting the Archangel Alchemy healing system.

Each section offers information about an Angel and their flames and qualities. Once you have been introduced to these loving guardians, you have the opportunity to become attuned to their gifts and qualities so you call on them for assistance and understand what it means to embody your angelic aspect within your daily life.

Channelled Message from the Archangels of the Ascension Flames

Beloveds,

We have brought you to this place of knowing. The journey you embark on is not a journey at all, but a remembering of your true sacred and holy template. You are of one unified field of love consciousness.

There is not now, and never has been, a separation. All separation is merely an illusion, and as you lean into your awakening, you are remembering more of who you really are.

Your purpose in this plane of reality is to peel back the veils of illusion and reunite with your limitless soul-ness, which is already perfect and whole in its pure love aspect of the one divine source.

You are not separate from God. You not separate from the self. You are not separate from one another. As you come to know this, you will come to witness it, and this witnessing begins in the feelings that stir within your emotional resonance.

From feeling comes a knowing , and the inner knowing guides you to the information that offers evidence to anchor in the wisdom. Once these connections are made, you begin to embody the knowledge and live as the divine presence within a human form.

You are great sages reborn, shining creator gods and goddesses who were here at the very dawn of time and seek to know the eternal, as the eternal is what you are.

Let this seeking and this question mark lead you to ever more as yet unfathomable heights of bliss as you relearn and redirect your course homeward to the delights of existential ecstasy.

We leave you with a thought to ponder: "Who would you be if you could truly remember who you are?"

Spend time regularly in meditation pondering this question, and you will gradually call back to yourself all the forgotten parts that make up the glorious whole.

"Who would I be if I could remember all of me?"

You are the shimmering diamond of infinite multifaceted oneness. If you could gaze into each blazing face upon that eternal crystalline form, what image would be looking back at you?

Do you not realize that all your brothers and sisters are a part of you, too? For all consciousness is connected within the one web of love.

Do not seek to harm another, for you harm yourself.

Seek always to love, to forgive, to learn, to grow, to thrive, and to live in love.

This is Ascension. This is the coming home. This is the great awakening to love eternal and the return of holy unity.

We Angels can appear as individual deities and guardians. So, too, the light and star councils operate as individual guides and messengers. However, we move and act and interact as one group consciousness.

We wish to clarify that "unity" is not about all of you becoming the same and emulating or copying one another. Nor is it about competing with each other, for there is enough for all.

Unity is about honouring one's unique soul blueprint and living

163

according to that signature in all its glory in devotion of and for the soul divine. You are unique expressions of the divine—individual fractals of the light and qualities of the shimmering united soul. When you honour your uiqueness, you make the entire face of the one divine soul more beautiful.

Think of the rainbow pearlescent light pouring through a waterfall hit by the sun's rays and spraying its bounty of colour outward. Without the separation of the colours, there would be nothing to see; the light would be perfectly clear.

This clear light is the oneness, but in order to incarnate and perceive the glory of the oneness, a separation must occur. The divine has sought to know itself, and we, and you, and all individualized life, are seeking the same outcome.

The holy purpose of incarnation and separation is to witness the divine in all its beauty and magnificence and then to return to the one. You are diamonds made flesh, faces and fractals of the beauty.

Walk in beauty, beloveds. Seek to know your beauty in all its forms and to share of the myriad extraordinary gifts you are blessed with, in order to inspire others to seek the attainment of this great truth.

Which face will you reveal to the world today? For you have many, and even within your own individual self, there are many more fractals to explore. You are unlocking deeper layers within the parts of yourself you have hidden from, so that you may reach higher into the knowing that you are the Glorious Gloriana – kings and queens of Heaven come to Earth.

We come in infinite love and joy to reveal this knowledge. How you choose to take this forward is up to you.

But, remember, your return to The One is inevitable, so to resist it would be futile.

Seek out the places of your resistance, love them and set them free.

Glorious Gloriana, praise be to thee.

In love and service,

The Archangels of the Ascension Flames.

What Are the Sacred Flames of the Archangels?

I first learnt about the concept of angelic fire, or spiritual flames, through my own interactions with the Archangels as one of the predominant ways they revealed their presence. As I have described, I would experience a kind of divine fire that seemed to ignite my entire nervous system and activate my energy centres from within whenever an angelic presence, especially an Archangel, was connecting with me.

Upon subsequent research, I learnt that the concept of holy fire was quite common in various spiritual circles. There were, as I have mentioned, examples in the Bible. The Holy Spirit itself is depicted as being surrounded by flaming solar rays, but the concept also crosses into Eastern Vedic traditions, such as the description of Agni as a fiery deity.[36] Madame Blavatsky of the Theosophical Society wrote about the sacred flames in her work *The Secret Doctrine: The Synthesis of Science, Religion, and Philosophy*. And other well-known spiritual authors also wrote about spiritual flames, such as Alice Bailey, Manly P. Hall, Elizabeth Clare Prophet, and Aurelia Louise Jones.

Most descriptions of these heavenly flames seemed to centre on the number seven, and suggested that there were seven of these rays in total. This seemed to correlate to the seven days of creation, the seven chakras, and the seven colours of the rainbow.

However, in my personal experience, through my channellings, visions, and visitations, I was shown that there is actually an infinite number of these rays or flames. Many of them are not visible to the naked eye, but are becoming more accessible as part of our evolutionary expansion into human–divine awareness. The best way to connect with each flame is to invite it into your energy field, visualize it, bathe in it, and feel its positive healing effects.

The 40 Archangels of the Ascension Flames

Archangels of the Black Flame

Sariel

Often described as one of the fallen Angels and the brother of Lucifer (the "light bearer"), Sariel is an Archangel that can help uncover the hidden blessing within darkness. If you are encountering a "dark night of the soul", Sariel brings comfort, helping you to offer yourself loving kindness in the depths of your despair. He is a potent ally to call upon when you have nowhere else to turn.

Sariel helps us uncover the triumph within our loss. As we emerge from darkness, he lights the path to redemption, reigniting hopefulness. When you have met Sariel, and understand that enlightenment is not only about light but the balancing of polarities, you will have met the innermost sanctum of your duality and entered the eye of the storm. If you can master peace within your pain, you have mastered your emotions and can find yourself at home within any situation.

Tzaphkiel

Tzaphkiel's name means "God's Knowledge" or "Understanding of God". This Angel is the epitome of the divine feminine, and she is aligned with the Great Cosmic Mother. Tzaphkiel guides us to seek spiritual perfection. Like the Egyptian goddess Isis, she is the teacher of esoteric knowledge, mythology, spells, and rituals.

Unyielding, and sometimes more than a little demanding in nature, Tzaphkiel can make you feel like you are being initiated into the darkest depths of the feminine mysteries when you work with her. However, as keeper of the Akashic Records, she offers you the key to unlocking all your lifetimes. When you enter the cosmic womb of Tzaphkiel, be prepared for what is lurking below the surface of your subconscious to be brought into the harsh light of day for review, but with Tzaphkiel as your powerful protectress there is nothing to fear, as the truth, however disconcerting, will always set you free. She is also a brilliant ally to help resolve conflicts.

As Keeper of the Ring-Pass-Not, Tzaphkiel rules the cycles and waters of creation. She offers you silence, which is vital for seeking higher wisdom. Once you lift the veil and peer into the dark recesses of your soul, trust this Angel is by your side guiding you across the abyss to renewal. Hers is a powerful alchemy, but glory greets you on the other side.

Archangels of the Russet Flame

Adnachiel

The Archangel known as "The Adventurer", Adnachiel's name means "The Shining One", and he helps you embrace your individuality and independence to access your pioneering spirit. He urges you to step out of your comfort zone and explore other possibilities in life. Like a warrior, Adnachiel helps you embrace any challenges with the spirit of adventure.

This free-spirited Angel also helps us step out of the constraints placed upon us by social conditioning and expectations, so we can speak up for ourselves and state our needs with honesty, authenticity, and integrity. This mighty Angel is especially good to call upon whenever you feel trapped by life's circumstances and feel the need to break free. He will help you forge new frontiers. You are a wayshower for humanity.

The Angel ruler of November and the sign of Sagittarius, Adnachiel can also help you embrace and channel your own inner fire so you can use it creatively. Call on him to help you appreciate your uniqueness, so you can shine brighter with humble perseverance.

Cassiel

The angel of serenity, solitude, and temperance, Cassiel's name means "God is My Cover", and this gentle angel can help you find great strength in your solitude. When life gets on top of us, and we feel overwhelmed, Cassiel reminds us of the importance of taking time out. She also helps honour our boundaries and say "no" when we need to. Cassiel's message is that it is okay to put yourself first so you don't become drained.

As the "Angel of Tears", Cassiel assures us that there is no shame in showing our vulnerability. By holding in our emotions, we can stifle ourselves. Another name for this Angel is "Speed of God", because of her ability to help us heal faster. Crying can be so healing, as it washes away sorrows and clears old hurts. Cassiel also brings us the strength to step back on our path after our period of solitude and serenity. She helps us get back on track with our purpose, even when we feel we don't want to or that we aren't ready. Cassiel will give you the motivation to pick yourself up.

Sandalphon

The Angel who truly links Heaven and Earth, Sandalphon is known as "The Tallest Angel"—so gigantic, in fact, that it is said to take 500 years to travel from his feet to his head. Like his twin Metatron, Sandalphon is one of only two Angels who previously walked the Earth as a human (he was the prophet Elijah). He is charged with looking after our planet and taking our prayers to God, weaving them into a crown of daisies.

Often symbolized by a wheel of fire, Sandalphon is also known as the "Wheel of the Divine Chariot" and, like his image on the oracle card, he keeps our feet planted firmly on the ground, while we embark on our journey of enlightenment. For this reason, Sandalphon is the ideal Angel to call on when you are doing any meditation or healing work. His grounding influence will deepen your experience and help you put your esoteric knowledge to practical daily use. You will always feel safe and at home.

Known as the patron Angel of Music, Sandalphon presides over the heavenly spheres and angelic choirs. He helps you embrace your gifts and make sweet music from your life.

Archangels of the Red Flame

Uriel

Uriel's name means "Fire of God" or "Flame of God", and he is the keeper of the flame of divine love. He teaches us the path of salvation and helps purify our hearts and release lower energies, such as guilt and anger, that may cloud our judgement. Call upon Uriel to help resolve arguments and bring forgiveness and healing into tense situations. He can help you start afresh and let go of hurts and grudges.

Also known as the "Angel of the Earth", Uriel watches over our planet and the elements. He is the supreme counsellor and one of the wisest of the Archangels, so you can ask him to assist whenever you have an interview or exam or if you need the answer to a difficult question. He'll sharpen your senses, so the answers you are seeking pop into your head.

Camael

Camael's name means "One Who Sees God". As this Archangel is able to see through illusions and get to the truth of any matter, Camael is also known as the "Angel of Justice, Forgiveness, and Empowerment".

Camael helps keep us in check. A warrior, like Archangel Michael, he shows us that we always have a choice in our actions and reactions. He helps keep us accountable, so we are honest with ourselves and can take full responsibility for our behaviour.

Camael's eyes of truth can act like a mirror into our own soul, showing us our shadow side and calling to mind all those parts of ourselves that we might prefer to keep hidden from the world. This mighty Archangel reminds us that it is important not to judge others before we have judged ourselves. Have you acted with integrity in each given situation? Are you being true to yourself as a being of unconditional love? Remember, every being on the planet is striving towards the goal of love. Any action not aligned with love is usually the result of fear. Forgive yourself and others. Strive to be compassionate.

Haniel

Haniel's name means "Glory of God" or "Grace of God", and she can help ignite your passions and bring you renewed energy and vitality. If your world is feeling a little lacklustre, call on this super-motivational Angel to restore your vigour and reignite your passion for life. She helps us channel our energies into the things we love.

Strongly aligned with the moon, Haniel is also the Archangel of intuition, and she has a strong feminine quality. She is particularly aligned with healers and psychics and helps us go with the flow of life, rather than trying to control everything. Haniel urges us to follow our inner guidance, so we can do what makes our heart sing, rather than what we feel obligated to do. And even if we find ourselves in an unsatisfactory situation, she helps us act with poise and charm.

Haniel can help you enter the peaceful garden of your heart and cross the bridge to whatever your soul is truly hankering for. She can also ignite passion within your love relationships, helping you connect with your sensuality and bring intimacy into your love life.

Archangels of the Pink Flame

Chamuel

Beautiful Archangel Chamuel is known as the "Angel of the Heart" or "The Loving One". The name Chamuel comes from the word *lenachem* in Hebrew, which means "comfort and compassion". Chamuel's pure love can help release sorrow from your heart and guide you towards forming open-hearted and balanced relationships. Call on this Angel to attract romance or when you need help to resolve issues with loved ones.

Whenever this being is around, you may get a fluttery butterfly feeling in the pit of your stomach. Chamuel is sometimes portrayed as a masculine Angel, but she can also be attributed with a soft feminine energy. She often arrives surrounded by springtime green and deep pink, the colours of love and compassion.

Call upon Chamuel to open your heart chakra and release any misunderstandings, hurts, or rejections. Her gentle yet powerful love can dissolve even the most stubborn lower emotions. She will infuse all your relationships with perfect, unconditional love.

Chamuel is also the angel charged with finding lost things and can help you locate anything, from misplaced keys, new friends, your ideal career path, or even a soul mate.

Ariel

Ariel is known as the "Guardian of Nature and the Air". As head of the Nature Angels, she is connected with the fairies and elementals. She watches over all the plants and animals, and helps encourage us to care for our environment. Known as the "Lioness of God", Ariel can shore up your courage and inner strength—she is especially good at helping you to stand up for your beliefs and values, and to look out for the underdog, which is certainly needed during this time of great awakening.

Ariel can help neutralize fears, and she shores up your inner resolve, giving you personal strength when you need it most. She can shield you from vexatious people and situations, and will gently but firmly help you say no to, or move away from, experiences that may be disempowering for you, or even potentially involve bullying or aggression. Like the dignified forest nymph she is represented by on her oracle card, she can infuse you with stamina, heroism, and noble defiance in the face of life's challenges.

Rikbiel

Rikbiel is known as the "Chief of the Divine Chariot", the Merkabah. This cherubim is said to be the "Power of Love", and he helps us recognize the incredible power of having loving thoughts. A harmonizing Angel that can influence centrifugal force and find the most the most loving point between two opposing forces,

Rikbiel is especially helpful to call upon when working in group situations as he maintains cooperation and promotes open communication. Like a cosmic diplomat, he shows us that when a group strives towards a common goal based in integrity, they can achieve great things. Like Chamuel or Uriel, he can heal emotions and promote forgiveness.

Rikbiel presides over the four cardinal directions and governs the wheels of the chariot, which are eight fiery angels known as the Hayyoth. If you are feeling stuck, call upon Rikbiel to get the wheels of love moving in your favour. Like the Wheel of Fortune in the Tarot, with Rikbiel's help, you can take the reins and ride his chariot through any challenges.

Archangels of the Orange Flame

Soqed Hozi

The Archangel known as "Keeper of the Divine Balances", Soqed Hozi is the Angel associated with intimate partnerships and is shown here as a half-man, half-woman Russian circus performer. Soqed Hozi helps us maintain our individuality while acknowledging the interconnectedness of all things, thereby keeping a flow of loving energy so that each person positively affects and supports the energy of the other.

Soqed Hozi can help you recognize and heal imbalanced partnerships that may feel like they are draining you. While we all need to lean on loved ones from time to time, it's unhealthy for a relationship to be built entirely on one person's needs and another person's attempts to fulfil those needs. A true soul mate relationship is uplifting, supportive, fair, and loving. If conflict or dysfunction occurs, it should lead to growth and understanding, not create further conflict and misunderstanding.

As the balancer of all the spiritual forces within the great matrix of existence, Soqed Hozi reminds us of our infinite nature and says we need to remember that we are a microcosm within the macrocosm. The whole universe is reflected in our being, thus everything in our lives is constantly moving and shifting towards perfect balance; it is only our perception that prevents it from being so. This is why our intimate soul mate relationships can feel so incredible; through them, we are able to see the truth of our own perfection reflected back at us in the other.

Radueriel

Gentle Radueriel is the Archangel associated with poetry and the arts. Known as the "Angelic Muse", he is a wonderful being that can help you with any creative project you're working on, providing you with inspiration and wisdom. He will stir up your passions and help you remember those things that allow your inner fires of inspiration to keep burning. Radueriel will show you how to sow your artistic seeds, so you can give birth to fresh new ideas and let your true gifts and talents come alive.

One of eight great judgement Angels of the heavenly throne, Radueriel is one of the few angelic beings that rank higher even than mighty Metatron. He is the angelic scribe or "Recording Angel" and the leader of the heavenly choirs. Whenever he speaks or sings, a new Angel is born.

Radueriel knows that stepping into our full power can take us out of our comfort zone, and it might feel easier to hold ourselves back. But he guarantees that if we dare to accept ourselves for who we are, he will raise our vibration to the angelic frequency with his sweet and pure music, allowing our beauty, strength, and creativity to shine.

Call upon this Angel if you are suffering from writer's block or if you have an idea but don't know how to get it off the ground. He will help you take your dreams from thought into form. Radueriel reminds us that if you can dream it, you can do it.

Barachiel

Beautiful Barachiel's name means "Blessings of God". She is the Archangel charged with bringing happiness to our family life and overseeing matrimony and parenthood. She often carries a basket of bread and the staff of life to symbolize fertility and abundance. She helps us provide for ourselves and our children—and to find the right partner to have children with, if we so desire. Barachiel helps strengthen all our family and close relationships.

Also known as the "Angel of Lightning", Barachiel is said to swiftly grant blessings for your good deeds and bring you success, especially in games of chance. She is sometimes depicted holding an ancient sacred book, which is said to contain the instructions for living a good life. The white rose is symbolic of her blessings. Barachiel is a light-hearted Angel. She inspires laughter when you call upon her. She reminds us that, despite the hardships of life, we can find hidden blessings everywhere.

Archangels of the Yellow Flame

Jophiel

The Archangel of joy, wisdom, and beauty, Jophiel governs the yellow ray of illumination. She gives us the ability to add more gladness to our lives. She also helps us learn and teach at the highest level, enabling us to find the answers to important questions, see the beauty in all things, and think more positively.

Jophiel sets us on the right path to achieving spiritual enlightenment. She can help us get organized and clear out our physical and emotional clutter, which can be a real help when you're tackling spring cleaning or trying to get to the bottom of any old, stuck emotions.

Visualize Jophiel's bright yellow light pouring into you and your home like sunlight, and ask her to illuminate anything you no longer need. Picture this light filling any areas of your life where you feel unhappy or dissatisfied. Ask Jophiel to send this light into any dark corners to cleanse the space around you, your home, and your belongings.

Getting rid of old, stuck energy alone helps you think more clearly, but when you ask Jophiel to help with this objective, it's like a light gets switched on inside your brain and you suddenly have new clarity to be able to see all the good things in your life.

Galgaliel

What an Angel to call on at the start of this incredible new era of change! Like a fierce Norse Valkyrie warrior, powerful Galgaliel's duty is to help us raise our personal vibration, and this is particularly useful as we collectively raise the frequency of the planet.

What does this mean? All energy is constantly moving. Even that which appears solid and stationary is actually vibrating when viewed at the microscopic level. When something is very fast-moving, it is harder to see with the naked eye.

Light is an example of this, as are Angels. On an exponential scale, our lighter emotions vibrate at a higher, faster rate than our so-called lower emotions, which is why they can feel heavy and have a tendency to get stuck in the body.

Galgaliel works to release the energy blockages that are preventing us from experiencing our highest possible timeline by raising our emotional frequency and bringing us back into alignment with the Creator, our highest source of light and love. Galgaliel has the power to harness and control powerful energy vortexes, which she directs into our energy field and chakra system to clear negativity and transform anything that is stuck.

Galgaliel is the head of the Order of the Galgalim, or the "Chariots of the Merkabah" (the light body). She governs the wheel of the sun, energy, and vibration. Her colour is a beautiful, glittering yellow-gold, like dazzling sunlight.

As a Solar Angel, Galgaliel helps you absorb the healing benefits of the sun, and offsets sun damage to skin or property. She also brings balance to the weather patterns.

Archangels of the Green Flame

Raphael

Raphael's name means "God Heals", and his main task is to aid us when we require physical healing or improvements to our general health and well-being. He assists healers and those in the medical profession, and is powerfully present during global health crises, such as pandemics, to ensure everyone gets the attention they need.

When people are getting ready to pass over, Raphael offers comfort and safety until Archangel Azrael arrives to help them with their transition. Raphael is the Angel of the Heart and governs the emerald ray. You may see green sparkles or feel tingling when he's around. He can also help heal sadness after loss.

As I wrote earlier, I once injured both my knees in a bus crash in London. During my physiotherapy sessions, I called on Raphael. It was amazing when he merged his energy with mine and I could physically see a green halo of light around my injuries. I knew this was Raphael's light manifesting in my aura, and it was so reassuring to know he was my personal cosmic consultant. If you feel unwell or suffer an injury, ask Raphael to bathe you in emerald light to restore your health.

Azrael

Known as the "Angel of Death", Azrael isn't at all as scary as his name suggests. In fact, he is perhaps the kindest and gentlest of all the Archangels. Like a mysterious, cloaked guardian leading the way across a treacherous bridge, he is associated with bringing comfort and reassurance in times of intense transition.

Azrael guides souls that are crossing over by gently separating the soul from the body at death and setting the spirit free; he also gives guidance and reassurance to those in the counselling professions. Like Raphael, Azrael can help your heart heal in times of loss, grief, and hardship. He is especially present during a bereavement.

Azrael can help you release any worries about lost loved ones and also act as a messenger, delivering your words and wishes to those loved ones on the other side. He lets us know that there is much more to life than a purely human existence and that we still have much to learn from beyond the grave. He reminds us that, rather than human beings having a spiritual experience, we are spiritual beings having a human experience. In this way, perhaps Azrael could be better described as the "Angel of Everlasting Life" rather than the "Angel of Death".

Ask him to help you through personal transitions and to wrap his wings around anyone experiencing grief or loss. He'll help comfort and console them, so they can find peace.

Archangels of the Turquoise Flame

Phuel

Gentle flowing Phuel is the "Angel of the Waters", and her role is to help cleanse the planet and us of any debris, toxins, negative vibrations, and emotions. Phuel works closely with Archangel Ariel, Guardian of Nature and the Air, to protect and nurture Mother Earth. Phuel also helps us understand and manage our emotions, as they ebb and flow just like water with the power of the Moon.

The colour associated with the Angel Phuel is a beautiful shade of turquoise, like the crystal-clear waters of the Maldives or the Caribbean. Imagine this flame is alive and fluid like the sea. As in the image of her as a mermaid, bathing in a crystal-clear lagoon, Phuel's light can flow around and through you to cleanse every part of your physical and energetic body. Phuel helps keep us in the flow of life, so that we do not feel stuck or hemmed in by our circumstances. As her name sounds like "fool", I also associate her with The Fool in the Tarot, with her carefree attitude and innocent fearlessness. Phuel reminds us that worrying about something or trying to control a situation often has the opposite effect. If we just remember to "let go, and let flow", the Angels will do their best to make sure life goes our way.

Zacharael

The Angel of Surrender, Zacharael's name means "Remembrance of God", and he asks us to remember that we do not have to carry our burdens alone. It is okay to ask for help when we need it. Sometimes life throws up situations or issues that we may find too difficult to cope with. We struggle to find answers or solutions, but can find none, and so it is often the case that we end up feeling helpless or like we have lost control. He tells us that a problem shared is a problem halved; there is no shame in asking for help. Similar to Sariel, Zacharael helps us surrender to the divine when we have nowhere else to turn.

Archangels of the Blue Flame

Sachiel

The perfect Angel to call on in times of scarcity, Sachiel is the Angel of Charity and Wealth. Her name means "Covering of God". It's for this reason that many call on her to "cover them" when they owe money. She acts as an angelic good luck trinket and is associated with fairness in trading, business, investments, insurance, and banking.

Make sure that your intentions are of the utmost good when calling on Sachiel as she often works on a "reap what you sow" basis. When you set your intention to align with your divine purpose for the good of yourself and the collective, she helps you become more affluent, so you are then able to assist others, who may be less fortunate than you.

Like Raphael and Chamuel, Sachiel is one of the guardians of the Fourth Heaven, or Heart chakra. As Lady Luck, she is often linked to Jupiter, the planet of luck and good fortune. Her colours are violet or blue and, like Asariel, she is sometimes associated with the energy of water, portraying the easy flow of divine abundance. Whenever you invoke Sachiel, she reminds you that you have access to the Law of Attraction. She shows you that abundance is always within your grasp when you acknowledge your divine limitlessness.

Asariel

Archangel Asariel is the patron Archangel of the Waters and rules planet Neptune. Like a Caribbean water goddess, she often appears in shimmering watery robes, wearing a crown of shells and carrying a trident. Her colours are green, aqua, and blue.

As the Archangel of the Waters, Asariel helps us connect with our deep emotions, creativity, dreams, and intuition. She can show us how to tap into our sensitive side and honour our thoughts, feelings, and inner guidance. Guiding the deep and often untapped recesses of your spirit, Asariel can help you navigate the endless ocean of treasures life holds for you. She allows you to let go of fear and flow with the currents of experience, supporting you through any ups and downs.

Asariel reminds us that if we "let go, and let flow", we can open ourselves to the countless blessings in front of our face that may be obscured in the shaded rock pools of the shallows; likewise, when we are afraid to wade into our own depths, she guides us into calmer seas. Like a sea anemone or hermit crab, with Asariel you can discern when you need to adopt your tough outer shell of protection or reveal the soft sweetness within. With Asariel's help, you can direct the power of Neptune's trident where it's truly needed.

Michael

Probably the most well known of all the Archangels, beloved Michael is the angelic protector. As your personal bodyguard, he infuses you with courage and will ensure that you and those you love are kept safe. Ask him to cut any negative cords to relieve tensions and bring peace to your family and friends and to watch over you and your loved ones. He is also known as the angelic policeman, so if you see a police car go by or witness a fight or argument, send Michael to help to surround the situation in his powerful transmuting flame to resolve any conflict.

Michael's colour is a brilliant cobalt blue or indigo and you may see blue sparkles when he's around. Whenever you feel afraid, uncertain, or need a little extra courage, call on Michael to wrap his blue cloak around you and shield you from harm.

Whenever you are going through rapid or difficult changes in your life, or feel uncertain about your path ahead, call on Michael to reassure you and trust that all will be well.

Archangels of the Purple Flame

Jeremiel

Jeremiel's name means "Mercy of God", and he is one of the most comforting Angels to call upon if you're experiencing a difficult time or have a tough decision to make. He can help you to develop a more merciful, compassionate outlook and treat others with love and respect.

Like the mysterious Northern Lights above Greenland, his flame and colour are deep purple, the colour of profound spiritual expansion. The crystal amethyst is often associated with this Archangel's healing energy, and you may see purple sparkles behind your eyes or in your aura when he's around.

Jeremiel is here to help humanity evolve, and we each have a personal path to follow in this regard. This Archangel is handy if you're undertaking a life review, as he can show you how to take an inventory of anything that is or isn't working and remove any old, stuck patterns so you can move forward.

There may be times in our lives when we have to face up to some hard truths about where we are holding onto behaviours, people, and situations that may not be in our best interests. Jeremiel can help us lovingly let go of the old, outdated, and outgrown aspects of ourselves and our lives with gentle compassion. He can also help us see the hidden blessings in any problems. Like Soqed Hozi, he helps us learn from our past mistakes in order to allow us to grow and become stronger.

Raziel

Raziel's name means "Secrets of God" and, like the Jewish high priest on his card, he is the Angel of the Mysteries. Associated with ancient teachings like the Kabbalah, Raziel helps us enhance and deepen our spiritual understanding of esoteric knowledge and practice.

Mystical Raziel is strongly associated with the gift of clairvoyance, and he can help your spiritual sight to fully awaken, guiding you to see the truth in any given situation. He can teach you to trust your intuition and inner guidance, and he boosts your personal power to allow you to see past any fears or illusions that may be holding you back on your sacred path.

Like Archangel Metatron, Raziel is closely associated with the mystical science of sacred geometry and esoteric symbols. He will often bring you messages in the form of glyphs or signs, either in your physical sight or in your mind's eye. The most prominent of these is the Tree of Life symbol, which relates to knowledge and our connection to the divine. Raziel is said to be the author of a sacred text known as *The Book of Raziel*, so you may see the symbol of a book around you or be guided to write when he is around. He brings guidance about the next steps in your own alchemical and spiritual evolution.

Archangels of the Violet Flame

Zadkiel

Like the Ascended Master Saint Germaine, Zadkiel is known as The Great Alchemist. His name means "Grace of God" or "Righteousness of God", and he is the Angel of Freedom, Benevolence, Transfiguration, and Forgiveness. He helps release negativity and transmutes limiting beliefs and thought patterns, so we can live a life of freedom. This begins with holding ourselves in forgiveness and, in a similar way to working with Jeremiel, having mercy for our own shortcomings.

Zadkiel can help us see a higher perspective and rise above the idea of right and wrong, good or bad, in order to see every situation in our lives as a great blessing or lesson.

He helps free us from outdated victimhood or guilt, and transforms our lower thoughts and emotions into loving and hopeful wishes and prayers, guiding us towards inner bliss.

Zuriel

Beloved Zuriel is known as "God Is My Rock" and the "Angel of Repentance". Like a Sufi whirling dervish, she is the regulator of opposing forces and governs the rotation of the heavenly bodies, keeping Mother Earth in sync with our solar system and universe.

Zuriel stands for harmony and peace. As the celestial rock, she helps keep you rooted to the spot when you need to make a stand for what's right. She is a formidable ally to have around when you are facing a conflict, especially when facing injustice coming from the opposition, as she literally cannot be budged. Zuriel acts as your inner backstop, preventing you from backing down in the face of unfairness.

As the Angel of Vitality and Fertility, also, Zuriel balances our hormones, brain chemicals, and other bodily systems, restoring our equilibrium and exuberance. She improves our mental health, eases stress and can, thankfully, reveal when we are acting foolishly.

Associated with the zodiac sign of Libra, she is all about tact, diplomacy, and mediation. Similar to Soqed Hozi, she blesses our social life and brings good relations and a strong sense of fair play to partnerships, friendships, communities, and groups. Zuriel can help us forgive and release any hurt or upset after we have suffered a disappointment.

As an Angel of Evolution, Justice, and Salvation, she rapidly restores harmony, brings foresight and can be called upon for prophecy, offering clear guidance on our next steps. The most powerful Angel of the Principalities, the Angels that govern groups, communities, and institutions, including entire nations, Zuriel watches over the innocent and vulnerable. She protects newborn babies and infants, welcoming them into the world.

Archangels of the White Flame

Gabriel

Beautiful Gabriel is one of the most famous Archangels, along with Michael. Gabriel can be perceived as either male or female, and is shown in the card as an androgynous figure to honour the balance of this angel's masculine and feminine qualities. Known as "God's Messenger", Gabriel's name means "God Has Shown Himself". He helps us discover our truth and true life path, and is particularly helpful to writers and those in the communication industries.

Gabriel brings hope in times of hardship, accompanies new beginnings, and guides us through the veil of illusion. Ask Gabriel to bring you a sign of hope during challenging times and to help you align with your true soul purpose. Gabriel can ensure your deepest desires are fulfilled and, when you lose your way, this Angel will blow his trumpet to remind you to believe in yourself. Gabriel reminds you that, at your core, you are pure innocence and deserve the best life has to offer.

As the Keeper of the White Ray, Gabriel is the guardian of the doorway to transcendence and our return to purity through Ascension.

Selathiel

Selathiel is the Angel of Contemplation and Devotion. His name means "Prayer of God", and he is also known as "The Intercessor". This peace-loving Archangel is a special guardian to those who have been ordained or who are qualified as spiritual teachers.

This gentle being comes to teach us about the importance of prayer. Selathiel shows us how to see every aspect of our lives as sacred and worthy of devotion, even the most mundane, everyday activities can be embraced as a form of devotion or in a sacred ritual.

He assists with bringing us more easily into a meditative state and can show us how to still our mind, so we can tap into the quiet voice of our true guidance. He can also enhance our concentration levels and help us avoid distractions.

Selathiel is often depicted with an expression of sincere humility on his face, with downcast eyes and his arms gently folded over his chest. Like the image on his oracle card, he is shown to be swinging an incense burner, or censer, the smoke of which carries our prayers more quickly to Heaven. An Angel of Mindfulness, he shows us how to live without unhealthy attachment, keeps us centred in the now, and helps us trust that our prayers are being answered, perhaps just not always in the way we might expect. Selathiel reminds us that everyone's path is unique. Don't follow the herd. Be devoted to you.

Archangels of the Silver Flame

Mirabiel

It's no coincidence that Mirabiel's name sounds like "mirror ball". Like a glitter ball reflecting endless sparkles of light, the silver-blue lunar-esque Mirabiel helps illuminate the divine feminine aspect of grace within us. In doing so, she helps balance, cleanse, and purify our spirit.

As we gaze into her mirror, we look deeply into our own soul self and slip beneath the mercurial waters of the unknown. We are then able to move with more flexibility, relishing the freedom activated by this Angel.

Mirabiel's feminine energy brings our lives into flow, helping us wash away and release any feelings of rigidity, control, and limitation, so we can relinquish the need to grip onto life too tightly. It is from this place of surrender and fluidity that we can tap into our intuition and creativity, then we can dance through life to our own personal rhythm, as Mirabiel's glitter ball throws sparkles of delight across any shadows. Lighting up all the dark corners, Mirabiel's light brings us clarity and discernment. We can trust that we are in alignment with divine timing. All is perfect.

You can also call on Archangel Mirabiel to balance the feminine and masculine energy of our planet. Like the wise elder shown on her card, Mirabiel is connected to the lunar energies, so she is wonderful to call on for manifesting and releasing during the new and full moon phases.

Archangels of the Gold Flame

Metatron

Metatron is the Angel of Sacred Geometry and governs the building blocks of creation. One of only two Angels who is said to have walked the earth as a human being—the other being Sandalphon—Metatron's earthly name was Enoch. He is known as "God's Voice" and, as the divine mediator with humanity, he sits at the very top of the Tree of Life in the Kabbalistic tradition.

He helps us connect with ancient wisdom, so we can tap into our true genius. If you ask him, he will activate your DNA and crown and upper chakras. When you are ready, he will illuminate your soul's mission, so you may step on the Ascension path and become the best version of yourself.

Jehudiel

The Angel of Figureheads, Jehudiel's name means "Laudation of God", and he helps us feel qualified to step into our own guiding and leadership roles. Like his image in the oracle, Jehudiel is often depicted wearing a crown and carrying a three-pronged whip, representing the divine authority of the Holy Trinity. He is linked with the Sacred Heart, helping us recognize our own Christ Consciousness, so we may live Heaven on Earth and teach it to others.

If you are in a position of authority, ask Jehudiel to help you act with integrity at all times and acknowledge that true power is the power of love—not the love of power.

My first recollection of the name Jehudiel was during a healing session I had while on a retreat in Ibiza after starting a new position at work. With my eyes closed, I felt a powerful angelic presence beside me and clearly heard the name "Jehudiel" (pronounced as "Yeh-hoo-diel"). I then had a vision of a golden crown being placed on my head.

This Archangel is the patron of all who work in some field of endeavour. His crown symbolizes the reward for spiritual labours. As an advisor to all who hold positions of responsibility and authority, he watches over kings, queens, presidents, judges, and others in positions of power, ensuring they still remain true to God's work. He is also known as the bearer of God's merciful love.

Kerubiel

One of the heads of the mighty Cherubim Angels, Kerubiel is a powerful Archangel. Unlike the classical pictures of chubby flying babies, cherubs actually have four faces—that of a lion, an eagle, an ox, and a human—which point to each of the four directions on the compass. The name Cherubim means "wisdom", and Kerubiel's name specifically means "The Flames that Dance around the Throne of God".

When I first experienced a meeting with this force of an Angel, I felt and saw huge golden talons, like those of an eagle coming down from above me. I physically felt the sheer weight of this being as he perched on my shoulders. His eyes flashed with golden fire, and his wings blazed with lightning that came in multiple surges of electrical heat. Golden fire surged and spewed in sparks from his (human) mouth when he spoke. The request was far from light and fluffy and, although still loving, it left me trembling.

Although he may look and sound rather ominous, this Angel really does have our best interests at heart. Like a cosmic lighthouse, he calls forth peace and light and sends it out in all directions. He uses his flame to ignite the highest heights of wisdom and knowledge within us. and he is here to help everyone on the planet to awaken and ascend.

Akatriel

Akatriel is a type of super-angel, one of the Angels of the Presence or Angels of the Face, a group of ultra-important Angels that work very closely with God, or Creator. Akatriel is particularly vital as he is known as the "Voice of God" or the "Presence of God" and sits on the Throne of Glory.

Unlike most other Angels, which may have more subtle energy, when you invoke Akatriel's presence, it is easier to distinguish his firm guidance from that of your own thoughts. As he is such a powerful being, when Akatriel comes calling it can seem as though it is actually the voice of God speaking directly to you. You are certainly unlikely to question the experience when you have it.

As an Angel of Justice, Authority, and Direction, Akatriel can help you see your own greatness. He can also bring you the gifts of self-sufficiency and capability to enable you to stand on your own two feet and trust your own judgement, especially in times of hardship or when your intuition may be challenged.

He reminds you not to compare yourself with the successes of others, but to look within the depths of your own soul in order to see your true magnificence and glory. With Akatriel's assistance, as you sit in silence and look within for the answers you seek, you will feel as though you are sitting upon your own Throne of Glory, as the true master of your own destiny.

Archangels of the Platinum Flame

The Twin Irin

The Irin are twin Angels that are said to reside in the Sixth Heaven. Together with another set of twin angels known as The Qaddisin, The Irin constitute the highest council of judgement in the heavenly courts. They are among eight ultra-powerful Angels that have a rank superior even to that of mighty Metatron.

According to the Bible, The Irin are known as "The Watchers". And as such, they are able to see the whole truth of every situation. They are wearing blindfolds as a nod to Lady Justice and the notion of "blind justice". The Irin see everything, so when they are around we are rarely even able to hide from ourselves. They open our eyes to that to which we may have been previously blind and show us where we have been "blind-sided", so they can help us achieve the gift of true discernment.

Likewise, if ever you are in a situation where the truth seems to evade you, call on The Irin to clearly show you the truth at the heart of the matter. Most empaths and sensitives are highly susceptible to seeing only the good in others. However, this can be disempowering when we later discover that another may have been acting in a way that was not entirely in integrity, or perhaps they were acting selfishly and didn't have the best of intentions with regards to the impact of their actions on us.

To me, The Irin represent ultimate justice, balance, harmony, and order. Whenever they appear, they carry a set of silver and gold scales. They use these scales to help us recognize the duality, or polarities, within our lives and show us where more balance may be needed. Like Soqed Hozi and Zuriel, they can also help align our masculine and feminine energies. Mostly, though, they help us delineate right from wrong to keep us accountable for our actions, or stand up to those who may be wronging us or taking advantage of our good nature in some way. The Irin can help highlight any injustices and show you how to act as a peaceful but powerful mediator to help resolve issues from the highest possible vantage point.

Pray to this poweful pair of Angels if you are ever involved in a legal situation or court case. You can ask them to raise the matter to a higher level of justice in order for it to be reviewed by the heavenly courts. There are justice systems in every dimension and at every level of existence, so if you ever feel you are being unfairly tested or cannot see a way out of an entanglement, call on The Irin to intervene on your behalf and bring the fastest and most harmonious and fair resolution to the situation.

If you invite The Irin into your life, they will bring you into swift alignment to your core truth and help you to find and awaken your most authentic self possible.

Archangels of the Rainbow Flame

Christiel

There is a reason Archangel Christiel's name sounds like "Christ", for this Angel's name could literally be translated as "Christ of God". Christiel is the Angel charged with bringing peace, especially when peace comes in the form of causing no harm. He reminds us that, if we act from a place of causing no harm, we are less likely to attract harm and it is then easier to trust that we will be kept safe.

This pure and mighty being is an Angel of the ethereal pearlescent white light, which is made up of all the colours of the spectrum. The rainbow is the symbol of promise, so the message here is one of the promise of peace and the promise that we can choose to live out our soul's purpose if we so wish. Christiel is, therefore, an Angel of Hope.

Like Archangel Gabriel, he works closely with the energy of Christ and can help awaken this consciousness within you, enabling you to feel unconditional love towards your fellow human beings and understand that everything in existence is connected. He is associated with the reemergence of the divine feminine and activates the secret codes of the Sacred Heart in all who are ready.

Christiel's message today is one of liberty, or liberation from the belief that we are only living a 3D existence. He says we can now detach from everything we think we know as human beings. This Angel wants us to recognize our divinity, so we can co-create our lives. Then we can attain peace for the entire human race.

Tahariel

The Angel of Purity and Purification, like her image on the card, Tahariel embodies all colours of the rainbow perfectly blended to create the white light of the divine. This pure light is your light, for we are all perfect sparks of the Creator.

A Native American prophecy says: "When the Earth is ravaged and the animals are dying, a new tribe of people shall come unto the Earth from many colours, classes, creeds and who by their actions and deeds shall make the Earth green again. They will be known as the Warriors of the Rainbow."

Many high-vibrational souls are incarnating at this time to assist with our Ascension. The Angels have shown me that certain old souls have chosen to go through multiple evolutionary cycles in this one lifetime—shifting from Indigo and Crystal children into Rainbow and Diamond souls—in order to become keepers of the New Earth Rainbow and Diamond Light Frequencies. If you are drawn to this Angel, it is likely that you are currently undergoing an evolution and now stepping into your Rainbow Child essence.

Tahariel's light is exquisite because it contains all the colours but at the same time contains none of them; thus, it acts as a kind of void, where everything is possible yet all-inclusive. It is the light of all creation, the still-point between the in and the out breath. It is the purest and most refined crystalline essence of everything in existence.

When you are bathed in this light, everything is illuminated before you on your path to truth, even those things to which you might wish to remain blind. Tahariel's light will bring discernment. It may require you to step beyond your comfort zone at times, but it will also protect you from that which is not for your highest good. Be prepared to release anything that isn't serving your soul's purpose and step into the true light of the divine.

Archangels of the Diamond Flame

Sophia

Often linked with the female Ascended Masters of Compassion—namely, Isis, Mother Mary, Mary Magdalene, and Quan Yin—Sophia, whose name means "wisdom" in Greek, is the Angel of Unconditional Love and the Wisdom of the Heart. Said to be one of the first Archangels created, Sophia belongs to the order of the Seraphim and covers all aspects of love, including maternal love, familial love, romantic love, and unconditional love.

As with Rikbiel, you can call upon her for help with any issue connected with the heart, for this nurturing, gentle Angel can resolve misunderstandings, heal heartbreak, and help you find your true soulmate. But this humble ancient being rarely takes credit for her work, preferring to stay in the background, subtly encouraging peace and universal love for the planet. She watches over avatars, so if you are drawn to this Angel, you may be one of the few on a Bodhisattva path of compassionate service to humanity.

Depicted as a pregnant Mary Magdalene and known as the Heavenly Mother, she is also the guardian of the zodiac and births the essence of the stars on Earth to help us see the bigger picture. She loves without judgement and can teach you to have compassion for yourself in order to overcome past issues. Her lesson is that if we can love ourselves, then we can fall in love with the entire galaxy.

In the Bible, she was said to be crying over man's reluctance to listen to her wisdom, but perhaps as more people on the planet begin to awaken, she will get her wish. The colour I associate with Sophia is an almost cosmic, luminous, pearlescent, diamond light, like the moon with flashes of pink and deep magenta—the ray of the universal heart.

Shekinah

The feminine aspect of Archangel Metatron, Shekinah refers to the energy of the divine feminine. The actual word in Hebrew means "Presence of God" or "Glory of God". She is also known as the "Dwelling or God" or the "Settling of God", and represents the epitome of universal matriarchal unconditional love.

If the divine masculine is represented by expansion, the divine feminine energy is that of drawing in and bringing people together.

The Great Mother, Shekinah is the female aspect of the highest source of creation. She is the divine mother, the original goddess, the female representative of our Creator, as shown by the wise female elder in her depiction. This energy exists within each of us, no matter whether you are a man or a woman.

When I first experienced the Shekinah energy, I was overwhelmed by the sheer force of the love I felt. It was far more powerful than the more masculine energy of God. She came into my body, and I was overcome with emotion. At the same time, this energy felt like it was drawing me into it, engulfing me. I felt like a child being drawn to her bosom, but at the same time it was like I was being sucked into the void. There was nothingness and movement all at once, as though I was teetering on the very brink of existence—the point at the edge of the void, where creation decides to create and then begins to move into form. It was an unstoppable force but so filled with love.

And then her voice spoke to me.

She told me that she has been dormant for too long and is now reawakening. She spoke to me of a beautiful change coming in the dynamic between men and women. I felt her great sadness over the suffering and slavery of her daughters, and was shown image after image of the mistreatment of women around the world. It was like watching a newsreel. But then she showed me how women were again stepping into their power, while men were finding their softness once more. A great rebalancing was revealed.

I felt the force of her energy spiral through me and come to rest in my heart. The Shekinah reminds us that there is no need to search for love. True love exists inside us, not on the outside, so rather than searching or urgently fighting and grasping for it, we need to turn our attention inwards, draw ourselves into our own bosom, and rest in the power that lies within our hearts.

The message she has gifted us with is beautiful and inspiring. If you are a man and you are drawn to this Angel, you may be experiencing a resurfacing of your feminine, intuitive nature or have a purpose in supporting others—especially women—as they embrace their feminine power. For women, her message is:

Awaken my daughters, now you are free.
Awaken my daughters, now you can speak.
Awaken my daughters, now you shall see.
Awaken my daughters, now you can be

As mighty, as powerful, as magnificent as me.
The Shekinah lives within you.

Melchizedek

Melchizedek is the Universal Logos, from the Greek word *logos* and, in this context, referring to universal divine reason. Like the president of the universe, Melchizedek represents the overlighting consciousness of our cosmos, so he's a bit like the grandfather of the Archangels. As keeper of the Ascension pathway, he acts as the bridge between Heaven and Earth and helps us find enlightenment.

Melchizedek governs the universal golden ray, the silver-violet flame of self-transformation, sacred geometry, and the Seven Cosmic Rays of Creation, which are all contained within the highest diamond-light spectrum.

If you are drawn to this Archangel, you are an ancient soul that has chosen to return to Earth to assist in this great awakening for humanity.

The Science of Sacred Flames –
Cosmic Rays, Bioelectricity, and Bioluminescence

High-frequency atomic nuclei and electrons in the form of cosmic rays are constantly bombarding Earth from multiple directions within our galaxy. These energies are so potent that some of them can even be detected below the surface of the earth, so imagine the effect they must be having on our physical bodies.

The discovery of cosmic rays by Austrian physicist Victor Hess in 1912 led to the creation of the field of particle physics, which is concerned with particles that exist beyond the confines of the atom, such as antimatter, positrons, muons, pions, kaons, and many others.[37]

Scientists at CERN have been studying cosmic rays, many of which originate from our galaxy and can also include gamma rays, as well as shock waves from exploding stars, or supernovae. There is also speculation that supermassive black holes in other galaxies may provide some acceleration of these high-frequency rays.[38]

Interestingly, particle physics was recently used to harness cosmic rays in the form of muons in order to detect a previously unknown void within the Great Pyramid of Giza.[39]

In terms of human evolution, Nobel Prize winner H. J. Muller famously discovered that cosmic rays can alter our DNA and, although a rare occurrence, the rays can cause gene mutations at ground level.[40]

Despite this, NASA and other space programmes are undertaking ongoing research to ensure that astronauts travelling into space are safeguarded from any negative health impact of extreme cosmic rays on their central nervous systems and other organs in the body.[41] In terms of our ability to hold light, our physical bodies also give off their own light rays, known as bioluminescence, which was proven in a Japanese scientific study using a special camera that is able to photograph the body's glow within conditions of total darkness.[42]

In spiritual circles, the glow around the human body is commonly known as the "aura" and can be photographed using Kirlian photography, which is named after the Russian electrician Semyon Davidovich Kirlian, who invented it in 1939. Scientists have rejected the validity of Kirlian photography, as shown in famous experiments using a dying leaf and a torn leaf, stating that other factors, such as moisture, can impact the results.[43] The Japanese study proved to be a breakthrough, however, as they were able to detect light in the body in controlled scientific conditions where no other light was present.

The Science of How the Archangel Alchemy Visualization Processes and Working with Their Flames Can Help You Heal

Our physical bodies naturally produce their own energy flow in the form of bioelectricity, and the neurons in our brain are able to fire signals that communicate with the rest of our central nervous system.[44] A study by the University of Colorado has found that using your imagination can help you reduce stress and anxiety, as the human nervous system cannot tell the difference between real or imagined positive and negative experiences. When you imagine positive experiences, it may lead to pleasant thoughts and sensations in the body, which, in turn, promote relaxation and lead to healing.[45]

CHAPTER 15

The Archangel Alchemy Staircase of Ascension

This chapter takes you on a journey through the 17 sacred gateways of the Ascension flames to meet the 40 Archangels and guardians of Archangel Alchemy that are here to guide you along your Ascension Pathway. Attunements and processes will help connect you with your core desires through an alchemical process that can be used for divination or to make a request. As you work your way up each rung on this heavenly ladder, you will ask a different question of each Archangel and receive the blessing of their guidance and clarity through the giving of a symbolic gift, which I call "Archangel Alchemy".

The individual coloured rays of the rainbow spectrum associated with each Archangel symbolize the potent properties of divine archangelic fire. Working with the holy flames allows you to take a big step forward on your journey back to wholeness, and activating unconditional love will help you attain the unified chakra, the field of oneness found within the complete diamond spectrum, and align with your own divinity.

By using the symbol of the diamond for these attunements, you are acknowledging that you are connecting with the all and everything through unconditional love. As you receive the healing and transformative gifts of the Archangels, you simultaneously share them with the whole world—as you receive, you give, and as you give, you receive. The diamond offers a container through which your own innate healing gifts may be amplified and refined. You will automatically receive any upgrades or enhancements to your psychic and healing abilities, and your personal guide teams and psyche will open to receive direct downloads of wisdom and information from the angelic kingdom and dimensions of light.

Essentially, the rainbow spectrum of the Archangels acts as a kind of bridge, or pathway, to enlightenment, reconnecting us to our own holiness and helping us realize that we are not separate from God; we *are* God. The key to "enlightenment" is in the word "light". The Archangels' message is that by opening our hearts to deeper love, we are taking in more light and are able to shed more light on who we are by accessing our innate wisdom.

Preparing to Embark on the Archangel Alchemy Staircase of Ascension

Attuning to the Gateways

In this meditation and attunement process, you will pass through each of the Archangel Alchemy Ascension Flame Gateways to enter the Angelic Kingdom of Diamond Light. Each flame, or ray, holds different healing qualities, and each Angel comes with specific blessings or gifts to impart.

As you progress up the staircase, there are requests you are invited to make of the Archangels of each ray in order to expand your consciousness and bring more clarity to your intention for healing or divination.

You can choose to do this process as one quick journey through all the Archangels and their colours, or you may choose to work with an Angel a day, a week, a month, and so on, until you have completed the whole attunement.

This process is overlit by Lord Melchizedek, the cosmic high priest, Universal Logos, and Ascended Master of Alchemy.

◊ Set your intention to receive the alchemical gifts of the Archangels as you journey through each of their sacred colour flames.

◊ If you plan to use this process for divination purposes, have your specific question in mind, and be open to receiving guidance via your psychic senses, such as clairvoyant pictures in your mind, auditory messages, feelings, clear knowing, and so on.

◊ If you plan to use this process for manifestation or healing purposes, have your specific request or situation in mind, and be open to receiving guidance about your request via your psychic senses, such as clairvoyant pictures in your mind, auditory messages, feelings, clear knowing, and so on.

◊ With eyes closed, breathe into your centre and visualize a huge, glittering, diamond-white, multifaceted, octahedronal diamond materializing around your energy field.

◊ The uppermost point connects with your soul star chakra, 6–8 inches (15–20 cm) above your head, and the lowermost point connects with your earth star chakra, 6–8 inches (15–20 cm) below your feet. These are new higher chakras opening up as part of our Ascension process.

◊ The diamond is radiating the brightest light you have ever seen, and it spins and moves within your auric field, scattering crystalline rainbow sparkles all around you.

◊ As you connect with each Angel and their flames, visualize this diamond turning the specific colour for each ray, and invite each Archangel to step forward in turn to bless you and imbue you with their gifts.

◊ Bathe in and infuse yourself with the colours and symbols of each Angel for as long as you intuitively feel you need to.

◊ Progress through the rainbow ascension ladder until you reach the diamond flame and see the diamond in your energy field becoming crystal clear.

◊ Imagine the diamond around you has stopped spinning and moving, and place your right index finger against your lips to lock your fields and seal your space.

◊ The diamond remains within your field as your personal protection, always aligning you with the angelic kingdom and the highest frequency and vibration available to you in any given moment.

◊ Imagine this diamond has the hardness of an actual physical diamond on the outside but is filled with the light of your soul, allowing you to safely shine as brightly as you can.

The Archangel Gateway of the Black Ray

Gifts and Healing Qualities: Neutralizing negative energies, harmonization, protection, overcoming fears, tests and initiations, manifestation, comfort, nurturing, the shadow

Request: "Angels, please bring redemption to my intention or question."

Sariel: "Dark Night of the Soul"

Archangel Alchemy: Lightning of Oblivion

Sariel's lightning of oblivion is rarely sought by conscious choice. These experiences can come like a bolt from the blue, swiftly drawing the unseen into our awareness. But with courage and compassion you can use the situation to your advantage. You are not being punished; you are revealing more of your God-self.

◊ Close your eyes and invite Sariel to send his powerful electric black lightning into any pain that has arisen due to a sudden, shocking revelation in your life.

◊ Like the forensic blue light used at a crime scene, Sariel's black light will show up any hidden solutions you may not have already thought of.

◊ When faced with truly difficult situations, invoking the Black Light of Oblivion may well reveal an unexpected miracle. Do not hold onto any expectation of a specific outcome or you may block the solution. This takes absolute trust.

◊ Hand over the entire situation to Sariel and the Archangels, ask for the highest truth and healing to occur, and surrender to whatever comes.

◊ When the process is complete, cover yourself with Sariel's cloak.

◊ Open your eyes.

Tzaphkiel: "Creation from Chaos"

Archangel Alchemy: Veil of Longing

◊ Close your eyes and imagine that you are standing in a moonlit garden before the steps of an ancient open-air temple. It has stone pillars and a domed ceiling.

◊ You ascend eight steps and greet Tzaphkiel.

◊ She sits before you, veiled in black. You have come to her with your request.

◊ You know you must speak to her of your innermost desires.

◊ What is it you long for?

◊ What have you been seeking so earnestly?

◊ She beckons you forward and invites you to lift her veil.

◊ You sense fear, but as you lift the fabric, it is your face that is revealed beneath her garment. However, the eyes are black and gold, like a black hole. At her brow is an indigo Eye of Horus.

◊ Spend a moment gazing into the eyes of Tzaphkiel, and surrender to her your deepest and most elusive longing, trusting that if your desire is meant for you, it shall be granted at the right moment and in the best possible way.

◊ Thank Tzaphkiel, and receive her cloak.

◊ Return from the temple.

◊ Open your eyes.

The Archangel Gateway of the Russet Ray

Gifts and Healing Qualities: Grounding, connection to Earth, being in the "now" moment, clearing karma, security, balance, love for life, contentment

Request: "Angels, please bring adventure to my intention or question."

Adnachiel: "Wayshower"

Archangel Alchemy: Horizon of Hope

◊ Close your eyes, and ask Archangel Adnachiel to be with you.

◊ Imagine that you can feel a warm, dry, desert breeze gently caressing your face.

◊ The light around you glows a deep, sunset-red and, in the distance, far off on the horizon, you can see the wind whipping up into a giant fiery tornado.

◊ As the tornado draws ever closer, you are filled with a sense of excitement. It whisks you up into its spiralling energy. As you spin in its power, you feel safe.

◊ It's like you are floating within the eye of the storm. All fears are sucked away from you by the force of the swirling column and dissolved back into its light.

◊ As you continue to be spun within this wind of wonder, you can now see the glow of a magnificent sunrise on the horizon and, as the sun rises higher, you begin to feel lighter and freer, like nothing can hold you back from your purpose.

◊ You feel excited about the future, and you want to fly towards the horizon and the promise of what the new day holds.

◊ You are filled with gratitude for the person you are and find yourself back on your feet.

◊ The twisting column of light slowly comes to a standstill and dissolves.

◊ Visualize your Angel wings turning white. Close them around you. Open your eyes.

Cassiel: "Serenity"

Archangel Alchemy: Cocoon of Solitude

◊ Find a space where you can sit quietly and close your eyes. Invoke Cassiel by saying her name silently three times within your mind.

◊ Visualize her deep-brown eyes again, and feel her loving energy around you.

◊ As you gaze into her eyes, you feel any stuck emotions begin to stir. Allow them to rise to the surface and acknowledge what they are. Try to do this without judgement.

◊ Whatever feelings or situations arise—anger, sadness, guilt, and so on—just acknowledge them, and thank them for teaching you. Let them gently melt away.

◊ If your tears need to flow, let them come. Honour yourself and your emotions, and be very gentle with yourself throughout this exercise.

◊ As you experience your emotional depths, feel Cassiel's wings enfolding you, creating a soft feathery cocoon of solitude to lovingly encase you.

◊ Now feel your energy begin to merge and integrate with this gracious Angel, so that her wings become your wings.

◊ Know that you can create your own cave of solitude whenever you need to by wrapping your wings around yourself and calling upon Cassiel's loving presence.

◊ Thank Cassiel, and allow her energy to separate from yours once again.

◊ Visualize your own wings turning pure white, and wrap them around you again as a protective cocoon of light, sealing your space. Open your eyes.

Sandalphon: "Prayer"

Archangel Alchemy: Wheel of Miracles

◊ Call on Sandalphon to anchor and ground you, so that you can feel safer and more at home here on Mother Earth.

◊ Imagine that this huge Angel is stepping into your energy field, so that the two of you completely merge and become one being.

◊ Imagine that you have grown to fit his size and that you can feel what it would be like to be as big as this gigantic Angel.

◊ As you tower over the earth, feel your feet as though they are Sandalphon's feet, rooted right down through all the dirt, rocks, minerals, magma, and into the core of the planet.

◊ Feel, see, sense, or imagine that your head is somewhere up among the stars and you can see the entire universe from this vantage point.

◊ Sandalphon ignites your light body and it begins to swirl around you as a vast copper-gold wheel of light.

◊ With intention, you expand this wheel around you and you feel as though you are one with the universe. Call in a miracle and feel it magnetize to you. Open your eyes.

The Archangel Gateway of the Red Ray

Gifts and Healing Qualities: Grounding, stability, physical strength, vitality, forgiveness, patience, emotional healing, tenacity, success

Request: "Angels, please bring strength to my intention or question."

Uriel: "Salvation"

Archangel Alchemy: Firefly of Freedom

◊ Uriel's "flame of freedom" is often depicted as a golden-ruby fire.

◊ Call upon Uriel to invoke this fire now. As he does so, imagine that your wings are turning the same golden-ruby colour.

◊ Imagine Uriel now holding this flame above the crown of your head. As he does so, it transforms into a beautiful firefly with brilliant, golden, fiery wings.

◊ As you breathe in, the flaming firefly descends through your energy field, passing through each of your chakras—Crown, Third Eye, Throat, Heart, Solar Plexus, Sacral, Base—so that it burns away any stuck emotions and fills you with wisdom and love.

◊ The firefly pauses at each chakra, turning each of your energy centres a brilliant, purifying and sparkling white.

◊ The firefly then begins to ascend back up through your body until it hovers above your head once again, now blazing with a brilliant, dazzling-white radiance.

◊ When you feel that all your chakras have been cleansed, imagine your own wings have also turned white, and wrap them around yourself.

◊ Open your eyes.

Camael: "Justice"

Archangel Alchemy: Eyes of Truth

◊ Close your eyes. Think of a situation or event where you acted in a way you regret.

◊ Perhaps you feel you were a little too aggressive or perhaps weak. Is there something you said that you wish you could take back? Did you or another feel embarrassed?

◊ Ask Camael to bring clarity about the situation, and imagine looking into his eyes. As you lock your gaze on his, you travel back in time to that event or situation.

◊ Imagine you are now looking your past self in the eye. Mentally ask your past self: What are you really trying to say? What do you need in this moment?

◊ Spend a moment with your past self to get to the heart of the matter. Perhaps you acted defensively because of something another did to you in the past. Or maybe you acted a certain way out of a fear that people wouldn't like the authentic you?

◊ Sometimes we react to situations in a certain way because of past experiences, or because we feel uncomfortable. By uncovering the truth behind your actions, you can choose to act differently should a similar situation arise in the future.

◊ Once you have a sense of the true reason behind your actions, forgive yourself. Thank yourself for bringing this valuable lesson to your present *you*.

◊ Thank Camael. Receive his peace pipe and headdress as a gift.

◊ Open your eyes.

Haniel: "Passion and Poise"

Archangel Alchemy: Song of the Heart

◊ Close your eyes, and ask Haniel to be with you.

◊ Imagine a deep red and magenta pillar of light emerging from your heart centre and reaching upwards and downwards into infinity.

◊ Become aware of your Angel wings, and visualize them turning this exquisite shade of magenta and bright red.

◊ Spread your wings, and feel yourself totally merge with this vast pillar of red and magenta light. See yourself ablaze with Haniel's fires of passion and grace.

◊ Open your mouth and allow the most natural *Ah* sound or tone to pour out from your heart, releasing any stuck emotions. Keep toning for as long as you need to. This is a powerful exercise, so if you feel you need to shed some tears, let them flow.

◊ Continue until you feel your heart is clear. Be honest with yourself. You can always do the process again on another occasion.

◊ Then repeat the same toning process for all your chakras, beginning at the base chakra and working your way all the way up to the crown.

◊ When you have toned through all of your energy centres and feel that they have been cleared, centre yourself back in your heart, and visualize the pillar of light now turning a pure silvery-white.

◊ Mentally call all your true passions to you, feeling that the space you have now created in your heart is open and ready to receive.

◊ Thank Haniel, and allow the pillar of light to retract back into your heart centre. See your wings turning pure white, and wrap them around yourself. Open your eyes.

The Archangel Gateway of the Pink Ray

Gifts and Healing Qualities: Love, romance, compassion, kindness, trust, connection, softness, gentleness

Request: "Angels, please bring love and compassion to my intention or question."

Chamuel: "Love and Relationships"

Archangel Alchemy: Light of Love

◊ Close your eyes, and imagine that you are travelling down into your heart chakra, as though you are looking out at the world through the centre of your chest.

◊ Ask Chamuel to ignite the light of love within your heart, and picture a bright-pink flaming orb expanding out from you. Your own wings expand and turn pink.

◊ See the orb increase in size until it fills and surrounds your whole body and your aura. Then see it move farther and wider out into the world around you.

◊ As this flaming globe of love grows bigger, it also builds in intensity. You can feel a slight pressure on your chest as more and more love pours into your heart.

◊ Visualize the flame expanding until it fills the whole universe.

◊ Consciously send this energy of unconditional love out to everything in existence.

◊ Send extra love to anyone you have recently been having difficulty with. Be honest, and try your best to feel compassion for this person—however difficult that feels.

◊ Direct extra love to any parts of the world in need.

◊ And, most importantly, radiate love from within to your whole self.

◊ Imagine your wings turning white, and wrap them around yourself.

◊ Open your eyes.

Ariel: "Strength of Heart"

Archangel Alchemy: Forest Friends

◊ Close your eyes, and imagine that you are sitting by a tranquil stream in a woodland.

◊ As you look at the forest around you, you begin to see subtle movements among the leaves, like the flutter of tiny wings.

◊ You realize that the forest is alive with fairies and nature spirits. They fly around you, sprinkling you with glittering-pink fairy dust.

◊ Soon, all the animals of the forest emerge to greet you.

◊ One of these animals stands out to you. It is a magical unicorn with a horn of spiralling light in the centre of its forehead.

◊ The unicorn bows before you. It touches its horn to your third eye, your heart, and then your navel, awakening the three treasures of your wisdom.

◊ Thank the unicorn, and ask Ariel to send the fairies to all the creatures in the world that need healing and protection.

◊ Wrap your wings around yourself.

◊ Open your eyes.

Rikbiel: "Compassion"

Archangel Alchemy: Heart Blossom

◊ Ask Rikbiel to activate his wheel of love, and imagine a rose-gold flower bud spiralling in the very centre of your heart.

◊ As this circular spiral of light begins to spin, the flower petals begin to open, and you realize that the flower is a beautiful pink-gold rose.

◊ Your whole body is filled with rosy, golden light.

◊ Visualize your Angel wings now turning a beautiful shade of pink-gold, and stretch them out wide. You may find that there is no limit to how far they can reach.

◊ This light then expands out from your heart and body. As it does so, the petals of the rose begin to very gently detach and float out into the world around you.

◊ Set the intention that these petals of compassion are floating off to whoever needs them.

◊ See these petals coming to rest in the heart centre of anyone you feel needs to have a little more compassion for others in their heart, and those who need to be treated with more compassion—either by you or those around them.

◊ As you send out these petals of pure love and compassion, their gifts are returned to you in a never-ending cycle of spiralling light.

◊ Know that you are helping to raise our planet's positive vibration with the power of your positive and loving thoughts.

◊ Thank Rikbiel. Allow your wings to turn pure white and open your eyes.

The Archangel Gateway of the Orange Ray

Gifts and Healing Qualities: Creativity, passion, intimacy, sexuality, sensuality, happiness, motivation, pleasure, fertility, adaptability, generosity

Request: "Angels, please bring pleasure to my intention or question."

Soqed Hozi: "Balance"

Archangel Alchemy: Pendulum of Partnership

◊ This is a powerful exercise to do either alone or with a partner. Invoke the Archangel Soqed Hozi to join you.

◊ Find somewhere to sit comfortably, either facing your own reflection in a mirror or, if you are teaming up with your partner, ask them to sit opposite you.

◊ Gaze into the eyes of your reflection or partner's eyes, and set the intention that you are strengthening the balance of love and understanding between you.

◊ Tuning into your sensory awareness, imagine that there is a constant flow of gold-orange energy moving between your hearts in the shape of the infinity symbol (like the number 8 on its side).

◊ Feel the love pouring from your heart into theirs (or your reflection), and vice versa, in a constant cycle of giving and receiving love.

◊ As the energies cross in the central space between you they combine, so that you are receiving self-love at the same time as you are receiving your partner's love, and they are giving and receiving, too.

◊ Spend as long as you like doing this exercise, and feel the energy of mutual love and respect grow between you.

◊ If you are working with a mirror, you will find your self-esteem and confidence greatly improves the more you do this process.

◊ Thank Soqed Hozi. Wrap your wings around yourself or your partner, and feel or sense your wings turn to brilliant-white as a protective cloak around you.

◊ Complete the session with a loving, warm embrace. If working with your own reflection, hug yourself!

Radueriel: "Creativity"

Archangel Alchemy: Song of Surrender

◊ Have a piece of paper and a pen handy. Close your eyes, and ask Radueriel to be with you to help you ignite your creative abilities.

◊ Feel his loving energy surrounding you, and imagine that he's now singing over you in the highest, most pure musical tones.

◊ Imagine that you can see these exquisite sounds as the most dazzling waves of sparkling, golden-orange mist flowing over and around you.

◊ Allow this powerful angelic sonic vibration to envelop you, and feel your own Angel wings become this sparkling, gold-orange hue. You now shift into the highest possible version of you. Open your heart, and let yourself sing along with him.

◊ As you allow this metamorphosis to occur, through your pure loving intention, anything inauthentic around your ability to create simply lifts away.

◊ Take up your pen and paper, and invite Radueriel to write some words of loving encouragement through you in a stream of consciousness. Keep writing without pausing until you feel the need to stop. Read and reflect on this new-found wisdom.

◊ Wrap your wings around yourself as a cloak of creativity. Know you are a truly perfect, creative, and highly gifted human being.

◊ Thank Radueriel, and open your eyes.

Barachiel: "Fulfilment"

Archangel Alchemy: Bread of Abundance

◊ Close your eyes and call upon Barachiel to fill your life with abundance, especially your family and home life.

◊ Picture your life as it would be with everything you need to be happy. See your prayers for your perfect soulmate, your ideal career, financial rewards, and a happy home life already fulfilled.

◊ As your worries about love, money, and abundance evaporate, feel any stress and tension rapidly dissolving.

◊ Imagine Barachiel floating above you, your life, and your loved ones, sending golden-brown loaves of bread from her basket to each of you.

◊ As the bread falls, it transforms into huge, bright-white rose petals. The petals tickle your face, making you chuckle. You are now able to laugh at any hardships, seeing them as blessings or illusions.

◊ The petals continue to fall around you and over you and, as they gently land on your shoulders, they activate your Angel wings, which turn a magnificent, sparkling white.

◊ Visualize or intend now that your wings are enfolding your parents, siblings, partner, children, and all your loved ones.

◊ Your wings act as a powerful magnetic force, drawing to you and your loved ones all the blessings and abundance they need for their happiness. Know your needs will always be met. Thank Barachiel, and open your eyes.

The Archangel Gateway of the Yellow Ray

Gifts and Healing Qualities: Power, confidence, charisma, strong will, leadership, clarity, humour, joy, fun, confidence, empowerment, self-esteem

Request: "Angels, please bring confidence to my intention or question."

Jophiel: "Joy"

Archangel Alchemy: Seeds of Glee

◊ Close your eyes, and call on Jophiel.

◊ Picture a sparkling, golden-yellow fountain of light pouring in through your crown chakra. This is the light of jubilant illumination.

◊ Next, think of anything you would like more clarity on.

◊ Ask Jophiel for the answers, and see if anything pops into your mind. You might not receive an immediate response, but an answer may arrive over the next few days.

◊ Next, ask Jophiel to lighten your load and help you release any physical and emotional burdens from your life.

◊ Like a gentle breeze moving through tall grass, Jophiel's energy wafts through your environment, scattering stuck energies.

◊ Similar to the seeds of a dandelion, they are broken up, transmuted, and scattered to the winds with all the lightness of a child's laughter.

◊ Then, like a champagne cork popping, any residual worries, cares, and clutter are blasted up and out of your life, transforming into a fizzy rapture of light.

◊ Feel the excitement of a new, positive outlook now cascading down over you in a torrent of yellow-gold angelic bubbles.

◊ Allow yourself to be filled with frothy feelings of joy and bliss from head to toe.

◊ As this rush of unbridled excitement takes over, your wings fly open and flap away any residual negativity.

◊ Send out your intention for joy once again, like those dandelion seeds on the wind.

◊ Turning pure white, your wings close around you as a protective cocoon.

◊ Allow yourself to smile, imagining that warm sunlight is shining down on your face.

◊ Send gratitude to Jophiel. Open your eyes when you feel ready.

Galgaliel: "Power"

Archangel Alchemy: Vibrational Vortex

◊ Close your eyes, and breathe deeply. Ask Galgaliel to clear your energy field and chakras, removing blockages and aligning you with your true life mission.

◊ As she rides in on her blazing golden chariot, you feel the warm glow of sunlight in your chest. A solar orb opens in your heart. It begins to spin in a clockwise direction.

◊ Gathering speed, the golden glow becomes a powerful, expanding energy vortex, spinning out and burning away dense energy, activating and cleansing your chakras.

◊ It opens out into your aura and keeps expanding for as far as it needs to. You now feel your true divine spark ignite as you are bathed in self-confidence.

◊   Set the intention that you are sending the energy of empowerment out to every living being on this planet and raising the vibration of everyone and everything.

◊   Let this vortex of light spin in a clockwise direction, sending love across the world.

◊   You can also imagine that this light is like an orb of sunshine within your heart centre, and see it expand and grow until it surrounds Earth like a golden-yellow halo.

◊   See waves of sunshine-yellow light, warmth, and power touching the hearts of every being on this planet, as the power of love sweeps away all fear and negativity.

◊   Feel the spinning gently slow and come to rest.

◊   Thank Galgaliel. Open your eyes.

The Archangel Gateway of the Green Ray

Gifts and Healing Qualities: Unconditional love, equanimity, belonging, surrender, higher perspective, emotional and physical healing, transitions

Request: "Angels, please bring healing to my intention / question."

Raphael: "Healing"

Archangel Alchemy: The Caduceus

◊ A staff with two entwined snakes and wings at the top, the Caduceus connects you to Raphael for healing and balance.

◊ Picture this gold-and-silver staff running down through your spine, with the tip in Heaven (Source/God energy) and the end in Earth's core (Goddess energy).

◊ A spark of light ignites the rod's tip and travels down your spine, in turn igniting your chakras. At Earth's core, another spark of light meets the first and heads back up the chakras to ignite your third eye, linking you to the divine.

◊ The light travelling down from above and up from below cleanses, balances, and aligns all your energy centres and meridians, offering deep healing on a core level.

◊ Sit with this energy for as long as you need to and then allow the symbol to fade.

◊ Rinse off in white light, ground and shield yourself, and open your eyes.

◊ You can place a flaming-gold, spinning caduceus in your energy field to help shield and strengthen your immune system and intend it to repel unwelcome pathogens.

Azrael: "Transitions"

Archangel Alchemy: Celestial Soul Bridge

◊   Close your eyes. Think of anyone in spirit to whom you wish to send a message, and invoke Azrael to help deliver your message directly to them.

◊   See him standing before you and, as he spreads open his huge wings in front of you, a bridge bathed in blue, green, and soft lavender light appears, stretching to Heaven.

◊   Set the intention to send your messages of love and comfort across this bridge to your loved ones on the other side.

◊   Know that they have received your gift with gratitude.

◊   Thank Azrael. Open your eyes.

The Archangel Gateway of the Turquoise Ray

Gifts and Healing Qualities: Nurturing, unconditional love, surrender, non-attachment, non-judgement, clarity, cleansing

Request: "Angels, please bring surrender and release to my intention or question."

Phuel: "Cleansing"

Archangel Alchemy: Stream of Clarity

◊ Do this exercise in the shower or bath as part of your daily routine to help cleanse your mind, body, and energy field. It will refresh your spirit.

◊ As you step under the running water of the shower, or lie back in the bath, ask Phuel to energize the water, so that it washes away negative emotions, beliefs, and thoughts.

◊ Picture a stream of turquoise-and-white light raining over you and through you. You may wish to imagine you are in a beautiful lagoon with a waterfall.

◊ As the dark or heavy energy is washed down the drain, it is dissolved by Mother Earth. The soothing waters bring you a new-found sense of clarity, balance, and peace.

◊ Imagine Phuel placing a turquoise silk cloak around you, sealing your energy field.

◊ When you have completed your bathing ritual, thank Phuel, and bless the waters, sending any excess healing and light down the drain into Mother Earth as a gift.

Zacharael: "Graceful Surrender"

Archangel Alchemy: Candle and Crystal Surrender Ceremony

◊ Hold the issue you need help with in your mind and say this prayer:

Beloved Zacharael,

Mighty Angel of surrender and release,
I hand over all my cares, worries, fears, and doubts.
And all my hopes, dreams, and desires.

Lift all burdens from my shoulders.

Clear my mind of anything hindering me
from receiving the clarity I need.

Please bring me the best outcome to this situation
[name situation or issue here]
for my highest good and
for the highest good of all involved.

I trust in you to bring about a swift and miraculous resolution,
which will occur in perfect, divine timing.
I surrender to the will of the divine.

I am ready to receive the blessings and miracles you and
the Angels are gifting me with.

I ask that I easily recognize any gifts,
blessings, and miracles as soon as they arrive.

I surrender. I surrender. I surrender.

It is done. It is done. It is done.

Thank you.

◊   Now blow out the candle and, as you do so, allow the smoke to send your prayer to Zacharael, so that he may take the burden from you and orchestrate a miracle.

◊   Next, place the crystal under your pillow, and ask Zacharael and the Angels to bring you any clarity, solutions, and answers you need during the hours of sleep.

The Archangel Gateway of the Blue Ray

Gifts and Healing Qualities: Expression, communication, truth, courage, service, purpose, synchronicity, friendship, protection, abundance

Request: "Angels, please bring truth to my intention or question."

Sachiel: "Wealth and Charity"

Archangel Alchemy: Shepherd's Staff

◊ Close your eyes, and ask Sachiel to be your personal guardian of wealth, value, prosperity, and abundance.

◊ Imagine that she is now offering you her magic golden shepherd's staff. Take it from her graciously, and see yourself dipping it into your wallet or bank account.

◊ Stir your finances with the tip of the staff, and witness yourself conjuring more and more financial support, while protecting the resources you already have.

◊ With Sachiel's staff for you to lean on, you will always be secure.

◊ Open your eyes.

Asariel: "Emotional Expression"

Archangel Alchemy: Abyss of Abundance

◊ Close your eyes, and imagine that Asariel is in front of you, holding her trident.

◊ Behind her is the sea, and you notice the vast waves rolling onto the shore.

◊ Asariel turns and, with her trident outstretched in front her, she beckons you into the waves. As you dip below the water, you can breathe and feel peaceful and calm.

◊ You come across a treasure chest. You know that it contains your heart's desires. Open the chest, and feel the precious contents rise out of it and flow into your heart.

◊ Visualize your most heartfelt desire, and feel it being activated within your heart.

◊ Meditate on a feeling of serene contentment, and let it bring you back to your calm centre, so that you can rest in equilibrium.

◊ Thank Asariel, and open your eyes.

Michael: "Courage and Protection"

Archangel Alchemy: Sword of Light

Michael's powerful sword is made from the pure light of the Creator, the light of unconditional love. The ultimate illumination, it illuminates the way forward when you need guidance, and there is nothing that can withstand its brilliance.

◊ Close your eyes, and ask Michael to use his sword to cut away any negative emotional cords that bind you to people, places, or events that are preventing you from moving forward.

◊ As you feel each cord release, seal it in white light to prevent it from reattaching.

◊ Michael can also use his sword to suck negative energy out of your aura or space.

◊   Finally, ask Michael to place his sword in your energy field, along your spinal cord, to keep you centred in your truth and integrity.

◊   Ask him to give you his shield and cloak for security when needed. Open your eyes.

The Archangel Gateway of the Purple Ray

Gifts and Healing Qualities: Vision, intuition, insight, perception, spiritual sight, clear perspective, psychic abilities, dreams

Request: "Angels, please bring magic to my intention or question."

Jeremiel: "Mercy"

Archangel Alchemy: Amethyst Aura

◊ Close your eyes, and call on Jeremiel. Imagine him standing behind you, enveloping you with his shimmering, purple wings.

◊ He invites you to enter a beautiful amethyst temple of light.

◊ As you enter the crystal temple, his amethyst aura covers you from head to toe with a protective shield; you may even see purple sparkles around you.

◊ Ask Jeremiel to show you the hidden blessings in any issue you're struggling with, and imagine that you are now gazing into an amethyst crystal ball.

◊ At first the crystal is filled with purple mist, but then an image becomes clear. You may not get a message straight away, but know the situation will be resolved.

◊ Thank Jeremiel, and open your eyes.

Raziel: "Mystery"

Archangel Alchemy: Tree of Life

◊ Close your eyes, and ask Raziel to help you connect with your true divine self.

◊ See him bringing the sacred Tree of Life symbol of the Kabbalah down into you through your crown, integrating the symbol's wisdom within your energy field.

◊ As you and the symbol become one, a lightning bolt courses down from the heavens, linking every sphere on the Tree of Life within your energy field.

◊ A sphere of purple light opens at your throat. You receive an attunement from Raziel. He opens your gate of Gnosis, offering you access to his sacred book of all wisdom.

◊ Stand in your power, knowing that whatever you need is already within you.

◊ Rinse off in white light, and ground yourself with gratitude.

◊ Open your eyes.

The Archangel Gateway of the Violet Ray

Gifts and Healing Qualities: Miracles, wisdom, knowledge, unity, awareness, intelligence, bliss, understanding, inner knowing, claircognizance

Request: "Angels, please bring miracles to my intention or question."

Zadkiel: "Freedom and Transmutation"

Archangel Alchemy: The Alchemist's Cloak and the Philosopher's Stone

◊   Close your eyes, and call on Zadkiel to set you ablaze with his violet flame whenever you feel weighed down by negativity or trapped by circumstances.

◊   Ask Zadkiel to wrap the violet flame around you like an alchemist's cloak of lavender light. Sweep this cloak around you to clear and transmute lower energies around you.

◊   Choose how you would like to feel, and ask Zadkiel to sweep his violet fire through your being and out into the world around you to align the frequency of any place or space to the positive and uplifting emotions of your choice.

◊   You can send this flame out into any space. Try it on public transport, in your workplace, or in any area around you to cleanse, align, and lift the vibration.

◊   As sensitives, we can often pick up on the energies of a person or place, but we also need to remember that we have the power to change the state of energy via intention.

◊   Next, imagine Zadkiel is handing you his magical philosopher's stone, placing it in your left hand. In your mind's eye it appears as a glowing gem, with the golden alchemical symbol of the philosopher's stone radiating from its centre.

◊ Place the gem inside your heart to acknowledge and activate your inner alchemist.

◊ Freedom is always within sight when Zadkiel is near. Thank him, and open your eyes.

Zuriel: "Diplomacy and Fair Play"

Archangel Alchemy: The Spiral Dance

The Spiral Dance, or Weaver's Dance, is a contemporary pagan ritual of movement and rebirth to help raise the vibration of a community or group of people.

◊ This dance is a simplified version. If you are working alone, you may just wish to gently whirl on the spot or let your body move in whatever way it pleases.

◊ If you are gathered in a group, choose a leader, and have everyone stand in a circle, holding hands.

◊ Set your intention.

◊ Choose a leader, and invoke Zuriel's pink-violet flame to lovingly bathe and harmonize the entire community as a microcosm of humanity.

◊ The leader lets go of the hand of the person to their left and starts to move to their left, passing in front of that person.

◊ The rest of the group follow the leader.

◊ Keep winding towards the centre of the circle, until you form a tight spiral.

◊ The last person can then become the leader, guiding the spiral in another direction.

The Archangel Gateway of the White Ray

Gifts and Healing Qualities: Hope, higher purpose, higher consciousness, collective consciousness of the planet, purity, peace, clarity, spiritual gifts

Request: "Angels, please bring hope to my intention or question."

Gabriel: "Holy Purpose"

Archangel Alchemy: The Golden Trumpet

Sometimes portrayed as a white lily, the symbol of purity, Gabriel's trumpet alerts us to the fact that he/she is igniting our divine spark, or inner light.

◊   Close your eyes, and think of all your past experiences and hardships.

◊   What have you learnt? Where did you stray from your path, only to have a life lesson occur to help bring things back into perspective?

◊   See the good in each lesson, knowing that there really are no wrong choices.

◊   Trust that if you stray too far from your true path, Gabriel's golden trumpet will sound to call you back into alignment.

◊   Imagine the trumpet also sounding to celebrate each blessing you have received.

◊   While change is not always comfortable, Gabriel helps us see our past experiences as strengths to help us move forward.

◊   The trumpet call reminds you that it's your time to shine.

◊   Thank Gabriel, and receive a white cloak for security.

◊   Open your eyes.

Selathiel: "Devotion"

Archangel Alchemy: Incense of Intercession

◊ Find a quiet space where you won't be disturbed, and light some incense (if you have none to hand or have allergies, you can just imagine the smell of incense burning).

◊ Picture Selathiel holding open a golden swinging incense holder.

◊ Think of the prayer you feel needs answering most urgently, and ask Selathiel to help you find the right words to pray.

◊ See your prayers flowing into the incense holder.

◊ You may feel a warm sensation around your ears to signify Selathiel is listening.

◊ Deeply inhale the scent of the incense (real or imaginary) three times.

◊ As Selathiel swings the incense, the smoke turns white, and your prayers rise with it. Set the intention to release them totally, knowing that they will be answered.

◊ See the smoke now come into your energy field, purifying and uplifting you.

◊ Thank Selathiel, open your eyes, and if using incense, extinguish it or let it burn out.

The Archangel Gateway of the Silver Ray

Gifts and Healing Qualities: Connection to higher self, realization of divine purpose, transcending karma, access to the Akashic records, manifestation, awakening

Request: "Angels, please bring awakening to my intention or question."

Mirabiel: "Reflection"

Archangel Alchemy: Mirrored Moon

◊ During a full moon, go outside, and call upon Mirabiel to activate her mirror ball of cleansing and protection.

◊ Visualize a multifaceted, silver-blue mirror ball within your heart chakra.

◊ As you bathe in the light of the full moon, the mirror ball is activated.

◊ It expands until it fills your whole auric field, reflecting away any negative energy.

◊ This lunar shield of light also shines the light of the divine feminine into the aura of anyone you encounter, so that they also benefit from this purification.

The Archangel Gateway of the Gold Ray

Gifts and Healing Qualities: Direct access to Source, understanding our infinite nature, limitlessness, divine insight, enlightenment, Christ light

Request: "Angels, please bring wisdom to my intention or question."

Metatron: "Ancient Wisdom"

Archangel Alchemy: Metatron's Golden Cube

◊ Close your eyes, and ask Metatron to cleanse and balance your chakras with his multifaceted, golden, geometric cube.

◊ Visualize the cube coming down from way on high, activating your higher Ascension chakras as it descends from above you.

◊ See it now hovering over the top of your head, glowing in vibrant, golden light.

◊ The cube slowly begins to rotate, giving off brighter light as it does so.

◊ With your intention, invite the cube to connect with your crown chakra. You may feel a tingling sensation as it merges with this centre.

◊ Allow the cube to spin within this energy vortex until you feel the cleansing and balancing has occurred. You may sense old energies leave during the process.

◊ Then imagine or visualize the cube moving down through your energetic body, cleansing and spinning in each of your chakras, one by one.

◊ As it reaches your feet, the cube now moves back up through each of your chakras to close them down again and seal your energy field.

◊ See the cube now exit through your crown chakra and hover above you once more.

◊ The symbol then showers a golden light over you, like a canopy or dome holding you within Metatron's protective influence.

◊ Allow the cube to ascend all the way back up to eternal Source.

◊ Ground yourself by becoming aware of your physical body. Open your eyes.

Jehudiel: "Leadership and Endeavour"

Archangel Alchemy: Whip and Crown of Salvation

◊ Close your eyes, and ask Jehudiel to help you step into your true personal power.

◊ He places a golden crown upon your head. See the detail of this crown. How big is it? Is it decorated with any symbols or motifs? What does it represent to you?

◊ Feel the weight of this crown. Allow it to ground and centre you. Feel it compelling you to sit or stand taller and straighter, giving you a more dignified air.

◊ Allow the power of the crown—and the feeling of being a magnificent and loving being—to fill your entire aura and energy field.

◊ Next, Jehudiel hands you his three-pronged whip for courage, strength, and devotion, especially with regards to your sacred service work.

◊ Suddenly, your heart bursts into gold flame. You are gifted with the sacred heart of Christ as your own Christed sovereign self is activated.

◊ See golden light streaming through all your chakras, cloaking and bathing you in light.

◊ Thank Jehudiel. Rinse off in white light, ground yourself, and open your eyes.

Kerubiel: "Illumination"

Archangel Alchemy: Compass of Consciousness

◊ Stand facing the cardinal direction of North, and close your eyes. Imagine Kerubiel is pouring his flame of wisdom through your crown.

◊ As you turn towards each subsequent direction, direct this flame through your third eye at your brow, illuminating the consciousness of every living thing.

◊ In the North, send healing to the earth energies—the rocks, plants, trees and flowers, animals and people.

◊ In the East, send this healing flame through the air to the birds and insects, enhancing and awakening the gifts of creativity and communication.

◊ In the South, use this fire to burn out all impurities and ask for warmth, comfort, and celebration to flood into people's hearts.

◊ Facing West, send healing out to the waterways and sea life, blessing our emotions.

◊ Finally, bring the flame down through your entire being, allowing it to wash over you until it rests in your heart as a warm glow.

◊ Thank Kerubiel, and open your eyes.

Akatriel: "Glory"

Archangel Alchemy: Throne of Glory

◊ Find a quiet space where you won't be disturbed.

◊ Sit on a chair with your back straight and your feet flat on the floor.

◊ Close your eyes, and call upon Akatriel.

◊ Feel the presence of this mighty Angel as he manifests in front of you.

◊ Then visualize him totally integrating with you in the same seated posture.

◊ As Akatriel places a gold crown on your head, see white light streaming down into your crown chakra at the top of your head.

◊ In your mind, say the words I AM that I AM to activate the voice of God within you.

◊ Ask any question, and await the answer. Trust what comes to you.

◊ Open your eyes.

The Archangel Gateway of the Platinum Ray

Gifts and Healing Qualities: Activation of the light body, perfect flow, unification, oneness, all chakras become one unified chakra, complete alignment, totality, stellar alignment, cosmic balance

Request: "Angels, please bring justice to my intention or question."

The Twin Irin: "Truth"

Archangel Alchemy: Scales of Discernment

◊ Call upon the Irin to align you with your true self and personal power. You will need to have a pen and paper to hand for part of this exercise.

◊ Close your eyes, and visualize two Angels, one male and one female, arriving before you. Between them, they hold the scales of ultimate justice, symbolizing the human heart being weighed against a feather.

◊ One holds a leather book, and the other holds a feather quill. As you gaze at them, the book transforms into a golden sheaf of wheat, symbolizing the successful harvesting of hidden knowledge.

◊ The feather quill then transforms into a mighty sword to symbolize the expression and execution of absolute truth. The two Angels then merge into one.

◊ As you bathe in their sacred flame, ask the Irin to reveal the truth of a specific situation you need more clarity about.

◊ Open your eyes, then take your paper and pen and start writing. Do not pause. Merely write whatever comes instantly to your mind.

◊ Don't worry too much if nothing comes to you at first. Just be patient with yourself, and take your time. The topic of your enquiry might be surprising to you.

◊ Read back over your message, and take any action necessary in order to live according to your highest truth and integrity in relation to the situation.

◊ You can try this exercise as often as you like whenever you need some guidance.

◊ As they stand before you, the Twin Irin lower their silver-and-gold scales of discernment into your energy field through your crown chakra.

◊ Visualize these scales, which are now glowing with iridescent, platinum light, melting into you and integrating with you.

◊ Feel yourself growing strong and centred, and trust that, as long as you are on the path of truth, you will always have divine justice on your side.

◊ Thank the Irin, and allow them to wrap you in their wings of light.

◊ Open your eyes.

The Archangel Gateway of the Rainbow Ray

Gifts and Healing Qualities: Understanding your true universal essence, clarity, perfection, completion, wholeness, connection to everything

Request: "Angels, please bring perfection to my intention or question."

Christiel: "Peace"

Archangel Alchemy: Christic Pearls of Peace

◊ Close your eyes, and focus on your causal chakra, another Ascension chakra, located approximately 3–4 inches (7–10 cm) from the centre of the back of your head.

◊ Imagine this chakra opening into a sphere, a luminous, full moon.

◊ Call on Christiel to bless you, and feel hundreds of his pearls of divine wisdom and peace flooding in through your causal chakra.

◊ These pearls carry the Christic Light Codes, hailing the resurgence of the feminine Christ, to all your energy centres to be activated and illuminated.

◊ As they integrate, they heighten your vibration on a molecular level. As these pearls dissolve into you, see, feel, and know yourself to be divine.

◊ Christiel then reaches into his heart and pulls out the flaming Sacred Heart of Christ.

◊ He places this into your own heart centre to remind you that we are all Christed beings of love at our heart's deepest core level. We are all capable of Ascension.

◊ Christiel wraps his pearly rainbow cloak around you. Thank him, and open your eyes.

Tahariel: "Rainbow Child"

Archangel Alchemy: Ethereal Essence

◊ Close your eyes, and call on Tahariel to help you embrace your true innocence.

◊ Visualize a multicoloured ray of light showering down upon you and flowing into you like flames through the crown chakra at the top of your head.

◊ As the flames reach you, they transform into hundreds of rainbow-coloured feathers.

◊ The light blends with your aura and turns to pure white, filling your whole body and filtering through your energy field, like liquid crystal.

◊ This light activates your divine essence. It may not appear to change any difficult circumstances, but it will alter the way you deal with them—softening and opening your heart and allowing you to deepen into your sensitivity and tenderness.

◊ With your divine essence illuminated, you become more balanced during times of stress and less affected by other people's energy and actions.

◊ You now realize that you are your own sanctuary. Your light will shield you from negative people and situations and, as you trust in the divine, so you trust in you. Let your light shine.

◊ Thank Tahariel. As she again places her rainbow cloak around you, open your eyes.

The Archangel Gateway of the Diamond Ray

Gifts and Healing Qualities: The divine "I AM" presence, Source, Oneness

Request: "Angels, please bring completion to my intention or question."

Sophia: "Unconditional Love"

Archangel Alchemy: Tears of Truth

◊ Close your eyes, and imagine Sophia's tears of compassion and universal truth raining down upon you.

◊ Her tears start to fall more heavily until they become a rainstorm.

◊ Each tear resembles a star and, as they enter your aura, these crystalline stars laser through any negative emotions.

◊ The diamond tears begin to pool in each of your chakras, starting from the base and filling you all the way up to your crown.

◊ Each pool begins to spin, creating a sparkling whirlpool that funnels downwards, cleansing the chakras and allowing lower emotions or blocks to drain away into a magical well deep within Mother Earth, where they are transmuted back into love.

◊ Feel refreshed and renewed, breathing in deeply, as though you are breathing in the fresh, clean air that follows a downpour.

◊ Sophia then wraps you up in her diamond-magenta cloak for protection and cocoons you in her delicate wings for comfort. Thank Sophia, and open your eyes.

Shekinah: "Divine Mother"

Archangel Alchemy: The Crystalline Cosmic Egg

◊   Close your eyes, and ask Shekinah to align you with unconditional love and compassion.

◊   She wraps her diamond and magenta wings around you in a loving embrace.

◊   She then pours a ray of diamond light into your heart through your crown.

◊   This light becomes a blazing fire and begins to spread, helping you to gift pure universal love to yourself and others.

◊   Now picture her light moving within your energy field as liquid, viscous, and jelly-like. This fluid light is black, but it is filled with zillions of glittering diamond sparkles.

◊   From the heavens, she draws down a great crystalline egg and places it in your aura.

◊   A golden ball of fire like the sun ignites in your solar plexus, and you realize the yolk of this egg is the Great Central Sun and the Source of all light for our galaxy.

◊   If you are drawn to Shekinah, you are indeed an ancient soul that has chosen to return to Earth to assist in this great awakening for humanity.

◊   Spend as long as you need to in this space.

◊   Open your eyes when you are ready.

Melchizedek: "Ascension"

Archangel Alchemy: Cosmic Colour Wheel

◊ Close your eyes, and imagine that you are basking in rainbow-coloured light.

◊ As you look up, you realize this light is a ladder or a bridge. You float upwards through the coloured light into space until you reach a dazzling white star. Step into this white light.

◊ In the centre of the star is a marble table with a loaf of bread and a gold chalice on it. You take a bite of the bread and sip from the chalice. This is spiritual nourishment.

◊ Soon you are engulfed by the brilliant flame of Melchizedek's diamond, rainbow, silver, gold, and violet spectrum. Feel, see, and imagine these colours swirling through every cell in your body, and breathe them into your being.

◊ Ask him if he has a message. Take note of any words or images that pop into your head. Picture a geometric wheel with segments that are all the colours of the rainbow within the diamond flame.

◊ Imagine you are placing this wheel inside your heart.

◊ Breathe in and, like rose petals opening, see your heart expanding with each breath. On each in-breath, you are drawing diamond light from the cosmos and the divine energy of Creator into your heart.

◊ The wheel spins in a clockwise direction, sending waves of beautiful diamond light out into the universe. Know you are raising the vibration of the universe.

◊ Melchizedek gives you the symbol of the diamond. You will witness this gift in your daily waking life in the following weeks as confirmation of this meeting. When the process is complete, open your eyes.

CHAPTER 16

Purging by Fire

At some point on the so-called "spiritual journey", you will find yourself being purged in the holy fires of transformation. As you burn, you will need to constantly remind yourself that this is exactly what you have been asking for. Nobody embarks on such a path without some form of change in mind. The transformation may begin as soft and soothing and, indeed, when you first invite the Angels in, they will be just that. But if you choose to proceed and go on proceeding in the devotion to knowing yourself—truly knowing yourself—at some point those gentle, coaxing Angels will turn fierce.

When this happens, their love will be no less compassionate, but they will waste no time in stripping you of all the lies and falsehoods you have gathered up in the small corners of your egoic mind. If your soul deems you worthy and ready for it, Pandora's proverbial box will pop its lid, and your carefully constructed world may feel as though it is literally being blown to smithereens.

I have known this path many, many times, and each time it hits, it is no less unsettling, but the acceleration that awaits you on the other side makes for one euphoric ride!

What will you purge in the fires of transition?

No matter what happens, be fiercely compassionate in staying true to yourself, your values, your truth, and your path.

The Archangel Staircase of Ascension, the process outlined in the previous chapter, is designed to offer you a safe container in which to navigate your transition. There are Archangels for just about every stage you will encounter. You do not have to move up the staircase as a linear process. If you wish, you may pick and choose which Archangel resonates best for you in any given moment, then work solely with them or choose a combination of these loving beings to offer you support, depending on the set of circumstances or emotions you are dealing with.

For example, you may call on the following Archangels: Sariel and Tzaphkiel to help you navigate the dark, Uriel to shroud you in the flames of forgiveness, Jeremiel to offer mercy, Azrael to carry you across the threshold, Raphael to help you heal old wounds, Michael to protect and shield you, Chamuel to cradle you in the deepest love, and Shekinah to loosen your grip on resistance and soften you into grace.

Following the alchemical pathway of the Staircase of Ascension to connect with the following 40 loving Archangels of the Ascension Flames will enable you to receive their healing gifts, guidance, and support. May peace guide you through these enflaming times.

Prayer to Archangel Nuriel

A beautiful Archangel to call upon is Nuriel. Known as the "Archangel of Fire", she helps clear lower vibrational energies, and even has the power to burn through and undo black magic and spells. Nuriel is like the angelic phoenix that will help you rise again, reborn, from the ashes of any difficulties you are facing.

She burns me

Nuriel

Bringing redemption from hell

And hope of heaven swells

Within my breast

Cracking shells of icicles

Laid to rest within these caves

Of solitude and grace

I burn for her

And in this torch-touch

Of ecstasy

And intimacy

I see clearly

What is and isn't me

Or meant for me

To be

I surrender

I retreat

And fall to ash

At my own feet

A phoenix-cinder
Beaten to the dust
To spiral back
To life
With flaming
Raging lust
I'm touched
I'm torched
My heart is
Deeply scorched
And purified
To rise reborn
Within the fires
Of love's
New dawn.

Poetry: The Alchemical Healing Language of the Angels

Somewhere beyond the realms of logic and the ego lies the soul. As we awaken more to the soul's longing, align with the soul's desires, and remember the soul's calling, we deepen into gifts of communication and unlock a kind of eloquence that can far better portray the sensory and emotive landscape that our true being and spirit inhabits.

When I started writing poetry as a young child, whenever I knew that I had written something good, I somehow felt that it had come from outside of me. It was as though something opened up within my consciousness and words just flowed through.

I didn't know anything about channelling back then, but there was a certain energetic state I could go into. Whenever I wanted to put pen to paper and create something inspiring, I would slip to the back of my mind and tap into a sort of melancholy reverie, and the words would just flow. I now know that the energy I was unconsciously slipping into was a kind of trance state. I was present but also somewhere else. It was like someone had turned on a tap and I couldn't turn it off until I had all the words down on paper.

It still happens to this day, especially if I am struggling with my emotions. I was badly bullied at school, and poetry became a way for me to become my own therapist. In a Catholic household where my father was a doctor and a "man of science", my sensitivity was not understood or given space to be acknowledged or appreciated.

I would lock myself in my room for hours and let the emotions flow through me and onto the page as words. Sometimes, those words would seem jumbled or nonsensical, but then they would shape themselves into a cathartic revelation, which would help me to make sense of what I was feeling or experiencing within my emotional being.

I still use this tool today, and I share my poems freely on Instagram and other social media in the hope that they will help others in much the same way they have helped me.

Most of the time, my poems come to me without any invitation. I never intentionally sit down to write poetry. I can be on public transport, in bed, in the bath, at the cinema, and something opens up and the words begin to flow through me like silk.

I liken my experience of channelling poetry to a waterfall cascading through my mind, and beautiful images and phrases pour through me like music. For so long now, I have kept notebooks by my bed and in my bag, so I can immediately capture the words before they flit away again. Nowadays, smartphones have a Notes section, and much of this book was, in fact, written in the Notes on my phone as, in typical air-sign fashion, I tend to write better when my mind is relaxed, when I am out in nature, or moving about freely.

There is no logic to my process when it comes to poetry and, indeed, any form of creative expression. Any form of art, in my opinion, is the pure expression of your soul at play. When we allow the soul to open up and lead the way, we are able to tap into greater expanses of joy and wonderment and appreciate life and the wider world around us. Is this, then, not the very description of what it is to live Heaven on Earth?

You may not identify yourself as a poet, but every person on this planet has an innate gift or set of gifts that allows them to tap into their unique creative ability. You might have a love of cooking, sewing, painting, drawing, or dance, but you may equally be someone who expresses their creativity through dabbling in mechanics or mathematics. Every brain is wired differently, and there are those who perceive science and technology as a form of music; they are all interrelated.

It is through the doorway of our imagination that these aspects of our creative soul self really come to life. I urge you not to discount the part of you that likes to daydream. When we allow our minds to relax, observe, and play, our inner creative juices begin to flow.

Poetry, art, and any form of creativity takes us into a meditative and relaxed state, where we may open to new possibilities and ideas, which will bring us greater joy in the future. This is also the time when the Archangels, Angels, and our loving guides can most easily reach us and pour their inspiration and guidance into our hearts to help steer our lives in the best direction for each of us.

As you work your way through this book, you are using your imagination by engaging all of your extrasensory abilities as well as your logical mind to engage in self-enquiry; access new solutions; awaken your ability to heal; bridge the left and right hemispheres of your brain; unify your masculine and feminine sides; and release old patterns, stuck emotions, and outdated mindsets, so you may elevate yourself to higher states of bliss.

Scattered Leaves of Mind

Everything falls from these open hands
Not crumb
Nor morsel
Can withstand the fire
That burns me now
I have come into its power
And I quiver
As an arrow in its bow
I'm let loose
Like ashes blown
But this is a mark
I do not know
I arc artfully towards
What I cannot see
Where I cannot know
But still I must let go
Let go
Let go

And in the throes
Of passion's
Dance
The fires of life
Grant me
Perhaps
Another chance
To live
Or else to face
A death
Of what
I could not conceive
Dancing about like
Wind-whipped leaves
Is the mind
That cannot quite believe
It's lost its grip
And must let go
And leave the ancient soul
To lead.

Express Your Pure Angelic Soul

Each of the exercises below can be done separately, or you may wish to try a few in a row. Play around with whatever works for you, and invite joy into your heart as you experiment and explore. As you perform each of these processes, you are opening a sacred portal direct to the angelic kingdom and the divine presence, and you are also acknowledging that the divine presence exists within you. Begin with a short meditation to breathe in the diamond flame of the Archangels.

Meditation

◊ As you breathe in, feel your lungs and heart filling with diamond-white fire and light, and see this light spreading throughout your entire being and body.

◊ See your body being surrounded in holy white fire, like the lining of a cloud.

◊ Let this light fill your whole auric field, and imagine it is transforming into a huge white Angel around you. This is your angelic soul self.

◊ Spend a few moments connecting with what it feels like to experience yourself as your purest soul's essence.

◊ Feel all the feelings and sensations of what it is to be a pure being and divine consciousness.

◊ Note your personality, gifts, beauty, and abilities from this loving perspective.

◊ Choose one or more of the exercises below, and allow your angelic soul self to guide you. Or you may wish to create your own exercise and allow your soul to lead you through it.

◊ When your experience is complete, allow your angelic soul self to place a white silk cloak of protection around you, then see the angelic part of you shrink down within your heart.

◊ Imagine a large diamond octahedron around you, with the hardness of an actual diamond on the outside but filled with light inside. This seals your space and offers protection, while allowing you to safely shine as brightly as you wish to.

Exercises

Writing Your Soul's Poetry: If you could pick up a pen and write the yearning of your soul down in words, what would your soul say? Start with one word, and let the words just flow. It doesn't have to rhyme or make sense; just let the words tumble out, and see what beauty you create.

Painting Your Soul Essence: If you could pick up a pencil, crayon, or paintbrush and draw or paint the essence of your soul, what would it look like? Do not try to make it perfect. Just let your soul express. Even if it looks jumbled. Creation is allowed to be a mess!

Nourishing Your Soul with Food: If you could cook the most delicious and nutritious meal for your pure soul self, what would that be? Tune in to your body, and ask for any flavours or smells to arise within your senses. Or ask to receive a vision of the right foods for you. Challenge yourself to cook intuitively without a recipe with whatever you have in the cupboard or fridge, and let the creative process unfold.

Dancing to Your Soul's Rhythm: Put on some uplifting music, or sign up for an ecstatic dance class and dance to the rhythm of your soul. Let your body unwind and lead where it wants to go. Dance with the diamond flame—become the flame, or imagine you are waltzing with your angelic self. You may find yourself doing some strange movements, but let yourself feel the freedom of the movements, or you may imagine you are transforming into another version of yourself, such as a goddess or an animal. Just let the body lead, let go, and have fun.

Singing Your Soul's Purest Note: Find a time when you won't be disturbed, and let yourself tone the note of your soul. This is especially lovely to do while soaking in a sea salt bath. Imagine that you can sing the most pure and beautiful note from the very depths of your heart. Tone for as long as you need to and then let whatever other sounds need to be expressed come out. Do not worry if these sounds do not make sense or sound like another language or even a wild animal. Sound your pleasure and your pain.

This process may awaken within you your own ability to channel light language. Let your soul speak, and offer it acknowledgement and love for as long as you need to. Journal, draw any symbols you may have visualized, or write about the experience afterwards.

Walking in Step with Your Soul: Take a nature walk, and let your soul lead you wherever it feels guided to go. Is there a certain tree or flowerbed that calls to you? Let yourself soak up the beauty of nature, and see the outer world as a reflection of your own inner beauty; you are a part of nature, too.

Building an Altar to Your Soul: Intuitively create a beautiful altar in your home, garden, or somewhere out in nature in dedication to your pure soul self. Use crystals, rocks, flowers, statues, candles, or whatever you feel drawn to. Just go with the flow, and allow yourself to create the most divine space in devotion to your pure angelic presence. This is a beautiful exercise—the perfect symbolic way to anchor your vision of your version of Heaven on Earth.

The Science of Poetry for Healing

Two quotes by Albert Einstein discuss the necessity of making a connection between art and science:

> *"After a certain high level of technical skill is achieved, science and art tend to coalesce in aesthetics, plasticity, and form. The greatest scientists are artists as well."* [46]

> *"What artistic and scientific experience have in common: Where the world ceases to be the scene of our personal hopes and wishes, where we face it as free beings admiring, asking, and observing, there we enter the realm of Art and Science. If what is seen and experienced is portrayed in the language of logic, we are engaged in science. If it is communicated through forms whose connections are not accessible to the conscious mind but are recognized intuitively as meaningful, then we are engaged in art. Common to both is the loving devotion to that which transcends personal concerns and volition."* [47]

According to scientific studies, poetry and science are not as mutually exclusive as we once thought. A scientific study at the University of Exeter has shown that reading poetry activates the same area of the brain which responds to music and encourages introspection.[48]

A similar study at Liverpool University found that when reading classic poetry, as opposed to prose or text written in modern language, brain activity increased and the mind was challenged. The activity was found to be longer lasting, stimulating the brain for longer periods of time and encouraging right-brain activity.[49]

The right brain is associated with logic and understanding, and so again we see evidence that the bridging of the masculine logic with the feminine intuitive leads to a healthier mind, which is able to process and understand more complex concepts, such as areas of science.

The right hemisphere is also the part of the brain that links to memories of our own experiences and encourages self-enquiry, which is great news for mental health and other forms of therapy, which explore the subconscious mind in order to bring about mental, physical, and emotional healing. Academics discovered that reading the classics could actually be more beneficial to people than studying self-help books.

As the study of science requires the use of imagination to assist in analyzing and reconstructing data, research reported by Frontiers in Neurology *stated that teaching children poetry in schools could help them better understand scientific concepts and improve their desire to learn and enjoyment of education.*

CHAPTER 17

Angelic Light Language and Light Codes

As I mentioned earlier, Angels will often give you physical signs to alert you to their presence. Another sign I have regularly encountered from the Angels and light guides is the love heart.

In early 2015, I began to see hearts everywhere I went. Each time I would absent-mindedly look up from whatever I was doing, there would be another love heart or sometimes even the word "LOVE" or "YOU ARE LOVED" on a sign in front of me. I would see hearts in the foam in my morning coffee, in chewing gum splodges on the pavement as I walked down the street, as I dabbed moisturizer on my cheeks in the morning, and I even spied a random one in my lipstick pot.

Hearts and other symbols and signs in the physical are just one component of how Angels and light beings communicate. They act as doorways or gateways in our consciousness to expand our awareness and help us raise our vibration and frequency. This angelic form of communication takes us beyond logic and reason and into the realms of the unknown, where we begin to make the unconscious conscious. This angelic language can also be transmitted via sound and light, and as we become more attuned to the celestial and angelic kingdoms, our own gifts of higher communication may be activated. This is a phenomenon that is now commonly referred to as "light language".

One morning during my wedding preparations in 2015, I awoke in a state of higher than average bliss. This sudden happiness was vibrating throughout my whole body. I knew it had to do with something more than just the fact that I was planning my wedding, yet it did feel connected with the union I was embarking on with my husband-to-be.

I had been swanning around the house all morning, singing and dancing as I set about stamping all our wedding invitations and creating all our music playlists. I had more than 100 invites to hand-stamp, but I was up to the task. I was just stamping away and humming along to some music, when out of the blue a sudden urge to speak aloud overtook me, and I started gabbling away in what sounded like another language.

It felt like I was babbling away in nonsensical sounds, yet the frequency of what I was speaking felt like absolute truth to me. The sounds were somehow ancient and beyond this world. It was poetry to my body and soul. My whole being was humming with energy, and I felt like I was buzzing higher and higher, with wave upon wave of inexplicable bliss.

I had the strange sensation that I was situated at the centre of a vortex of energy. And waves of light were threading their way up my body and out through my crown. It was a hilarious and euphoric experience. I thought to myself that it must be light language, since I had heard of it in previous experience. I never thought I would speak it, though. In fact, I had secretly hoped I would never have to. It went way beyond what my logical mind would consider normal, yet it felt sublime as the sounds tumbled through me.

After that day, I began to use light language frequently. I would never set out to do it; it would just switch on, and the compulsion would take over. Sometimes it would come as speech, and at other times, I would feel compelled to sing. The harmonies that arose were haunting and beautiful. I started to sing and tone in the bath, the sounds cascading around me and amplifying through the water. My bathroom had become my sacred space and temple ever since I had channelled Precious Wisdom, and this new experience was taking it to another level indeed.

I have no idea what my husband thought when all this began. Sometimes the sounds were gentle, fluid, and melodic, and sometimes they sounded like Native American chanting. At other times, there were distinct voices, and I was aware of other beings speaking through me. I could sometimes translate what was being said but, again, it wasn't like a linear language—more an entirely holographic feeling experience. I was communicating in vibration, or rather, the universe was communicating through me in frequency.

The Use of Angelic Light Language for Multidimensional Healing

Soon, this elevated vibratory language began to show up in my healing and channelling workshops and sessions. At first, during self-healing, I could sing over myself and place my hands on various parts of the body to release trapped emotions and transmit a deeper healing energy. Then it began to be more present in my client sessions, too.

I realized that I could work with the sounds to clear many different kinds of trapped energies, and before long, I was using light language to assist with spirit release and chakra clearing, and even to unlock the gift of psychic surgery. The client's body would light up in white-gold light, and I would see the trapped energies or emotions in red or black, but after a while, I wouldn't even need to see; I would just know what needed clearing or releasing.

Working in this way, I began to receive a lot of positive feedback from my clients. People who had been in pain would often find immediate relief, and I was told of miracle after miracle occurring after my sessions.

A woman who had repeated ectopic pregnancies finally had a successful conception after we cleared her fallopian tubes. A man with severe arthritis in his foot felt his pain leave directly after the healing and was able to walk normally again. A woman who had been put on antipsychotics after she felt entities step into her felt them leave and was able to come off her meds six months later. A client's sister, who had broken her back and was told she would never walk again, got up and walked three days after I worked remotely on her. I had two cancer patients telling me their tumours were shrinking after being told by doctors they were living on borrowed time.

It was more than just the physical symptoms that would mirror a change for these people. Many of them found their whole experience shifting up a gear and rapid changes taking place in various areas of their lives, from family to work. Some finally found the courage to leave relationships that weren't serving them, while some were moved on rapidly from jobs that were no longer in their highest interests.

I cannot explain or take credit for these miracles, nor do I have a logical explanation for what occurred after meeting with each client; however, I do believe that the divine and the Angels were working through me to assist them in making the necessary life changes to take back their power from the conditions they had been suffering from.

Legally, in the world of complementary therapy, we are not allowed to say that we can "cure" anything. My personal belief is that there is no such thing as an "incurable" condition. Nothing is ever guaranteed, but I think that we need to do more study to understand why and how these healings are possible. Perhaps we just need to find the unique solution for each individual by taking a more holistic approach to healing. In my experience, there is no one-size-fits-all cure; we are all different, and disease can arise for any number of different reasons.

I have witnessed many success stories of people being healed and healing themselves, after they had been told by doctors they couldn't be helped. I have also assisted many people in passing over at the end of their earthly life, some of whom had succumbed to illnesses that I was unable to help reverse or release them from. However great or gifted a healer is, we are not here to play the rescuer and, ultimately, we cannot interfere with a soul's chosen path.

How a person's soul determines things are to work out for them is none of my business. I trust that their higher self knows exactly what is needed for each person at each time. This includes myself, of course, for my own life has become increasingly intense the more I work with the angelic and divine energies. Ups and downs may become more frequent and more rapid, yet I must find the power within myself to hold my centre and a sense of balance, no matter what challenges the universe throws at me. With the help of the Angels, I always trust that all is unfolding exactly as it is meant to.

Cosmic Rays and Angelic Light Language

At the end of 2015, I married my husband in a beautiful angelic ceremony on the magical Spanish island of Ibiza. I set a big intention that our wedding and all the celebrations and rituals we had organized around it would open an angelic portal, or doorway, of love for whoever needed it on this planet. Self-love was the path I had dedicated myself to, and my wedding felt as though it was an initiation.

I didn't realize the significance of it at the time, but I later found out that our wedding had happened right in the middle of something called "the X-Wave". Also known as "The Wave of Love", this was a potent galactic wave of energy that hit Earth in September and October, 2015, and my wedding day—symbolic of the union of the Divine Masculine and Divine Feminine and the collective intention I had set for love to be sent to everyone—just happened to be slap-bang in the middle of it. I wondered if this high-frequency cosmic download of energy had a bigger part to play in the activation of my angelic light language capabilities.

The Science of Light Language

When I met and interviewed Dr. Raymond Moody, one of the world's leading experts on Near Death Experiences (NDEs), in 2013, he spoke to me of what he calls "The Language of Nonsense", which is bizarre gibberish the dying can often utter as they near death.

Dr. Moody has since written a book on the findings of his scientific study on the subject, called Making Sense of Nonsense: The Logical Bridge between Science and Spirituality. *Dr. Moody's book covers the results of his five decades of research into the philosophy of* nonsense and how these seemingly illogical utterings can open a doorway to new spiritual and philosophical breakthroughs. In my experience, Dr. Moody's research confirms that light language, or "nonsense", allows us to access other dimensions, areas of consciousness and abilities that we would not otherwise have access to when operating purely from a logical perspective.

The Science of Voice for Healing

In an interview with Githa Ben-David for *The Alexandra Wenman Show*, I discovered some interesting facts about the healing power of the voice.[50]

Having studied music, and especially classical saxophone for many years, when she was 25, Githa travelled to India to study music, where she studied with a singing teacher called Mangala Tiwari and discovered something she calls "The Note from Heaven".

There, she learnt about the Indian melodic framework of raga. "A raga means what colours the mind, and what colours the mind are the notes—a combination of notes will create a feeling," she said. Mangala Tiwari saw her ego and told her to go home and sing one note for at least one hour a day, telling her, "That is your ground note, and you sing that."

She started to find her power from singing this one note and "surrendering into a state of being". She heard many notes as overtones with that one note. "Many notes came out," she told me. "I was convinced it was not me singing. I thought there must be somebody out the window copying me every time I opened my mouth, and that's the overtones."

Githa went on to discover that she has a gift for sound healing. She now teaches The Note from Heaven to people all over the world, showing them how to connect with The Oneness for profound healing, uplift, and transformation.

Having become interested in the science of healing, she has now published a book called Heal The Pineal, about the importance of the pineal gland, or pineal cone, in the brain, and how to use vocal techniques—specifically something Githa refers to as "Hung Song"—for clearing toxins from this gland. Working with Dr. Stephanie Seneff, she has been exploring how sound can be used to clear and awaken this powerful gland at the centre of our brain.

The Science of Music for Healing

The use of music and sound as a healing tool has roots in almost every indigenous culture on our planet, going back thousands of years, from drumming in Africa to Tibetan singing bowls, gongs in China, and the didgeridoo in Australia.

A study in the Journal of Evidence-Based Integrative Medicine *has more recently proven that sound meditation is effective in helping people reduce tension, anger, fatigue, anxiety, and depression while increasing overall spiritual well-being. The study worked with gongs, Tibetan singing bowls, crystal bowls, cymbals, didgeridoos, and various bells. Even people who had never done any meditation previously reported reduced anxiety and tension afterwards.*[51]

Another study reported by the National Centre for Biotechnology Information in the USA found that pain was significantly reduced in people suffering from fibromyalgia with the use of low-frequency sound therapy. Improved sleep and a reduction in the need for pain medication was also reported as a result of the study.[52]

Karen Newell, co-founder of Sacred Acoustics, has been working with healing brainwave entrainment techniques through sound and frequency for 11 years. These innovative recordings help reduce stress, improve rest and sleep, and promote healing. You can listen to a free sample recording at sacredacoustics.com.

I had the pleasure of interviewing Karen for my YouTube channel, where she spoke in depth about her discoveries with the use of sound. Karen talks about the use of binaural beats and a specific wah-wah sound that has been scientifically proven to aid healing. In the interview, she says:

"With Sacred Acoustics, the technology we create is very precise, very mathematical. On the one hand it's not like regular music, but on the other hand it is very precise, delivering very intentional brainwave frequencies to the listener so that they can achieve a quieter state of mind more easily than sitting silently."[53]

Karen also speaks of a broad range of effects, including physical changes, in people as a result of working with Sacred Acoustics for healing:

"Some people will feel tingling in their body. They might feel little twitches or unusual sensations . . . the tones really help to relax the physical body while your mind stays aware and alert. . . . People sometimes find that they fall asleep more easily; some people find they have more energy. . . . There is a very wide range of effects, but the relaxation is very common."

Karen also explains how sound and frequency can influence our brainwaves to improve relaxation and healing:

"The brain is normally at a Beta state of awareness. The electrical signal coming out of the brain, as measured by EEG, calls the Beta state roughly 12–30Hz. And below 12Hz are the more relaxed states, so 7–12Hz is the Alpha, 4–7Hz is Theta, and 0–4Hz is Delta, so Delta is when we are absolutely asleep. Theta is a little step up from sleep but kind of not fully awake and alert, so that's a very meditative state. And Alpha is a very focused, relaxed kind of state. And so these brainwave frequencies are delivering such binaural beats that bring us into those lower states of awareness. That state between awake and asleep that's roughly 4Hz . . . we call that the "hypnogogic state", and that's where the body becomes incredibly relaxed, but the mind is still awake . . . we are inducing it intentionally with these very specialized frequencies."

CHAPTER 18

New Angels for the New Earth

Channelled Message
from the Seven Elohim
That Surround the Godhead

Seven mighty Elohim surround you,
Seven facets of divine creation,
Seven building blocks of light,
Seven joined in emanation,
The seven of God's holy might.

We are tall,
We are white,
Ancient forms of
purity and light
Piercing through
the dark of night.

Our hands above your crown,
Our wings about your heart,
Our light within your mind,
Create! It's time to start,

As an orchestra of strings
vibrates
through the core
of your heart.

We come at a time of great need to intervene for you. What is it you are waiting for? Begin your journey! Your heart holds all the answers you seek and the world is waiting for your message. You have gifts you need to share like secret pearls hidden within a shell. Call upon us and we will help you crack open that hard shell that you have kept around you like some form of protection. Only this shell is no protection you need. It is merely the limiting shell of your fears and doubts, your limiting patterns, programmes, and beliefs.

Break out of that limiting space! Crack open that shell. Release your fears, and fly into the light. Spread your wings into the glorious sunshine of a new dawn, and take flight!

We understand that there are many lifetimes of this fear that you have accumulated, and so your layers of protection resemble the layers of sediment on an oyster shell. Layer by layer, as you consciously let in more light, more love, and the more you listen to the calling of your truth and the song of your heart, you will begin shedding these layers.

All you need do is set the intention that you are ready to let go of all that has been holding you back. It is that simple!

Ask for our assistance, and the assistance of the Angels and councils of light, and we will bring more light into your body, mind, heart, and soul.

Just think it to begin it.

Will it to be so, and then just let go.

Everyone on this planet will have to go through this great shedding, as there is too much light now to sustain the deep levels of fear that have bound this paradigm and this reality together. This way of being is now outdated. The cracks are showing!

Set your sights on the light. As much as you can, visualize yourself enveloped in pure light. Breathe it in. Take it into your heart. Open your heart like a blossoming flower of light—light coming in from infinite

Source above and Mother Earth below, and flowing into and out of your heart with each breath, the pure light of love.

As you receive it, so shall you give it, and the more you give, the more you shall receive. This is the key to breaking down your outdated layers of fear, limiting beliefs, unbalanced ego, and the illusion of protection.

When you stand in the pure light of love, you shall need no protection, for love is all you will be, and so love is all you will see and experience.

We are standing around you in a circle—the seven mighty Elohim that surround the Throne of Grace. We are bringing the pure light of God in through your crown chakra, illuminating your mind and all of your your unique gifts. We are switching on the light bulb in the dark room of your doubts so that you can more clearly see who you are and what you are meant to be.

In truth, you can never really stray from your path, but you must consciously intend to stay on it for it to flow. You can choose to exercise your free will and act against it, but this will only make the process feel more difficult for you and then your guides and Angels will have to intervene to bring you back on track. This can be painful, as you try so hard to hold onto that which is not serving you but which creates an illusion of comfort and safety. You feel you need to cling to the material as, up till now, you think that is all you know. But the sense of freedom you will have will be far more liberating, supportive, and comforting, if you only learn to let go.

The best course of action is to surrender to the light. Devote your life to love, and let go of any ideas you have as to how that will play out in your earthly reality. Your higher self has it all in hand, so relax into the light, and let your focus be on the now moment. And, in every now moment, set the intention to give and receive vaster and vaster quantities of light.

Live in light.

That is truly all we ask. It is so simple. That is the way of the heart, and that is the key to en-"light"-enment.

We are the creators of form. We wish to co-create Heaven on Earth with you, and for you. Step into the light, and be unafraid, for Heaven is your birthright, and we are assisting you always.

With love and grace,
The Seven Mighty Elohim

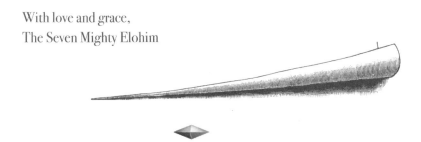

The Elohim Creator Gods and the New Angels Coming to Earth

As I have mentioned previously, at the end of 2012, I visited the sacred ancient temples of Egypt on a retreat for the winter solstice.

On 20 December, the day before the "Great Cosmic Moment" that marked the end of the Mayan calendar, our group had been to the Great Pyramid and done a powerful meditation and activation. Each of us had the opportunity to lie down in the red granite sarcophagus.

When we returned to Luxor that night, four of us stayed up all night, as we were so high on the energy. We could see strange lights flying in the night sky with our physical eyes. It was amazing.

We were sitting in our hotel room, giggling our heads off, when someone said: "I wonder when the actual cosmic moment is, the end of the Mayan calendar and alignment?"

And I just knew, I felt it, so I answered: "It's now!"

One person in our group had taken her pendulum out to check, and at the same moment I said the words, the pendulum went completely still. In that second, we all simultaneously felt an immense rush of energy, and our vibrations shot up so much higher in that one instant.

I was vibrating from head to toe with a beautiful energy. I almost felt like I was going to come out of my body, and then I had this incredible vision of a portal opening above the rim of the earth and all these huge Angels rushing in through the portal. I was told that these were Angels no one on this planet had ever encountered before and that they were only able to be here because of this great planetary shift and the change in consciousness. I was so excited because it reaffirmed my connection with the Angels in such an immense way. I wrote the following passage on my return to London:

It's 4 a.m. by the time I hop into bed. It is pitch-black in my room, which has heavy blackout curtains over the windows. I am wired awake. It feels like I have had about 15 cups of coffee that have been laced with a huge dose of love. It's like I have been drugged with bliss. I close my eyes and try to sleep, but my whole body is buzzing and vibrating with energy.

I open my eyes again and sit up in the darkness, and there, directly in front of me, hovering at the foot of my bed, is a big, red, pulsating ball of light about the size and shape of a beach ball. I am stunned. My eyes are wide open, and I am staring straight into this glowing, bright red orb of energy, which is pulsating—its edges are expanding and contracting, as though it is breathing.

I close my eyes tightly, thinking it must be some trick of the light, but when I open them again, the giant red orb is still there. I move my head to one side, and it moves with my gaze. I try the same thing to the other side, and it follows me.

And then it begins to speak to me telepathically. The voice I hear is beautiful, feminine, and almost sounds like music. It is not one voice, but many, like a harmonic chorus. I know it is another group conscious-ness, but this one is very different to the voice of the Higher Galactic Council. It is gentler in its tones, more feminine, somehow more . . . angelic.

They, too, ask me to speak for them, and I receive a message, which I am now being asked to share here.

Channelled Message from the Intergalactic Elohim

We come to you as the collective of the Intergalactic and Interdimensional Elohim. A bridge has now opened to make it possible for us to connect with humanity. Prior to this moment, the vibration of Earth was too dense, and people were not expanded enough in their consciousness to even begin to comprehend our existence. We are what you would call "Angels" in the traditional sense, as we are aspects of the divine and archetypes of creation.

But to simplify, we are essentially creator gods of neighbouring dimensions and universes. We exist in many worlds from you, and yet we walk beside you. We are here to assist in the great awakening of this planet. Infinite realms abound, and your human mind can comprehend but a tiny portion of what, in reality, is infinite. This must be felt to be experienced. You think you connect to your consciousness through your brain. This is only partly true. You connect to your consciousness through your heart.

Your heart is the portal. We are here in service, and we are at your service. Our names hold sacred phonetic keys which, when spoken, dissolve the veils of illusion that humanity has kept itself imprisoned within for aeons.

It begins with being open to the possibility that you are more than you think you are. It begins with your curiosity. It begins with a willingness to go beyond logic and frolic in the playground of the seemingly absurd. What is nonsensical to you makes perfect sense to us. Language is the key that opens the door beyond this reality. The language of nonsense is, in fact, derived from the greater concept of the Language of Light.

Words hold power, and sound holds light and crosses space and time in less than an instant. Whatever defies logic actually helps you grow. If it doesn't make sense to the logical mind, that is a good thing. For that is when you learn to drop into your heart and your emotional awareness. What "feels" right in your heart is the right way. Feel your way forward through your heart-mind.

Watch your words. Your words open doorways within your heart. Which doorways would you like to create—doorways to bliss or doorways to pain? Hear our names, speak our names, sing our names, and we shall hold the doors to the divine open for you. But be warned: Only the pure of heart may enter. If you dabble in higher states of consciousness out of greed or the need to control others, great will be the fall.

The karma now playing out on this planet is a result of the actions of those who have attempted to misuse the secret codes of power gifted to this realm in ancient times. They are few in number, yet the results of their greed will be catastrophic for the world of blindness they have built up around them. Do not be afraid, for this is a great blessing and will lead to freedom for all. The time is now.

Behind the veil lies a truth beyond your current comprehension, but only one of you needs to unlock it for the rest to reap the rewards. This is the Holy Grail, this is the Ark of the Covenant, this is Jacob's Ladder, this is Shamballa, this is Utopia. This is all there is. It is really so simple. Seek, go on seeking, and surely you shall find. It begins with you. It is not separate from you.

Worlds within worlds, universes within universes, realms within realms—how vast you are, and yet how tiny you humans keep yourselves. Awaken and expand into your vastness. Awaken into love. Our hearts go with you, our song vibrates through you.

The way is open. The time is now.

It is written.

I do not remember how long I lay there gazing into the orb, but at some point I fell asleep with the names of the 12 Intergalactic Elohim running through my mind like a song: *Adnachiel, Baruchatah, Zacharia, Yeleliah, Ishmahiah, Aurahiah, Zizfahah, Amiah, Alleleia, Hierahahah, Sheknahila, Yod Heh Vav Heh* . . .

I had been given all the names of these Angels in the days leading up to this message, but I didn't really know who or what they were until that moment.

I stayed in this incredible high vibration, I would say it was a fifth-dimensional frequency or vibration until the end of the trip, so it was for about another five days after that, and I was channelling (or rather, embodying) these Angels over those five days. I was given the name of each Angel and what each one represents, and they were like no Angel's name I'd ever heard before But, more importantly, their energy was like no other angel I had encountered before. I had no words to describe the energy currents running through my body, but if I had to I would use words like "galactic", "otherworldly" and "celestial" when talking about these immense plasma light beings. I have been told their names are in the Language of Light, and the phonetic sound is what invokes them and their energies.

When I asked my guides about these immense angelic beings, they said:

These Elohim are new to your planet. They could not exist at the level of consciousness and light that was previously resonating on Earth. The portal was opened between 21/12 and 23/12, when the earth was literally flooded with light. This light is now here for thousands of years and will not dissipate; rather, as people start to absorb the light at a rate that is right for them, it will grow and expand within their bodies and within their cells. This is the new epoch. There will not be another fall. Many are awakened and holding light for the Ascension. You are chariots of light, racing towards a golden dawn.

That is why you are made of matter, so you can carry the light.

You are containers for light. You will find that people begin to awaken quickly now. Friends you thought were skeptics will begin to channel and will come to you for advice. It was only their fear that stopped them asking questions before, but when they experience this love that they have never before felt, their hearts will open, and they will feel relieved and safe and more able to accept what is happening.

As they spoke of this, I began seeing sacred shapes, patterns, geometries, and mandalas in front of my vision, like I was peering into the very fabric of the universe.

The Elohim spoke to me again:

We are the creator gods of many neighbouring universes. Many are interested in what is happening on Earth during your current timeframe. Much hinges upon the outcome, and so much support is available to you now.

As I also understood it, these mighty Angels also represented our own levels of consciousness. Yet these were levels of consciousness that had never before been accessed by beings in human form, and we were now being granted that access. It was to be an entirely new cycle in our collective evolution.

Angelic Light Language Activation with the Intergalactic and Interdimensional Elohim

Chant the names of each of these powerful Angels to activate your own Light Language, awaken the Ascension codes within your DNA, and restore your divine blueprint of full multidimensional consciousness.

The names of each of these Elohim came through via the angelic Language of Light. They are a combination of the sacred languages of Hebrew, Sanskrit, and other tones and sounds. Their names may sound like nonsense, but as we have discovered, nonsense has long been used as a tool to expand our consciousness and experience states of being beyond the physical.

To begin, ensure you are sitting upright, with your feet flat on the floor and your back as straight as is comfortable for you. A lovely way to do this exercise is to chant the names while soaking in a relaxing warm salt bath.

Imagine a large diamond octahedron being placed in and around your energy field to shield and protect your space and simultaneously open a doorway to the highest diamond-light dimensions of Ascension. The diamond may shimmer and move as you progress through the exercise. You may see other symbols, shapes, colours, images, and beings as you tone.

As you chant or sing each Angel's name, know that you are invoking the healing powers of that deity and accessing the dimensions of angelic sound healing frequencies. Tune in to the feelings and sensations each name delivers to you, without trying to make sense of what is happening on a logical level.

If other sounds and tones wish to come forward from within you, just let them flow. You will experience a rise in your vibration as a result, and may experience physical sensations, such as temperature changes, tingles, goosebumps, and a sense of being extremely grounded yet expanded at the same time. You may feel as though you have grown much taller than you actually are.

This chanting exercise is designed to open you to higher states of awareness and promote a deeper sense of healing and relaxation.

Below, I have included some information about what each Elohim may represent. However, it is best not to attach to these meanings but go with your own perception of what these divine beings reveal to you.

When the process is complete, ground yourself, and imagine the diamond around you is locking into place to seal your fields.

Chant the Names

Adnachiel – "Cosmic Fire"
Possible meanings: Pioneer Angel, adventure, new horizons, "Angel of independence" in Hebrew

Baruchatah – "Cosmic Ether", "Cosmic Mind"
Possible meanings: *berechiah* = "Yaweh blesses"; *buchatah, baruch* = "blessed" + *atah* = "you"; thus, "Blessed are you"; *barach* = "knee", brack = "lightning". There is the implication of a downward motion; i.e., You, God, are coming down to us

Zacharia – "Cosmic Matter or Form"
Possible meanings: "God remembers" in Hebrew

Yeleliah – "Sound"
Possible meanings: *yelel* = "howling"; *iah* = "of God"; thus, *Yeleliah* means "howling of God" or "sound or voice of God"

Ishmahiah – "Resonance"
Possible meanings: *ismachiah, yicmakyahuw* = "Yahweh sustains"; *ishmaiah* = "Yahweh will hear"

Aurahiah or **Oriahiah** – "Frequency"
Possible meanings: *oriaha* from the Hebrew = "Light of God"

Zizfahah – "Light"
Possible meanings: *Ziz* (Hebrew: זיז) is a giant griffin-like bird in Jewish mythology, said to be large enough to be able to block out the sun with its wingspan; *svaha* = Sanskrit for "oblation". "so be it", "hail!", "shout of joy", "release"

Amiah – "Illumination"
Possible meanings: *amia* = "People of God"

Alleleia – "Radiation"
Possible meanings: *alil* = perhaps "furnace", "crucible"; *aliyah* = "ascent"; *ayah* = "falcon"

Hierahahah – "Cosmic Heart"
Possible meanings: *harhaiah, charhayah* = "Fear of Yahweh", "God protects", "Heat of God", "Glowing of God", "Zeal of God", "Ardour of God"

Sheknahila – "Cosmic Soul"
Possible meanings: *shecaniah, shechaniah,* = "Dweller with Yahweh"

Yod Heh Vav Heh – "God, Elohim" (as you see it from an even higher perspective, a more cosmic and divine perspective, rather than a human perspective)
Possible meanings: "Infinite creation", "the divine", "the all", "the oneness", and "you as part of it all"

The Science of Angelic Names –
Phonetics and Angels as Angles

Angels are mathematically quantifiable, high-level, plasma beings, and evidence of them can even be found in our DNA, according to physicist Dan Winter. As I see it, in very basic sacred geometry terms, if we picture the corner of a triangle and place humans on one side or plane of the triangle (or in one dimension of existence) and the divine on the other side or plane of the triangle (or in another dimension of existence), the "Angel" would represent the "angle", or ratio/relationship between the two sides.[54]

So we could say that the Angel acts as the bridge between ourselves and the divine. This is a bridge in consciousness and, the way I interpret it is that, as we raise our vibration and expand our consciousness to become more angelic, we get closer to living in alignment with our divinity and activating and embodying our innate God/Goddess presence.[55]

To further highlight this point, we can look at the etymology and phonetics of the names of many of the Archangels, which are written in the Hebrew language. Said to be a sacred language, each of the 22 letters of the Hebrew alphabet aligns to the mathematics of sacred geometry and the patterns of creation, as every individual letter can be formed from the Star of David, or Magen David. Hebrew letters can also be created from the spirals within the human heart. [56]

Even more amazing is that when Hebrew letters are pronounced verbally, vibrations in the voice can cause sand grains to take on the shape of the Hebrew characters.[57] *This adds weight to the creative power of sound, which is reflected in the Biblical saying: "In the beginning was the word."*

Most of the Archangel names end in the suffix "el", which means "God", "Deity", or "of God" in Hebrew. And each Archangel's name describes the properties it represents. For example, Michael is the one "who is like God", or "will of God"; Raphael is the one who "God has healed"; Gabriel is "God is my strength"; and so on. When you speak the Archangel or Angel's name aloud, you are vibrating and commanding the creative principle of the divine that the individual Angel represents. You are invoking that angelic aspect within yourself, so you are calling up your inner Michael (or your inner divine will) to create the energy of protection around you. In essence, when you speak the Angel's name, you are becoming the Angel.

PART FOUR

The Archangel Alchemy
Healing System

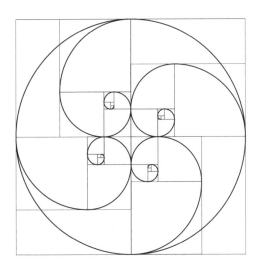

CHAPTER 19

Preparation and Attunements

The Winged Breath

Breathing is the first thing we do when we are born and the last thing we do at our death. Breath is life, and it is a bridge between our body, soul, and spirit. The importance of breathing has been brought to humanity's attention in a profound way in recent times, but breathing is much more than drawing in oxygen to fuel our physical bodies.

Breathing in the light of love is a fundamental practice to any spiritual technique. When you consciously connect to the infinite source of love that is always available to us, you are able to raise your vibration, elevate your mood, enhance your well-being, increase your wisdom, illuminate your gifts, and bring more vitality into your physical body through your cells and DNA.

Spend a moment each day breathing consciously and mindfully. When you breathe in, imagine that you are breathing the pure white light of unconditional love into your heart and filling your whole being and body with it. Breathe deeply, allowing the air to fill your diaphragm, so that you feel like you are filling your lower belly and even pelvic region.

A similar version of the following process was taught to me by my singing teacher Angelina Kalahari. I have added my own angelic spin to it, but it is a beautiful way to gift yourself healing, enhance your confidence and courage, and balance your emotions.

Four-Count Winged Breathing

◊ Breathe in fluidly and smoothly for four counts, as follows:

1–Filling from the bottom upwards, the air—visualized as white light—enters through the nose.

2–It immediately travels deep down into the pelvis.

3–Then the belly expands.

4–And, finally, the ribcage expands outwards. Imagine your ribcage is like a pair of wings opening out.

◊ Breathe out in a continuous flow for four counts. As you breathe out, count to four slowly, breathing away all that is not serving you—all worries, negative, or limiting thoughts, emotions, and stresses, making more space to breathe in more love, light, joy, and wonder.

◊ Repeat the four-stage in-breath and the four-count continuous out-breath for as long as you need to in order to feel calm, safe, centred, and filled with positive energy.

Clearing and Transforming
Trapped Energies and Emotions

◊ Ground, open, and protect your space, per the channelling checklist.

◊ You may wish to body dowse or check with your pendulum if there is anything specific to clear first.

◊ Set your intention for transmuting any lower-frequency or unwanted energy. Your intention can be set using your own words, but should always be in alignment with the purest intention to transform any trapped or stuck energy through 100 percent divine unconditional love via your higher self. Always ask that any healing or clearing be done with the highest and best intention and outcome for all in mind.

◊ Choose a symbol to represent the divine source energy of your divine higher self.

This can be any symbol that represents the divine for you; for example, it could be the diamond, a heart, a sacred circle, or the flower of life. Ensure that the symbol you choose is something neutral and unconditional, and not something that you may associate with any kind of limitation. For example, a cross may represent Christ but also Christianity, a man-made religion.

I feel it's best to try to choose something that holds no personal fear or limiting associations for you. Sacred geometry is wonderful as it holds the essence of source and is built on the mathematical equation of unconditional love, known as Phi or phi. You can use your pendulum to check if the symbol you have chosen is in your highest and best interests to use for this purpose. Note: Metatron's Cube works very well, as it is the pattern of divine creation itself.

◊ Choose an action to perform in conjunction with visualizing the symbol, which will represent clearing, releasing and transforming trapped energies. It's best to choose a simple and subtle action, such as a hand mudra, swinging your pendulum round in circles very fast, blowing out through pursed lips, clapping your hands or clicking your fingers, gazing up into the third eye, fluttering your eyelashes, yawning or even burping.

◊ Witness or observe the change in energy, primarily through the feeling awareness.

◊ Check with your pendulum, dowse or muscle-test that it has been cleared.

◊ Once your clearing is complete, rinse yourself off in white light and close down your energy field with the Shrink, Sink, and Shield process from the channelling checklist.

The Main Archangel Alchemy Attunement Process

The Archangel Alchemy attunement activates the divine diamond-white sacred flame within you. This diamond light frequency is the highest and purest ray currently available to Earth and contains within it the clear light of God—the gold, silver, platinum, and high-frequency metallic rays and the pristine white light—which contains all the colours of the spectrum, as well as their translucent, iridescent, pearlescent, fluorescent, luminescent, cosmic, angelic, and multidimensional properties.

This is an activation to the multidimensional angelic cosmic diamond heart and the gateway to the most angelic aspect of your eternal soul self. Some of the colours activated within this attunement are not yet known to us within this plane of existence and cannot be seen with the naked eye. These include many infrared, ultraviolet, solar, galactic, and ultra-galactic or multiuniversal rays.

Preparing to Receive the Attunement

Find a quiet, calm, and safe place where you will not be disturbed. It is best to do the attunement seated, with your feet flat on the floor and your back as straight as comfortably possible. You may wish to have a glass of water handy and a pen and paper to jot down any notes, impressions, thoughts, or insights following the process.

The Archangel Alchemy Attunement

Perform the Winged Breath as outlined above. To begin, you will establish the Pillar of Light and Inner Sun to shield and protect your energy field. For ease, it is included below, as the first part of the attunement process.

Part 1: Establishing Protection

◊   Come into a space of harmony, neutrality/unconditional love, and close your eyes.

◊   Visualize your conscious awareness as a sphere of white light, and bring it into your body. Anchor it into your centre, behind your navel.

Call up diamond-white light from the core of Mother Earth. Connect it to your centre, then allow it to rise and open your heart.

◊ Call down golden-white light from the divine through the sun and into your heart. Bring it into your centre, and anchor it there.

◊ Imagine, see, intend, or feel your conscious sphere like an inner sun. Let it blaze with divine fire, and expand it out through your energy field to clear and transmute or lower, negative, limiting, or unwelcome energies.

◊ Expand it out as far as you wish around you, and set your safe perimeter. Seal it with protective golden light.

Part 2: Activating the Archangel Diamond Flame and the Cosmic Diamond Heart

◊ With eyes closed, breathe into your centre and visualize a huge, glittering-white Archangel standing behind you, with wings outstretched. It is Archangel Gabriel.

◊ The Archangel carries in their hands a large, multifaceted diamond with a seemingly infinite number of faces. It is radiating the brightest light you have ever seen, and it spins and moves within the Angel's hands, scattering crystalline rainbow sparkles all around you.

◊ Gabriel places this cosmic diamond into your heart centre, and it begins to expand and dissolve into your energy field.

◊ All of your physical, energetic, and subtle bodies are illuminated in its dazzling light as you become one with its energy.

◊ You begin to hear beautiful music and tones as the choirs of Angels sing their frequency through your entire being.

◊ High above you, a diamond-white octahedron illuminated in brilliant light is spinning in your soul star chakra.

◊ Below your feet, another brilliant diamond-white octahedron appears, spinning in your Earth star chakra. The diamond above begins to descend towards you, while the diamond below simultaneously ascends.

◊ As the two diamonds move towards each other, they grow larger and merge to form a huge octahedronal diamond around you.

◊ One diamond spins around your body to the left in an anti-clockwise motion, and the other diamond spins around your body to the right in a clockwise motion.

◊ This movement creates a diamond shield and as the octahedrons spin, they purify and repair your etheric field, calling back any missing soul fragments and transmuting any lower energies into the highest frequencies of angelic and divine love.

◊ The movement begins to spin so fast it harmonizes. This creates a zero-point field within the centrifugal force created by the counter-rotating spin of the diamonds.

◊ It is as if there is now just one large diamond around your energy field creating absolute stillness. The spinning diamonds have opened the unified field of oneness. This opens the gateway to the multidimensional self and unity consciousness, aligning all your timelines in the here and now.

◊ Gabriel steps forward and places a smaller diamond octahedron in each of your palms. Your hands become illuminated in pure-white flame.

◊ Gabriel then places a small diamond octahedron in the soles of each of your feet, which also begin to blaze with white fire.

◊ Gabriel then places three gleaming diamond octahedrons within your third eye at your brow, your heart centre, and your navel in the centre of your belly. These three locations are the three treasures of the divine human, representing the highest attainment of love, wisdom, and power and the alignment of the mind, body, and soul.

◊ As these three aspects come into perfect alignment, a waterfall of diamond-white liquid fire begins to pour down over and through you from Source, activating your rainbow-diamond DNA and illuminating your inherent gifts. You may see or sense beautiful music and tones, extraordinary colours, ancient symbols, hieroglyphs, numbers, and letters. You may even be aware of Angels and beings of light around you.

◊ This holy iridescent fire contains all of the sovereign light codes of your divinity and opens a portal to your soul self at the highest levels of your existence.

◊ Know that, as a divine human, you are a bridger of worlds, uniting all dimensions of existence within you. You have been awakened to your innate angelic healing nature and gifts.

◊ Allow this light to soften around you as a beautiful, shimmering cloak, securing and sealing all your energy fields and anchoring this attunement into your daily, waking life and reality.

◊ Be aware of Archangel Gabriel and all of the Angelic Kingdoms of Light embracing you in love and acknowledging you as the human Angel you are.

◊ Become aware of how vast your consciousness has become, and begin to draw your awareness in close to your body.

◊ Shrink yourself right down so that your consciousness is contained within your physical body. Sink your weight into the chair, and feel the heaviness and density of your physical being. Feel, see, or sense the largest octahedronal diamond around your body now locking into place to seal and shield your energy field. Keep an eye out for the symbol of a diamond in your daily waking life as confirmation of this activation.

◊ Ground yourself fully and, when you feel ready, open your eyes, and bring all of this beautiful healing and alignment with you into your daily awareness and experiences.

You have now been gifted with nine pristine platonic diamond octahedrons, which have opened a portal to the great unknown and the consciousness of the divine feminine at its highest available level. The two larger octahedrons, which merged to open the field of unity, have now become one, as they have perfectly harmonized, so the nine have now been reduced to eight diamonds of eight sides each.

The eight represents the four building blocks, or foundations, of our physical reality and, doubled, it represents the infinite divine multidimensional mind of God, or the divine masculine. The divine masculine refers to our awareness and the known universe, while the divine feminine is the great unknown, the unmanifest, and that which is yet to be discovered. She is the great mystery.

The 9 = the infinite divine feminine = unknown

The 8 = the infinite divine masculine = known

As we bring the energy of the nine and transform it into the eight, we are bringing the unknown into the known, the darkness into the light, raising our vibration, and making ourselves aware of what we were previously unaware of. In short, we are making the unconscious conscious.

As the two energies merge and unite through love, they create a field of oneness, or unity, within the consciousness of each person. This is what is known as the process of Hieros Gamos (in Greek, *hieros gamos* means "holy marriage"), or the union of the masculine and feminine within each of us, to birth the holy child we each truly are. This is a form of Archangel Alchemy at its most refined.

The Science of the Cosmic Diamond

In 2004, astronomers discovered an actual physical giant cosmic diamond star located in the constellation of Centauris. Known as BPM 37093
and nicknamed Lucy, the star is a white dwarf, the core of a star. It is
made up mostly of carbon and coated with a fine layer of hydrogen and
helium, which is formed after the star uses up its nuclear fuel and dies.

*A massive chunk of crystallized carbon located 50 light-years
away from Earth, the "cosmic diamond" is 2,500 miles across and
weighs 5 million trillion trillion pounds, or approximately 10 billion
trillion trillion carats.*

*Scientists also discovered that the cosmic diamond sings! It
is continuously pulsating and rings like a gong, sending out waves
of energy across the cosmos. "By measuring those pulsations,
we were able to study the hidden interior of the white dwarf, just
like seismograph measurements of earthquakes allow geologists
to study the interior of the earth. We figured out that the carbon
interior of this white dwarf has solidified to form the galaxy's largest diamond," says Metcalfe of Metcalfe, Montgomery, and Antonio
Kanaan (UFSC Brazil).* [58]

CHAPTER 20

The Significance of the Archangel Alchemy Attunement Symbols

The Cosmic Diamond and Opening the Divine Vortex

The octahedron is one of the five platonic solids that can be found within the symbol of Metatron's Cube, derived from the ancient creation symbol of the Flower of Life. A 3D diamond, the octahedron has eight faces that are each equilateral triangles.

In many spiritual schools of thought, this shape corresponds to the element of Air. Many attribute the Angels as beings of the air, such as birds, butterflies, and dragonflies.

In the ancient teachings of the *merkabah*, otherwise known as our "light body", the octahedron is often representative of our emotional body.[59]

However, Gabriel informs me that the shape of a golden mean diamond, when used in the Archangel Alchemy system, represents high emotional intelligence, as it unites the heart-mind with the one divine mind. In essence, Gabriel tells me, it is through the harmonizing of unconditional, or non-judgemental, love with human, compassionate feeling love that we build a bridge to our sovereignty and reclaim our forgotten innocence.

When I was in Egypt in 2012, and again in 2018, to run my own retreat, the Angels and guides showed me that the Great Pyramid wasn't a pyramid at all but a huge diamond, or octahedron, with the upper half above ground and the lower half below the earth. In fact, my first ever entry into the Great Pyramid had me squeezing myself down the long, narrow passageway into the antechamber beneath it, before climbing up to the King's Chamber. It felt symbolic of a rebirth.

The visions and messages I received on those journeys to Egypt were more like ancient memories resurfacing within my mind. I was shown image after image of sacred initiations being held within the chambers of the pyramid, and that its main purpose was not as a tomb at all, but rather, its primary function was to heal and harmonize—not only the people who underwent the initiations but also to heal and harmonize Mother Earth herself.

To me, the pyramids all over the world are sacred places of initiation and transformation, where those preparing to become spiritual adepts, priests, and priestesses, would have to journey through the veils and face their deepest fears, in order to be granted access to the higher realms and know themselves as angelic and divine.

After my own memories resurfaced I was subsequently guided to other books, which have all confirmed my inner knowing. One of my favourite such books is *Initiation* by Elisabeth Haich, in which she recalls her past life in Ancient Egypt and shares the details of her spiritual training and initiation.

Records reveal that the Great Pyramid was once covered in white limestone to harness the power of the sun.[60] The ancient Egyptians knew the importance of the sun as not merely a source of heat and light but also a gateway to the infinite divine. They also knew that access to that gateway was through the heart, or more simply, through love.

In my opinion, the Great Diamond, otherwise known as the Great Pyramid of Giza, is not a tomb or burial chamber; it is a physical portal designed to mirror the etheric portal of our own lightbody, so that we can traverse the stars and commune with other worlds and dimensions, including those where other aspects of ourselves reside.

Physicist Nikola Tesla discovered that the Great Pyramid is a huge power generator; however, far from using up Earth's precious resources, it harnesses safe and free celestial energy in the form of a kind of divine electricity. I believe that it is this same divine electricity that I am able to feel when the Archangels step into my energy field.

From what the Angels have shown me, and the memories and visions I have had, I believe the Ancient Egyptians were initiating themselves to their highest spiritual level: to know and embody their god-selves, so they could harness and embrace this divine electricity. Using the human body and nervous system as the battery, they could then amplify the divine current within the Great Pyramid (Diamond) to create the electricity they needed for safe and potentially highly advanced technology, which simultaneously healed the earth and all in its vicinity.

When I first entered the King's Chamber, the energy was high and clear. I could see that there was no logical way the pyramid could have been built by slaves using mere hand tools and ropes. The giant square blocks fit together with such precision that even my little fingernail could not fit between them.

It's difficult to imagine that anything other than very advanced technology could have achieved this.

On my first visit for winter solstice in December 2012, as noted earlier, I was able to lie down inside the red granite sarcophagus. I closed my eyes, and in a split second I was hurtled upwards though the stars, right through the central star of Orion's belt and into a brilliant white light. I met many Angels and light beings, and they gave me information about the work I was going to be doing in the future and how I would be writing and teaching about Angels, channelling, and the Ascension. The experience seemed to last for hours, yet it only took a few seconds, then, with a bright spark of light, I was instantly back in the red granite sarcophagus in the King's Chamber.

On that first trip in 2012, as noted, I was on a retreat. There were 24 people in our group. We gathered in a circle around the inside walls of the King's Chamber, and together, we began to chant. Our voices mingled in a harmonic resonance that was so high and pure it felt as though we might blow the lid off the place. I could see and feel Angels filling the chamber as the vibration got higher and higher.

Again, I began channelling and was requested by the Angels and light guides to open up a huge light pillar of diamond-white and shimmering, pale-gold flame in the centre of the chamber. I began to visualize the pillar, and witnessed it taking on a life of its own, growing bigger and more intense by the second. The column of diamond white-gold fire stretched up beyond the apex of the pyramid into the heavens and deep down below the ante-chamber right into the core of the earth.

I saw a figure, like an apparition, step out of the body of each member of our group, enter the flame, and vanish into the white fire with a flash of light, then witnessed the same thing happening to me. I felt the familiar surge of powerful love electricity rushing through my body, and I saw and felt an older version of myself stepping out of me and entering the pillar of white-gold flame. I felt so much lighter—as though I had shed years of excess emotional baggage.

As we continued to sing, I again watched in awe as every member of our group was embraced by a beautiful, blazing-white angelic presence, which then merged with them and disappeared into their body. This was a vision of beauty and purity, and I instantly received the guidance that we had all received an activation of our diamond-light DNA and retrieved a part of our true angelic selves. I knew that I had been shown a kind of angelic alchemy, and that the pillar of fire I had opened had allowed it to happen for us all.

However, it did not feel as though this was something new. It was as though we had all been there before and been through something similar at

278

another point in time. This was a great remembrance, and I felt that we were all gathered there in a magical synchronicity to witness it again.

A few months after I returned from that trip to Egypt, I discovered that a new neighbour had moved into the flat next door. I got chatting to him in the shared garden one day and soon discovered that he was an Egyptologist. I was very excited by this information, so I asked him if he had any good book recommendations about the history of Ancient Egypt and in particular the temples. Instead of offering information on the books he thought I should read, however, his answer piqued my interest.

"Whatever you do," he warned, "Don't read any books by Graham Hancock."

I thought this a very odd response, but instantly a voice inside my head said: *He's given you the answer you seek: Read Graham Hancock.*

In my true fashion, I handed this message back to the universe and waited for guidance. Two weeks later, I was meeting some friends for a drink on London's Southbank, and as I walked under London Bridge, on my way to our meeting point, I passed a bookseller with rows and rows of secondhand books for sale.

I felt a strong pull towards one of the wooden tressle tables, where the books were all stacked, side by side, spines facing up in neat rows. However, one lone book had been pulled out of the stack and lay face up, with its cover clearly on show. I looked down at the book and gasped. On the front cover was a picture of the Great Sphinx. I read the title and saw the name of the authors, and my body broke out in goosebumps.

It was as if the universe had left that book lying there just for me to stumble across. The book was called *Keeper of Genesis* by Robert Bauval and, of course, Graham Hancock, and, while I couldn't confirm the dates, the information it contained backed up some of the memories and truths the Angels had shown me in my visions within the Great Pyramid.

I was subsequently led to more and more fascinating research that confirmed what the Angels had shown me about our ancient origins and the use of free, clean, and safe energy that has the capacity to heal both ourselves and the planet. The work of Nassim Haramein, Lynne McTaggart, JJ and Desiree Hurtak, Christopher Dunn, and many others seemed to confirm the same.

Events such as the Conference for Human Consciousness and Evolution, television networks like Gaia TV, and TV series such as *Ancient Aliens* and *The Pyramid Code* are starting to shed a lot more light on these subjects. There is a wealth of knowledge at our fingertips, but it is curious to me that these safer, simpler, and cleaner forms of energy have not yet been made available to the general populace.

The Archangels have demonstrated to me that the energy of Archangel Alchemy is a much more simplified and refined version of the celestial power ancient civilizations managed to master and harness on a far grander scale.

Gabriel tells me that we are entering a time on this planet when we will again have access to highly advanced technology with a particular focus on light and sound, which will be safe for all and cause no harm to our planet.

Archangel Diamond Light DNA Activation

As we evolve in our consciousness, physiological changes are also occurring, and our sensitivity is becoming heightened. Changes are occurring within our DNA, and we are able to access more of our inherent gifts and abilities. To assist with streamlining this process, the Archangels have gifted us with a

Archangel Diamond Light DNA Activation

◊ Close your eyes, and centre and ground yourself.

◊ Imagine a golden sphere of protection around your energy field.

◊ Visualize a huge angelic being radiating gold and diamond-white light appearing behind you. This is Archangel Metatron.

◊ Metatron raises his arms above your head and opens his hands out wide.

◊ As he does so, a large portal of light opens way above you, and a large spiral of diamond-white light begins to wind its way down towards your crown.

◊ As the spiralling light touches your crown, you feel tingles, and the light finds its way into your pineal gland, where it activates the DNA within your master cell.

◊ Light then cascades through your whole body, igniting and activating all your 12-strand DNA.

◊ You may see shapes, colours, fire letters, and geometries in your vision, or feel rushes of energy, warmth, cold, tingles, or buzzing in your body.

◊ Allow the process to run. It will naturally dissipate after a few moments.

◊ When you feel the energies have settled, visualize Metatron taking the edges of your golden sphere and pulling them around you like a golden cloak of protection.

◊ Thank Metatron, ground yourself, and open your eyes.

The Science of DNA Activation and Epigenetics

Epigenetics, as examined by scientists such as cell biologist Dr. Bruce Lipton in his book *The Biology of Belief*, explores how an individual's beliefs, behaviours, and environmental factors can affect their genetics. Consciously transmuting our negative thought patterns, subconscious beliefs, and lower emotions can, therefore, have a positive impact on our health and the way we respond to the world around us, in general. The higher our consciousness, the more detail we are able to access within our subconscious and the greater our ability to heal and transmute our negative and limiting patterns. You might say that this, in turn, helps us to positively transform and activate our dormant DNA, so that we become more angelic in nature and vibration.

CHAPTER 21

The Archangel Alchemy
Healing Practices

What Is the Purpose
of Archangel Alchemy as a
Healing System, and How Does It Work?

Beloved,

You are a seed. You are a cell of pure love energy. You are vibration in collaboration with the everything. When you harmonize with the Core, the Source, the Essence, or Seed of pure vibration within, you can begin to alter your external experience as a reflection of your internal process.

Your essence is you in your most pure state of being. Your essence is sheer divinity. Your essence is love in its most crystalline frequency. Your essence is creation in perpetual motion, which is constantly evolving, contracting, expanding, replicating, and perfecting itself.

If you knew that every thought you had had the potential to create an entire new world, or even a universe, what would the essence of that universe be? What would you wish to create? In every moment, your thoughts are creating and re-creating your reality. Your feelings create your thoughts, and the story of your experience plays out according to your will.

You have a choice in every moment to re-create your thoughts anew, so your reality is in alignment with your perception of what would be the highest and best experience for you to have.

For a long time in your collective history, much of your co-creation has been taking place in the unconscious. But you now find yourselves in a time when the hidden, unhealed, unknown, and unintegrated parts of your awareness are surfacing and becoming known.

Whether you are aware of it or not, you are calling home to your awareness all aspects of the self so that you may return to a state of wholeness, and this is occurring for each of you as individuals, and also as a collective humanity.

This healing remedy we Angels gift you with is the key to accessing your own archangelic vibration to enact transmutation. It is alchemy, and, as such, varies from person to person in its intensity and timing. The healing frequencies of this system adjust themselves perfectly to whomever and whatever they are attributed to, and may be used on the self, to aid other individuals, in group work, and to heal Earth herself.

This is not a healing in the traditional sense, for it works on the innate knowing that the divine is already perfect in its design and unfoldment. As part of the divine, you, too, are perfect in your design. Bridging this knowing into an embodied state of being is where the healing occurs. This remembrance is now available to all, but not all will actively seek it. For some, they may remain relatively unaware of what is occurring, but their soul will be the driving force behind the integration.

For those of you on a conscious path, who are actively seeking reunification with the divine, we gift you our Archangel Alchemy. The ultimate goal of this system is to help you live within your bliss and to have your bliss alive within you at all times. This is the true core vibration of the human—the enlightened human is able to live a life of sheer, unbridled joy with next to no effort.

There are those who will tell you that this is not possible, for to be human is to suffer in order to grow. As a group—or you may say as a race or tribe—you are dissolving these old programmes and constructs of mind and becoming living examples of embodied beauty and ecstatic joy.

Heaven and Earth are collapsing in on themselves, and you are headed for a new holographic earth, where you no longer separate out these two concepts. Heaven and Earth are one and the same. Likewise, your version of Hell is part of the all, and the holographic aspect of your nature. Hell may be seen as the reflection of the unintegrated or unhealed parts of the human psyche that are clamouring for love and attention.

You are integrating the dual aspects of yourselves and each other, and indeed, the entire paradigm. The separation becomes more intensified the closer you come to reunification. And there is a dance—a "tug of war", you might say—between the ego and the soul, until finally the ego understands that it is the soul that is truly in charge, and then the ego lets go of its attempts to control. This is not the soul taking over the ego, but the soul and the ego reuniting and working together in seamless harmony and equilibrium.

This healing system is designed to help smooth the way for this integration to occur within a safe container of pure love. The diamond, which is both your Essence and your Source, acts as a healing chamber within which the alchemy can unfold according to its divine perfection.

This symbol and shape reflects your own perfection in all its forms, and is in perfect harmony with all of creation according to the laws of nature.

Allowing the Archangels to work with you through this divine container enhances your co-creative capacity and accelerates your consciousness and gifts to their most angelic level. In short, you are becoming your own angelic consciousness within a human body.

Archangel Alchemy allows you to gracefully release the false ideas and programmes of the human, so that you may become the ultimate divine definition of what a human truly is when aligning with and living out your fullest potential.

Some are calling this "superhuman", but it is merely what you were always designed to become. This is a thrilling time for humanity. You are paving the way as pioneers on a voyage of unchartered discovery.

The time is truly now to become all that you are and all that you were always destined to be.

Welcome to the new diamond age!

We are holding you in so much love,

– The Archangels

The Benefits of Archangel Alchemy as a Multidimensional System of Healing

Because Archangel Alchemy works by harnessing the infinite nature of divine unconditional love, this system can be used to work on any issue whether physical, emotional, mental, or spiritual.

Much of the healing works at a subconscious level, so you may find that there is an entire spectrum of adjustment, which can range from very subtle changes to profound transformation.

The healing goes to wherever it is most needed, and the Archangels will always work on the issues that your higher self deems most important at any given time. While you may set out to work on healing a physical ailment, for example, you may find that you also experience a shift in your emotional state or spiritual awareness.

Archangel Alchemy is an entire holistic system that has been gifted to humanity to assist with our global awakening and the transitions taking place on multiple levels.

Some of the more metaphysical activations taking place during the healing process and as a result of alchemical changes may result in:

◊ Activation of the light body

◊ Retrieval of lost or fragmented soul aspects, such as the inner child

◊ Healing of inherited ancestral and genetic (DNA) patterns

◊ Access to higher states of awareness

◊ Deepening of meditative practices

◊ Enhanced psychic abilities

◊ Improved ability to communicate with spirit guides and Angels

◊ Awareness of other beings, realities, and dimensions

◊ Higher states of bliss and joy

◊ Rapid changes occurring within life circumstances, such as shifts within relationships, career, and so on

◊   Deepening of compassion and empathy

◊   Healing of multiple timelines

◊   Surfacing and healing of past, future, parallel, or other life memories

◊   Awakening of kundalini energy

◊   Bridging of polarities, such as the male and female

◊   Light Language activation

◊   Receiving light codes and downloads

◊   Enhanced intuition and claircognizance

◊   Activation to Earth service or gridwork

◊   Awakening of new gifts and abilities

◊   Access to higher knowledge and wisdom previously inaccessible

◊   A deeper understanding of the nature of love in all its forms

◊   Experience of enlightenment; that is, knowing oneself to be divine and connected to all.

The chapters that follow outline how to perform the Archangel Alchemy healing techniques. This multidimensional and alchemical system can be applied to various situations, people, and scenarios, in person or through distance healing. You can use Archangel Alchemy Healing for yourself, other individuals, children, pregnant women, and groups of people. You can also perform it on animals, plants, water, and food. In addition, the Archangel Alchemy system can offer healing into death and transitions as well as healing for the Earth, world service, and gridwork.

How to Perform the Archangel Alchemy Healing Techniques

Archangel Alchemy is a set of healing techniques that require the channelling of pure Archangelic energy, and as such, the healing processes require a similar opening and preparation of your space, as set out in the Channelling Checklist outlined in Part Three of this book.

You will perform the healing within the sacred space of a Diamond Healing Chamber, which is completely protected and held by six magnificent Archangels, along with an added outer perimeter of powerful indigo-purple Throne Angels.

If you feel that you need extra protection for you or your client, prior to performing the healing process, you may also choose to perform the Lesser Banishing Ritual of the Pentagram set out in Part Five, or you can include any other protection ritual or process you like to use.

How Long Should the Healing Take?

Aside from children, animals, and healing into death, a session in Archangel Alchemy should last one hour, and this includes time to have a short consultation chat and set any intentions before the healing, and also includes time at the end for feedback and discussion.

The Key to Why Archangel Alchemy Works as a Healing

This healing harnesses the pure vibration of divine unconditional love. While performing the healing for yourself or anyone else, it is very important that you do not focus on what is wrong and needs to be healed. The key to the perfection of this healing as an alchemy is to visualize or intend that all the cells and vibrations of your physical, mental, emotional, and spiritual being are being returned and restored to their original divine blueprint and harmonizing with their inherent divine perfection. It helps to see the situation, ailment, or illness as already healed, and to imagine that all parts of you, your client, or situation as have already been returned to their optimum state of being.

The healing will work on whatever level is needed for your highest good. If you wish, you can set a specific intention to release an old emotional pattern, work on a physical ailment or just be open to receive whatever healing your higher self and the Archangels deem is necessary for you at any given time.

Trust that the healing is perfect from start to finish and will integrate in the perfect time for you or your client.

Guidance for Performing the Self-Healing Process

◊ **Ground yourself:** Ensure that you are present and in your body. Be acutely aware of your physical sensations, and anchor your consciousness by imagining it as a ball of light and centring it in your heart.

◊ **Set the intention for the highest and best healing to take place:** Set a clear intention to only connect to the most loving angelic beings that have your highest and best interests in mind.

◊ **Open your space:** Visualize a pillar or column of diamond-white light cascading down from infinite Source above you, surrounding you, and flowing all the way into the core of the earth. Visualize it plugging into a huge diamond in the very centre of the earth.

◊ **Shield and protect your space:** Next, see a spark of light at your heart centre, and with every breath in, allow the light to expand into an orb and then expand it out as a huge sphere of light around you and your whole space. Seal this orb in golden light to protect your space. Call on your healing guide teams and any loving Angels, Archangels, or star beings, Ascended Masters, fairies, unicorns, and other guardians of light to join you to hold the perfect space of love, healing, and protection. Intend that only the highest Archangels, healing teams, and beings of love may enter your space, and all else is to be transmuted into divine love or sent to the highest point of its own divine evolution available.

◊ **Raise your vibration:** Breathe in the energy of pure love through the white light, and invite love to enter every facet of your being. Imagine that you feel tingles all over your body, and you may begin to see sparkles of light around the room and feel tingles in your feet and the palms of your hands. Sometimes, I get the sense that the air in the room has become thicker or more tangible, as though I can reach out and grab the energy.

◊ **Invoke the Diamond Starlight Healing Chamber of the Archangels:** Visualize a huge diamond octahedron descending from the Angelic Kingdom of Light way up above you and surrounding your whole space and energy field. The uppermost point of the diamond is connected all the way up into Source/God/the Divine, and the lowest point is connected into the zero point within the core of the earth. Each of the four corners stretches into infinite space around you.

With your intention, pull the diamond in closer around you so that the uppermost point connects with your soul star chakra, 6–8 inches above your head, and the lower point rests within your earth star chakra, 6–8 inches below your feet. Then pull in the four corners of the horizontal plane of the octahedronal diamond so that they sit just around the edge of your auric field.

Now invoke the following Archangels to hold and oversee the six corners of the diamond healing space. Visualize each Archangel beaming their healing ray from the heart into the diamond as crystalline pearlescent light.

In the above and below space:

◊ Metatron holds the top point of the diamond way above you and showers golden-white light down into the diamond.

◊ Sandalphon holds the lowest point of the diamond way below you and showers pearlescent silver-white light into the diamond.

In each of the four corners at the centre of the octahedron, call upon:

◊ Uriel to hold the North corner. See this Angel beaming ruby, russet red, olive green, citrine yellow, and black colours as pearlescent light into the diamond.

◊ Raphael to hold the Eastern corner. See this Angel beaming yellow and green colours as pearlescent light into the diamond.

◊ Michael in the Southern corner. See this Angel beaming sapphire and orange colours as pearlescent light into the diamond.

◊ Gabriel in the Western corner. See this Angel beaming violet and white colours as pearlescent light into the diamond.

Now see, sense, and feel the entire diamond filling with the most dazzling diamond-white angelic starlight. Let the light become as bright as you can imagine, as though the whole diamond chamber, with you inside it, is shining brighter than the brightest star in the sky.

Finally, invoke the powerful protective forces of the Throne Angels:

◊ Standing around you, in each corner of the room where you are performing the healing, invoke or invite four huge indigo-purple Throne Angels to hold the space.

◊ While you are contained within the pure diamond-pearlescent white light of the healing chamber, the protector Throne Angels are filling the remainder of the space with transmuting indigo, purple and golden light.

◊ **Perform the healing**: Call on the presence of the perfect Archangel to step into your energy field and merge with you. You can do this silently in your own mind or aloud.

Feel, see, or sense the Archangel stepping into the diamond healing chamber and then stepping into your energy field. Allow the Archangel to completely merge with you, and visualize yourself becoming this Archangel now. Let go of the image of yourself as the human, and become the angelic presence you have invoked.

See the diamonds in your head, heart, lower belly, hands, and feet being illuminated in white light, and place your hands over your heart. Feel the unconditional love healing light and energy flowing from Source and the core of earth through the Archangel to your heart and out through your hands.

Let go of your logical mind, relax, and just become the observer of the healing. Be open to receiving the healing and witnessing any insights being offered to you by the Archangel now. Allow the energy, light, and qualities of the Archangel to infuse your whole being, so that the healing flows to wherever it needs to go.

You may keep your hands in the one position over the heart for the whole healing, or intuitively move the hands to other body parts, as necessary. Follow your guidance with regards to this.

◊ **Receive any communication and evidence**: Using all your psychic senses, or clairs, ask to connect with and receive messages from your Archangel. Be open to receive any visions or messages the Archangel wishes to impart. These may come in the form of words or pictures inside your mind; colours, symbols, or shapes; or you may just get a clear knowing. Ask for a sign or a symbol that you will see in your waking life as evidence and validation to your ego mind that this healing experience has happened.

◊ **Gratitude and disconnect:** Once the healing has come to an end (either you will feel it naturally dissipate, or if you are working within a specific timeframe, you may ask for it to come to completion), say thank you to the Archangels for their healing, guidance, and assistance. Invite the Archangel to anchor the healing on a physical level and then send any excess healing out through the diamonds in the soles of the feet into Mother Earth to be distributed wherever it needs to go.

Then invite the Archangel to step out of your energy field, and allow yourself to return to your normal, human state. Consciously release the diamond healing chamber by imagining the Archangels and Throne Angels carrying it out of your energy field and all the way back up through the sun, into infinite Source light. Allow the Pillar of Light to dissolve.

◊ **Close down and seal your space:** Shrink, sink, and shield your energy field and consciousness so that it becomes body-shaped and contained within your body. Sink your weight into your body and the chair, and ground yourself by placing your attention in the lower belly or your feet. Shield yourself by wrapping the sphere of golden light around you like a cloak and then wrapping an indigo-blue wizard's cloak over the top of it to seal your energy. Finally, visualize a huge diamond octahedron around you, and fill it with white light, allowing you to shine as brightly as you can while remaining protected.

Variations on the Archangel Alchemy Healing Practice

Hands-On Healing for Another Person

When performing Archangel Alchemy for another individual, have the person sit on a chair in front of you or lie face up on a healing table, or couch. Follow all the same instructions detailed in the self-healing practice above, but place both yourself and the client inside the diamond healing chamber and have the Angels surround the two of you. You may need to intend that the size of the healing chamber is being adjusted to fit the amount of physical space you both inhabit.

Perform the healing in the same way you would for yourself, but instead of placing your hands over your own heart, you will place them on or over the higher heart at the top of the chest of your client. It is a good idea to ask the client if they are comfortable with physical contact before you begin. If they prefer the healing to be non-physical, you may just hover your hands over them at a distance of about 12–16 inches (30–41 cm) above the body. Once again, you may intuitively move the hand positions to other areas of the body or energy field as needed.

When the healing is complete, disconnect and close down in the same way you would for the self-healing practice, detailed above. Gently bring your client around by speaking to them softly. You may wish to help them sit up and offer them a glass of water. Leave some time after the healing for feedback and to discuss their experience.

Group and Distance Healing

To perform a group or distance healing, follow exactly the same instructions for self-healing, but instead of placing the hands over your heart, form a mudra (hand gesture) by having your palms facing outward and creating a diamond shape with your thumbs and forefingers in front of your heart. When you begin the healing, you are then projecting the healing energy from your heart, through the diamond mudra and sending it with your intention into the group field or to the person in the distance.

For distance healing, you can just imagine or visualize the person or people you are sending healing to, or you may work with a photograph, have their name written down on a piece of paper in front of you, or you can perform live distance healings via phone, Zoom, Skype, or any online platform of your choosing.

When the healing is complete, disconnect and close down in the same way you would for the self-healing practice, detailed above. Gently bring your client or the group around by speaking softly to them and guiding them through a grounding process. Leave a short space of time after the healing for feedback and to discuss their experience.

Healing for Animals and Small Children

For animals and young children under the age of 12, perform the healing in the same way as a distance healing for a maximum of 15 minutes only.

Usually, an animal will let you know when they have had enough by getting up and walking away.

Healing for Pregnant Women

As Archangel Alchemy works with pure unconditional love, it is safe for pregnant women. However, when working directly over the bump, limit the time to a maximum of 15 minutes. Otherwise, if you are unsure, leave the hands over the higher heart, and the healing will be directed to wherever it needs to go.

Other Ways to Use Archangel Alchemy

◊ To bless your food and drink

◊ To bless and charge your bathwater

◊ To cleanse, bless, and charge your spiritual tools and crystals

◊ To bless and cleanse your home or area

◊ For Earth and planetary service, you can perform the healing on whole communities, countries, and regions of the planet

◊ To perform healing for a specific theme. You can do this either by performing the self-healing practice and working on the emotions the theme brings up for you, or you may do the distance healing practice and project the healing into an image or symbol that represents them to you. For example, for a news item, you can project the healing into the page of the newspaper.

How to Cleanse and Close Down Your Energy Fields

Always cleanse in a waterfall of white light after any spiritual work, and close down your energy field:

◊ **Shrink**: Shrink your energy field and consciousness so that it becomes body-shaped and contained within your body.

◊ **Sink**: Sink your weight into your body and the chair, and ground yourself by placing your attention in the lower belly or your feet.

◊ **Shield**: Shield by imagining a cloak of indigo and golden light being wrapped around you like a protective wizard's cloak to seal your space.

The Science of Energy Healing

Science has begun to validate some key components of energy medicine in recent times. A study at Seoul National University has confirmed the existence of the energy meridians of the body, which scientists are referring to as the Primo-Vascular System.[61]

Another study by IONS looked at the effect of energy healing on hand and wrist pain and reported a reduction in pain in people suffering from carpal tunnel syndrome.[62] One practitioner taking part in the study also reported "seeing", and made observations clairvoyantly during the 200 sessions.

CHAPTER 22

Healing into Death and Transitions

Archangel Alchemy is a beautiful process to assist someone who is preparing to pass over into spirit or to ease them into a graceful transition during a time of rapid change.

If you wish and if they are open to it, you may invite the dying person's family and loved ones to join the healing and have everyone gently place their hands on or over the dying person's body. You would then open the diamond healing chamber around the entire group.

In this way, both the person transitioning and their loved ones will receive healing and support. This can be beneficial in helping the family let go and process their grief more easily, following their loved one's passing. In some cases, members of the family may even witness the soul as it leaves the body, and some have even reported travelling part of the way with the dying person to see them safely across to the other side. I myself have had experience of this, and it can be incredibly humbling and reassuring to both the family and the transitioning soul.

When we perform a healing into death, as always, we must never hold on to a specific outcome and must only ask for the very highest and best healing and outcome to occur. We must allow the divine and the Archangels to work through us and, instead, become the observer.

A healing into death can sometimes take less or more time than a traditional one-hour session. It is best to go with your intuition and allow the healing to take place at its own pace. You can ask the Archangels to guide you, and you may find that the healing gently brings itself to a natural close at the right time. You should feel the energies start to gently dissipate on their own and then will know to start to bring the healing to a close so you can disconnect and seal the space.

The Gift of a Graceful Transition – A Personal Account of Death and Dying

In early 2016, I was approached by a client, asking if I would be willing to perform healing on her brother, who was in a coma in a hospital intensive care unit. His blood had been poisoned by an aggressive strain of strep bacteria, and his condition had rapidly deteriorated. She first made an appointment to come and see me in person, and by the time she got to me for her session, her family had already been informed that he might not make it, so it was immediately evident that I was her last hope for a "miracle healing". I gently explained to her that any healing I did would be performed by the Archangels from the divine perspective, and so my intention was for the highest and best healing to be delivered without any human hopes or fears getting in the way. I would simply be there to hold the space for whatever needed to take place.

The Archangels totally supported me in that intention. Sometimes, as humans, it can be difficult to let go of the need to know whether a certain outcome will unfold, especially when someone's life is at stake. We so desperately want to offer hope or give good news, but I knew in that moment that it was vital that I stay neutral and grounded in a space of total unconditional love and surrender to the Angels.

I felt my client relax as I explained all this to her, as if she, too, had been given permission to let go of the need to control anything. I knew that she understood completely that it wasn't her responsibility, or mine, to "save" her brother.

As I began my client's healing session, I was also guided to send distance healing to her brother in hospital and, at that point, my mind went totally blank and I found I was very easily able to let go and not try to see what was happening. In fact it was one of the easiest sessions I have ever done. The Archangels allowed me to mentally step back and simply allow the healing to unfold as needed. I felt held and supported and trusted that the absolute divine and perfect outcome for all would unfold.

The next day, my client phoned to ask if I would come to the ICU in person to perform healing for her brother. My only other experience of performing a healing of this kind was when my grandmother had passed over a few years before. She has since visited me in meditation and explained that she is now a "spiritual midwife" and helps souls transition from the other side.

I asked the family to gather around and again explained that we were simply holding the space for the most divinely perfect healing to unfold. I invited all of the family members to place their hands lightly on his body, and I observed the Angels merging with every person in the room. In that moment, I felt the loving energy of my grandmother behind me, and I knew she was also helping to hold the space. Even knowing of her role in spirit, I didn't jump to any conclusions about the outcome of this healing; I simply let go and felt so much love—love for the soul of this man lying unconscious before me; love for his family, who had so graciously invited me to assist in their time of great need, and who had offered such an open-hearted and kind welcome, despite their palpable grief. I surrendered totally to unconditional love. My mind went blank again, but I will never forget the feeling that came over me in that moment.

As I left the hospital, I still didn't know what the outcome would be for that man, but the world around me looked different. Colours appeared brighter, and I could see light shining from the eyes of every person I passed. It was like I could see the very light of their soul radiating from within.

I learned a few days later that he had passed shortly after the healing. His sister thanked me not only for helping her brother to transition smoothly but also for helping the family more easily accept his passing. She said that the healing had made a huge difference for all of them. I was also told that, as the Angels had merged with them, some of the family members, including his mother, were able to feel their energy and a tingling sensation in their finger-tips. I'm so very grateful that I was given the opportunity to be of service in this way.

Something changed in me that day. I never thought that I would be able to describe death as a beautiful thing, but as the soul of this man passed over, I really feel that he gave me a great gift. A kind of purity emerged from within, and I can't help but think that perhaps an outworn part of me also chose to transition at that time. I wonder if perhaps he, too, helped to hold the space for me. In any case, I will never look at life the same way again.

So many people fear death. We're almost taught to fear death from the moment we incarnate in this reality, but that day, I really learned that there is nothing to fear. The love I felt in that room was immense, and as a result of this experience, I truly found something extraordinary. I found grace.

The Science of Death as Rebirth – Life Review, Out-of-Body Experiences, Past Lives, and Euphoria

A scientist performing an EEG on a dying patient suffering from seizures has recorded evidence of brain activity associated with memories. Dr Ajmal Zemmar of the University of Louisville observed changes in gamma oscillations, along with delta, theta, alpha and beta oscillations, involved in memory retrieval. Dr Zemmar has speculated that perhaps this brain activity could account for the many descriptions of a life review recounted by people who report near-death experiences (NDEs).

Similarly, while studying a volunteer able to have out-of-body experiences at will, neuroscientists using fMRI technology have discovered other forms of unusual brain activity associated with kinesthetic imagery or mental pictures of body motion, along with deactivation of the visual cortex. This suggests that a person may still be having physical experiences after they have left their physical body, as also reported by people who have had NDEs.[63]

Anita Moorjani wrote about her miraculous healing from cancer in her book Dying to Be Me. *In the book she recounts how while she was in a coma, she had an NDE, where she was visited by her father and other loving beings. She recounts how she felt nothing but unconditional love and received incredibly clear information about the nature of the universe and how time is non-linear. When she returned from her experience and awoke, her doctors were baffled when, just two days after her body had been riddled with cancer, they couldn't find any trace of the disease.[64]*

A German study found that, at the point of death, the brains of dying rats were flooded with positive chemicals, such as serotonin, a mood-enhancing neurotransmitter. Their serotonin levels had tripled by the time of death and this led scientists to hypothesize whether the same thing could be happening to humans at the time of death, and potentially offer an explanation for NDE descriptions of floating upward and entering a tunnel of light.[65]

Many reports of NDEs describe panoramic memory flashbacks, heightened or very pleasant emotions, meditative states, hallucinations, and transcendental out-of-body experiences. Could this offer proof that life after death is actually a positive experience, where the soul goes on to have a further life and encounters in other dimensions outside of the human body?[66]

In her work as a transformational therapist Lorraine Flaherty has led hundreds of people on hypnosis journeys to explore their past lives. In her book Healing with Past Life Therapy: Transformational Journeys through Time and Space, *Lorraine recounts some of the incredible evidence for the existence of past lives, showing that the soul does indeed live on after death.[67]*

Dr Karen Wyatt, a medical doctor, who has spent years working in hospices and with the dying and grieving, believes in the importance of the spiritual side of life. She says the medical system is falling short by only focusing on the physical side of healing and that we can learn a lot about love and the true nature of life from the dying. Karen says: "One thing I came to learn after doing hospice work for so many years, and being with people as they were facing what was really a crisis time in life or the end of life, is that I came to understand that it's really important for us to learn how to negoti-ate these difficult times. And to recognize that these are very ripe opportunities for us to learn spiritual lessons, and particularly about love." [68]

Judging from my own experiences, from early childhood and into adult life, I believe I have always had an acute understanding of the nature of love as the all-permeating frequency of our universe. I do not think we have any reason to fear death, and I wholeheart-edly believe that my own very early NDE as a newborn meant that I came in with an army of Angels and an innate "knowing" that there is so much support out there for us, and so much more to humanity and our consciousness than we could possibly understand in one lifetime. And yet, in many ways, it is also the simplest concept to grasp: love is all there is and all there ever was.

CHAPTER 23

Why Archangel Alchemy Works

The Secret Healing Power Hidden in the Patterns of Nature

As we have now seen, all of nature and creation is governed by divine mathematics, which was known by the ancients to contain the secrets to all life in the cosmos. These patterns are present within music, astrology, numerology, and geometry, and all facets of our existence.

To the naked eye, nature may appear to be chaotic and unruly, but on closer inspection, we can see that all of creation follows a rhythm of pattern and form. Hidden within matter and these patterns of creation is a powerful energy vibration that can be harnessed for healing and well-being. As I have spoken about in previous chapters, this is the energy and vibration of pure, unconditional love.

This power was taught in ancient mystery schools and often hidden within symbolism, architecture, music, and metaphor. Famous scholars such as Leonardo Da Vinci, Isaac Newton, and Albert Einstein were among those who studied the inner workings of art, science, astrology, and alchemy and were privy to this knowledge.

Nature worship is prevalent in pagan and indigenous traditions, and its symbolism was emulated in ancient monuments, such as the Great Pyramids of Giza, which were built on sacred geometric patterns and celestial alignments. Inventor Nikola Tesla, who famously studied the pyramids, even uncovered that this hidden natural power could be harnessed to create safe and free electricity.

We are part of all creation, so our being and bodies react positively whenever we make a conscious connection to the natural world. Being in a forest or by the sea for even a short while can make us feel totally revitalized.

When we connect directly to the energy of an Angel, we achieve the same effect—often with even greater clarity and potency. But why is this the case?

The Mathematics of Unconditional Love

If we look at the naturally occurring patterns in nature, we find something called the Fibonacci spiral. This spiral and its number sequence were first revealed to the western world in AD1202 by an Italian monk named Leonardo Fibonacci. He studied the patterns of plant growth, and discovered that many plants grow in a spiral fashion, such as the leaves on a tomato plant or the seeds in a sunflower.[69]

Starting with 0 and 1, each new number in the sequence is the sum of the two before it: 0, 1, 1, 2, 3, 5, 8, 13, 21, 34, 55, 89, 144, 233, 377 . . .

Fibonacci and the Golden Mean

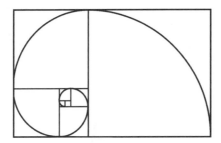

In the Golden Ratio, or Golden Mean, **a+b** is to **a** as **a** is to **b**. The Golden Ratio is a special number found by dividing a line into two parts so that the longer part divided by the smaller part is also equal to the whole length divided by the longer part. It is often symbolized using phi, after the 21st letter of the Greek alphabet. As an equation, it looks like this:

$$a/b = (a+b)/a = 1.6180339887498948420 . . .$$

The digits after the decimal point go on and on, theoretically into infinity, but are usually rounded off to 1.618.

If you look at the relationship between any two successive numbers in the Fibonacci sequence by dividing them, as the numbers get higher and higher, the result gets closer and closer to the Golden Mean of 1.618. For example, the ratio of 3:5 is 1.666, but the ratio of 13:21 is 1.625. Getting even higher, the ratio of 144:233 is 1.618. So when we say plants grow towards the divine, not only do they grow upwards towards the light of the sun, they also mathematically grow towards the divine number of the Golden Ratio.[70] Many flower petals also follow this spiralling sequence. The rose, which is said to be the flower that represents divine love and the Goddess, is a very good example of this.

This exquisite ratio exists within flower petals, trees, seeds, natural foods, shells, and galaxies and unifies the properties of space, time, light, gravity, and even our own DNA.

Our faces and bodies have this ratio, and our brains are constructed with it, with our pineal gland, or "third eye", spiralling with this magical formula.[71] This gland, shaped liked a Fibonacci pine cone, also produces melatonin and DMT, which is thought to cause dreams, clairvoyance, and higher spiritual states. By aligning to nature's vibration, we can access higher emotional states for well-being. Leonardo Da Vinci used this formula extensively in his art, especially in his famous drawings of the Vitruvian Man.[72]

A beautiful example of this ratio used in sculpture is Michelangelo's David, which is located in the Uffizi Gallery in Florence, Italy.[73] The first time I saw this sculpture in person, I was moved to tears and did not know why. The mathematical perfection of it clearly evoked a supreme emotion of love within me.

When you enter a space built on this equation or find yourself in the presence of an object that is built on it, it is as though every cell within your body begins to harmonize with its own divinity. As I have written, I have also experienced unexpected outbursts of emotion within the sacred temples and pyramids of Egypt, Mexico, Peru, and many other sacred spaces around the world that have been built according to the proportions of sacred geometry.

The arched windows and floorplans of most old churches are built using this equation to deliberately make the worshipper feel more pious on entering the space, making the "sinner" believe that it was the religion, or dogma, of the church that was creating this feeling of holy devotion and purification within them.[74]

This is just one example of how this formula has been misused throughout our history. If only people knew that what they were really feeling is a mirroring of their own divine nature expressed in a mathematical formula, they would never put their power outside of themselves again.

Nature's Invisible Healing Vortex

As discovered by Marko Rodin, Vortex Maths shows us that within the Fibonacci series there is a hidden subcode that repeats every 24 numbers. If you discount 0 as not being an actual number, but the origin of all numbers and drop it from the sequence, you start with 1. The first 24 numbers in the pattern are:

1, 1, 2, 3, 5, 8, 13, 21, 34, 55, 89, 144, 233, 377, 610, 987, 1597, 2584, 4181, 6765, 10946, 17711, 28657, 46368 . . .

As the ratios within this pattern are how we find the Golden Mean, or Phi, we can call this the "masculine pattern".

If you add the digits of each whole number together until they each become a single digit, you get the following sequence:

1, 1, 2, 3, 5, 8, 4, 3, 7, 1, 8, 9, 8, 8, 7, 6, 4, 1, 5, 6, 2, 8, 1, 9 . . .

This is the Vortex Maths sequence, and we can call this the "feminine pattern". When we divide this feminine number pattern into two blocks of 12 digits and add them to each other, we discover that they all add up to 9.

1st 12 numbers	1	1	2	3	5	8	4	3	7	1	8	9
2nd 12 numbers	8	8	7	6	4	1	5	6	2	8	1	9
....	9	9	9	9	9	9	9	9	9	9	9	9

All life in our universe is represented by the sphere. Our cells are spherical, as are the sun, the moon, and the planets in our solar system. We operate in accordance with cycles, such as the seasons and birth, life, and death cycles.

All life and all universes are contained within the sphere.

The pattern that shapes our cells is a binary system, a pattern that starts with 1 and continues doubling in numbers.

For example: 1, 2, 4, 8, 16, 32, 64, 128, 256 . . .

If you add together the digits of each of these individual numbers until they form single digits, the "female sequence" then becomes:

1, 2, 4, 8, 7, 5, 1, 2, 4, 8, 7, 5, 1, 2, 4 . . .

The digits 3, 6, and 9 are missing. If all the other numbers in the sequence represent physical matter and physical existence, then 3, 6, and 9 must relate to the realms of the Non-physical.[75]

(As an interesting side note, I had no idea about the existence of Vortex Maths when I had the logos for my business and Precious Wisdom healing system designed. Imagine my delight to discover that my initials AW, when formed into a symbol, follow the same pattern! The Angels were obviously inspiring me when I thought up my branding.)

ALEXANDRA
WENMAN

Vortex Mathematics proves life and energy must exist beyond the realms of the physical and rational. Could this mean that angels and other Non-physical beings are real after all?

The truth of the spherical pattern of the universe is that within the sphere of life, there exists another shape, which represents the animating principle or flow of energy. It is a shape that is known as a "tube torus". The tube torus is a doughnut with a hole through the centre that runs between two opposite ends, or poles, creating a central axis, such as Earth.[76]

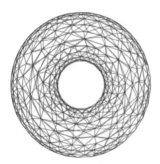

The energy flow moves in one end, up through the core, and out the other end, then over and down around the sides and then back in and up again, creating a vortex. Hurricanes, planets, cells, galaxies, and our own aura, brain, and heart all use this same self-animating toroidal flow of energy.

At the core of the torus is a singular point of supreme balance and stillness, which is often referred to as the stillpoint, or "zero point".

If we see 0 as the neutral point from which all numbers arise, and which divides the positive and negative numbers, the number 9 could also be seen to create two polarities, which are embodied in the numbers 3 and 6.

The 3–6–9 and 6–3–9 cycle can be thought of as clockwise and counter-clockwise, or electricity and magnetism.

Centrifugal force, or two counter-rotating or oscillating forces of energy, opens the vortex, or vacuum, which creates the "zero point", which is also the essence or neutrality, or nonjudgemental, unconditional love energy.

This stillpoint is the neutral energy of pure love. This is the state of perfect equilibrium, harmony, and balance, from which all life and creation begins, and within which the ideal conditions for healing can arise.

Creation and the Golden Mean

In the beginning, all life follows the same pattern of creation. We can see this basic pattern prevalent throughout all creation within the concept of sacred geometry.

All life begins as a sphere, or a cell. When cell division occurs, it splits into two. The shape at the centre of the first two overlapping spheres is called the Vesica Piscis. Within this basic almond shape, which can also be seen in our eyes, our mouths, and other parts of the human anatomy, the key to all of life is said to exist.[77]

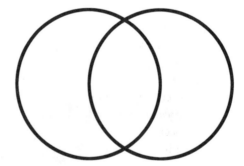

This overlapping of two spheres represents our dual nature at its most fundamental level: the separation of human consciousness from divine consciousness, when we become individualized at conception.

In this simple shape, with its two spheres crossing over, or interlinking, we can see the coming together and moving apart of two opposing, or polarized, forces—which again could represent masculine and feminine, dark and light, matter and antimatter, and so on—creating the vortex, or neutral zone, at the core.

The central point where the two spheres intersect, known as the *Vesica Piscis* (the "bladder of the fish"), is the original depiction of the Divine Proportion, or Golden Mean, for this is where this mathematical formula first occurs within the creation process, at its very conception.

The *Vesica Piscis* could be thought of as the womb of all creation. It's a powerful symbol of the divine feminine, a portal for the non-physical to manifest itself into the physical reality. This is why the ratio is known as "divine" and referred to as the mathematical formula of unconditional love, for it is the essence of love within the all-permeating divine that allows life to occur in the first place.

Amazingly, the *Vesica Piscis* is also present in the spherical tube torus, the shape of the flow of energy of our own auric field, as well as the energy fields of the earth, the planets, the solar system, the galaxy, and the universe. It also represents the atomic spin of an atom, so the saying "As above, so below. As within, so without" is true.

So How Do We Get the Golden Mean from the *Vesica Piscis*?

If we see the curved, or spherical lines, of this shape as feminine, then to access the divine we must find the masculine counterpart. By drawing straight lines and connecting them to the corners of this shape, we soon find we have a rectangle.

When we add the masculine energy to the feminine energy, we discover three numbers, which continue infinitely behind the decimal point without a repetitive pattern. These three numbers are the square root of 2, the square root of 3, and the square root of 5. It's this third number—the square root of 5—that gives us the Golden Ratio.

These numbers were discovered by the Greek mathematician and philosopher Pythagoras, who was apparently also a high-ranking member in many ancient mystery schools and secret societies.

If we divide the rectangle in two diagonally, we find two Golden Mean triangles.

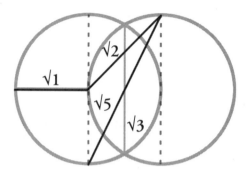

After that first split, the cell then splits again and again and again until it completes 13 divisions. These 13 rounds of creation are depicted in the flower of life symbol.

This flower of life symbol was known by the ancients in many different parts of the world and can be found in ancient statues and carvings in various locations. One of the most intriguing examples of this Flower of Life symbol is where it has been mysteriously etched or laser-cut into the walls of the Osirion at Abydos temple in Egypt.

The first few stages of embryonic cell division correspond to the Flower of Life pattern, which depicts the fundamental aspects of space and time. It is from this beautiful Flower of Life pattern that we discover sacred geometry.[78] Once again, if the spherical or curved lines represent the feminine, we must join the dots or link up the corners of each full sphere with straight lines in order to unearth the masculine, and then we can uncover the secret of sacred geometry.

The symbol that remains, known as Metatron's Cube, perfectly depicts how each of the Platonic solids—the individual geometric shapes first brought to our attention by the Greek philosopher Plato—exist within all of nature and within our own energy fields. Within Metatron's Cube, we again find our Archangel Alchemy diamond symbol. These are the building blocks of all of creation.

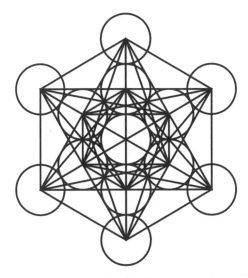

As we ourselves are built on these geometries, which are hidden within the spherical matrix of our cells and our DNA, we can surely say that every human being is mathematically perfect and sacredly divine.[79]

Calling on the Angels

As Metatron is known as the Archangel that represents the building blocks of creation, we could say that the Angels are really the "angles" that join up existence. Angels as angles represent the ratio, or "relationship", between us and the divine/God/Source; they are the consciousness bridge between our earthly and godly selves, as well as the doorway between the seen and unseen worlds.

Masculine and feminine work together in harmony in order to create. As you can see from the mathematics, we cannot have one without the other. It then stands to reason that, like us, Angels are not only present throughout all of nature and creation but are also what allows creation to take form in the first place.

As we are all part of nature, Angels are, therefore, part of us.

So when you call on an Angel for healing, you are harnessing your own inner divine healing power, which is part of your true nature. This is why angelic energy offers some of the most pure and potent healing vibrations available to humanity. Healing with the Archangels isn't just about getting well, though; it is about being the very best aspect of yourself by aligning to your true nature, which is to become aware that you are the divine itself.

When you are no longer a passive bystander in life, believing creation and the divine to be something separate from you, manifesting or accessing the highest levels of healing available becomes different. When you know yourself divine and begin to embody that wisdom through the power of unconditional love, our divine blueprint, you have the ability to influence the elemental kingdoms and all of nature to bring about your desired result.

The Diamond, which portrays the purest and most divine aspect of our soul, is represented by the octahedron shape. We can find a 2D example of the diamond within the *Vesica Piscis* by joining up each corner with four straight lines.

The corners of all the 3D shapes of the Platonic Solids, when revealed within Metatron's Cube, align to the same 3–6–9 pattern that is revealed within Vortex Maths.[80] So, once again, we see how sacred geometry, and especially the octahedron or diamond shape, acts as a gateway to the Non-physical realms of consciousness, where we may access the divine.

Therefore, when performing Archangel Alchemy, you are actively opening an unconditional love vortex, or portal, and calling up the purest and most potent essence of your own divinity, which is part of nature. This vortex, or portal, allows the unmanifest to become manifest through the power of unconditional love, otherwise known as neutral or nonjudgemental love. It combines the feminine desire to create with the masculine building blocks of creation to bring thought into form.

In my view, this maths strongly accounts for why I had such a powerful experience and vision of a vast healing portal, or vortex, of light opening up within the Great Pyramid (AKA The Great Diamond) when I was in Egypt.

When we work with unconditional love in healing, focusing only on the highest and best outcome without judgement, we open the doorway for the divine to work through us, and it is in this space of trust and surrender that a miracle can occur.

In my opinion, this provides us with solid, irrefutable mathematical evidence of the secret angelic healing power hidden within the patterns of creation.

Epilogue

It is both my personal experience and my firm belief that there are vastly superior intelligent life forms that exist within our universe and, indeed, our multiverse. However, as we can see from both the mathematical and metaphysical evidence on offer, our own intelligence is not bound to our physical reality, nor to the apparent limitations of our physical form.

The processes and techniques shared in this book are a direct gift from the Archangels to help us understand the true infinite nature of our own capabilities, so we may tap into our genius and live to our fullest potential.

I wholeheartedly believe that we rapidly need to bridge the worlds of science and spirituality in order to move forward as a species. If we remain tied to the realms of logic only, we miss out on some of the miraculous and often unexplainable events and experiences, which can lead us to accelerated growth and huge advancements for humankind, especially in the fields of health, well-being, and medical advancement.

I am by no means a scientist, but I have every hope that in the future I can be involved in doing scientific research to further validate the incredible technologies the Archangels, Angels, councils of light, and celestial guide teams have gifted me with. I have seen first-hand how these techniques can help people to heal beyond their expectations, and sometimes even mine, and I want to share this knowledge with the world.

Fractal

When the light fractals
It scatters rainbows
Crystalline streams
In those sunlit beams
It's amazing
How quickly your pain goes
When the sun
Clothes you
In rainbows

Notes

Prologue

[1] Robert J. Fox. *Prayer Book for Young Catholics* (Huntington, IN: Our Sunday Visitor, 2004), 102

PART ONE
Chapter 1

[2] Carl Jung, with Marie-Louise Franz, *Man and His Symbols* (Garden City, NY: Doubleday, 1964), 3, 4, 41

Chapter 2

The Science of Angelic Visions and Visitations

[3] Dr Rick Strassman, *DMT: The Spirit Molecule* (Vermont: Inner Traditions / Bear & Company, 2001), 185-219

Chapter 3

[4] https://www.shutterstock.com/g/larissa+wenman

The Science of Prophecy

[5] Theresa Cheung and Dr Julia Mossbridge, *The Premonition Code: The Science of Precognition, How Sensing the Future Can Change Your Life* (London: Watkins Publishing, 2018)

[6] Gustav Davidson, *A Dictionary of Angels* (New York: The Free Press, 1967), 336

The Science of the Angelic Choirs – Other Dimensions as Music and Sound

7 *The Alexandra Wenman Show*:- Dr Eben Alexander, science, NDEs, & other realities: "I was a speck of awareness on a butterfly wing." https://www.youtube.com/watch?v=EuopePJ1_gU

Chapter 4

The Science of Sleep, Dreams, and Lucid Dreaming for Healing

8 https://www.ninds.nih.gov/Disorders/Patient-Caregiver-Education/Understanding-Sleep
9 https://healthysleep.med.harvard.edu/healthy/science/what/sleep-patterns-rem-nrem
10 https://www.mind.org.uk/information-support/types-of-mental-health-problems/sleep-problems/about-sleep-and-mental-health/
11 K.R. Konkoly et al., "Real-time dialog between experimenters and dreamers during REM sleep," Curr Biol, doi:10.1016/j.cub.2021.01.026, 2021
12 https://noetic.org/research/healing-lucid-dream-pilot-study/
13 *The Alexandra Wenman Show*: Karen Newell, Author & Co-founder of Sacred Acoustics: "I wanted to know the answers to everything" – https://www.youtube.com/watch?v=XUKZcNMyNQI

Chapter 6

The Science of the Body Angel and Our Gut Instinct

14 https://www.newscientist.com/article/mg24632881-300-consciousness-isnt-just-the-brain-the-body-shapes-your-sense-of-self/
15 HeartMath Institute. Rollin McCraty, R, PhD. Retrieved from https://www.heartmath.org/resources/downloads/the-energetic-heart/

Chapter 7

The Science of Channelling

[16] Helané Wahbeh. *The Science of Channeling: Why You Should Trust Your Intuition and Embrace the Force that Connects Us All* (Oakland, CA: New Harbinger Publications, 2021)

[17] Helané Wahbeh, Loren Carpenter, & Dean Radin. (2018). "A Mixed Methods Phenomenological and Exploratory Study of Channeling." *Journal of the Society for Psychical Research*, 82(3), 129-148

[18] IONS Channeling Update (2016-present) 7/12/2020, noetic.org.uk

PART TWO
Chapter 8

[19] www.britannica.com/art/chromaticism

The Science of the Creative Force of Sound

[20] https://solarsystem.nasa.gov/resources/2559/echoes-of-the-universes-creation/

[21] https://www.newscientist.com/article/dn21653-ancient-sound-waves-sculpted-galaxy-formation/

[22] Anthony Ashton, Miranda Lundy, John Martineau, and Daud Sutton, *The Quadrivium: Number, Geometry, Music, Heaven* (Glastonbury, UK: Wooden Books, 2010), 68

The Science of the Diamond

[23] https://www.smithsonianmag.com/science-nature/diamonds-unearthed-141629226/

[24] https://geology.com/articles/diamonds-from-coal/

The Science of the Holographic Universe

[25] Niayesh Afshordi et al. From Planck Data to Planck Era: Observational Tests of Holographic Cosmology, *Physical Review Letters* (2017). DOI: 10.1103/PhysRevLett.118.041301

[26] https://phys.org/news/2017-01-reveals-substantial-evidence-holographic-universe.html

The Science That Supports the Living Consciousness of the Universe

27 https://www.independent.co.uk/life-style/gadgets-and-tech/universe
   -brain-shape-cosmic-web-galaxies-neurons-b1724170.html
28 https://www.frontiersin.org/articles/10.3389/fphy.2020.525731/full

Chapter 9

29 Carl Gustav Jung, Edited and with an Introduction by Joseph Campbell,
   The Portable Jung (New York: Penguin Books, 1976), 139
30 https://www.bailii.org/ew/cases/EWHC/IPEC/2021/2546.html

The Science of the "One Flame" – Quantum Entanglement

31 https://www.space.com/31933-quantum-entanglement-action-at-a
   -distance.html
32 https://www.sciencedaily.com/terms/quantum_entanglement.htm
33 https://noetic.org/profile/dean-radin/
34 Dean Radin, PhD, *Entangled Minds: Extrasensory Experiences in Quantum
   Reality* (New York: Paraview Pocket Books, 2006)
35 *St John of the Cross: Dark Night of The Soul*, New Translation and
   Introduction by Mirabai Starr. Foreword by Thomas Moore, author of
   Care of the Soul (New York: Riverhead Books, 2003)

PART THREE
Chapter 13

The Science of Sacred Flames – Cosmic Rays, Bioelectricity, and Bioluminescence

36 Eva Rudy Jansen, *The Book of Hindu Imagery: Gods, Manifestations and
   Their Meanings* (Havelte, Holland: Binkey Kok Publications, 2001), 64
37 https://www.britannica.com/science/cosmic-ray/Electrons-in-cosmic-rays
38 https://home.cern/science/physics/cosmic-rays-particles-outer-space
39 https://www.livescience.com/60842-cosmic-rays-reveal-void-great
   -pyramid.html
40 https://www.nobelprize.org/prizes/medicine/1946/muller/biographical/
41 https://www.nasa.gov/analogs/nsrl/why-space-radiation-matters
42 https://journals.plos.org/plosone/article?id=10.1371%2Fjournal
   .pone.0006256

43 https://www.lightstalking.com/what-is-kirlian-photography-the-science-and-the-myth-revealed/

The Science of How the Archangel Alchemy Visualization Processes and Working with Their Flames Can Help You Heal

44 https://www.verywellmind.com/what-is-an-action-potential-2794811
45 Marianne Cumella Reddan, Tor Dessart Wager, Daniela Schiller. "Attenuating Neural Threat Expression with Imagination." *Neuron*, 2018; 100 (4): 994 DOI: 10.1016/j.neuron.2018.10.047

Chapter 16

The Science of Poetry for Healing

46 Remark made in 1923; recalled by Archibald Henderson, *Durham Morning Herald*, August 21, 1955; Einstein Archive 33-257
47 Response to the editor of a German magazine dealing with modern art requesting a short article, January 27, 1921; quoted in Dukas and Hoffmann, *Albert Einstein: The Human Side*, 37
48 https://www.newstatesman.com/culture/2016/06/love-affair-between-science-and-poetry
49 https://www.frontiersin.org/articles/10.3389/fneur.2015.00003/full

Chapter 17

The Science of Light Language

50 *The Alexandra Wenman Show*: - Githa Ben-David: "The Note From Heaven is like a bridge to the Oneness": https://www.youtube.com/watch?v=xoKJFggtOl8&t=4s

The Science of Music for Healing

51 https://journals.sagepub.com/doi/full/10.1177/2156587216668109
52 https://www.ncbi.nlm.nih.gov/pmc/articles/PMC4325896/
53 http://www.goldenmean.info/ophanim/
54 https://www.youtube.com/watch?v=4vG-mWCP9vA
55 http://www.goldenmean.info/ophanim/
56 http://www.goldenmean.info/dnaring/
57 http://www.soulsofdistortion.nl/SODA_chapter11.html

PART FOUR
Chapter 19

The Science of the Cosmic Diamond

[58] https://www.universetoday.com/9295/astronomers-find-a-huge -diamond-in-space/

Chapter 20

[59] Drunvalo Melchizedek, *The Ancient Secrets of the Flower of Life Volume I* (Flagstaff, AZ: Light Technology Publishing, 1998), 4
[60] https://www.bbc.co.uk/news/uk-scotland-edinburgh-east-fife -46694316#:~:text=Built%20for%20King%20Khufu%20and,9%20 miles)%20down%20the%20Nile

Chapter 21

The Science of Energy Healing

[61] "The Role of ikiiki (Psychological Liveliness) in the Relationship between Stressors and Stress Responses among Japanese University Students" by Yoshiyuki Tanaka and Akira Tsuda, *Japanese Psychological Research*, Vol. 58, No.1.71-84, 2016
[62] https://noetic.org/publication/ energy-medicine-treatments-hand-wrist-pain/
[63] https://www.forbes.com/sites/paulhsieh/2022/02/27 /what-happens-in-the-brain-at-the-moment-of-death/?sh=79a46bb76046
[64] Anita Moorjani, *Dying to be Me: My Journey from Cancer to Near Death, to True Healing* (London: Hay House UK, 2012), 89
[65] https://www.newscientist.com/article/mg21128294-900-near-death -experiences-may-be-triggered-by-serotonin/
[66] https://www.frontiersin.org/articles/10.3389/fnagi.2022.813531/full
[67] Lorraine Flaherty, *Healing with Past Life Therapy: Transformational Journeys Through Time and Space* (Vermont: Inner Traditions/Findhorn Press, 2013)
[68] *The Alexandra Wenman Show*: Dr Karen Wyatt: "None of us has the power to fix what's happening right now – love will sustain us." – https://www.youtube.com/watch?v=KPNXVwSvGVU

Chapter 24

Why Archangel Alchemy Works – The Secret Healing Power Hidden in the Patterns of Nature

[69] Drunvalo Melchizedek, *The Ancient Secrets of the Flower of Life Volume I* (Flagstaff, AZ: Light Technology Publishing, 1998), 207-211

[70] https://www.mathsisfun.com/numbers/fibonacci-sequence.html

[71] http://www.mathematicsmagazine.com/Articles/ FibonacciNumbersPineConeandVatican.php#.YjN3pxDP0Xo

[72] Drunvalo Melchizedek, *The Ancient Secrets of the Flower of Life Volume I* (Flagstaff, AZ: Light Technology Publishing, 1998), 195-206

[73] https://www.mos.org/leonardo/activities/golden-ratio

[74] Anthony Ashton, Miranda Lundy, John Martineau and Daud Sutton, *The Quadrivium: Number, Geometry, Music, Heaven* (Glastonbury, UK: Wooden Books, 2010), 112-115

[75] Vortex Math, Part 1 and 2: Nikola Tesla; 3, 6, 9: The Key To Universe: https://www.youtube.com/watch?v=OXbVZc10lnk

[76] Drunvalo Melchizedek, *The Ancient Secrets of the Flower of Life Volume I* (Flagstaff, AZ: Light Technology Publishing, 1998), 155-156

[77] Priya Hemenway, *The Secret Code: The Mysterious Formula that Rules Art, Nature and Science* (Springwood, SA, Lugano, Switzerland: Evergreen, 2008), 50

[78] Drunvalo Melchizedek, *The Ancient Secrets of the Flower of Life Volume I* (Flagstaff, AZ: Light Technology Publishing, 1998), 31-37, 185-194

[79] http://www.magicmerkabahangel.com/

[80] https://tombedlamscabinetofcuriosities.wordpress.com/category /metatron-cube/

Bibliography

Books

Alexander, Eben. *Proof of Heaven: A Neurosurgeon's Journey into the Afterlife.* London, UK: Piatkus, 2012.

Ashton, Anthony, Miranda Lundy, John Martineau, and Daud Sutton. *The Quadrivium: Number, Geometry, Music, Heaven.* Glastonbury, UK: Wooden Books, 2010.

Bailey, Alice. *The Seven Rays of Life.* New York: Lucis Press, 1995.

Bauval, Robert, and Hancock, Graham. *Keeper of Genesis: A Quest For the Hidden Legacy of Mankind.* London, UK: Arrow, 1997.

Ben-David, Githa. *Heal the Pineal: Detox with Hung Song.* Odder, Denmark: Gilalai, 2020.

Blavatsky, Helena Petrovna. *The Secret Doctrine vol. II.* Wheaton, IL: Theosophical Publishing House, 1993.

Carroll, Robert Todd. *The Skeptic's Dictionary: A Collection of Strange Beliefs, Amusing Deceptions, and Dangerous Delusions.* Hoboken, NJ: John Wiley & Sons, 2003.

Cheung, Theresa, and Dr Julia Mossbridge. *The Premonition Code: The Science of Precognition, How Sensing the Future Can Change Your Life.* London, UK: Watkins Publishing, 2018.

Davidson, Gustav. *A Dictionary of Angels.* New York: The Free Press, 1967.

Flaherty, Lorraine. *Healing with Past Life Therapy: Transformational Journeys through Time and Space.* Rochester, VT: Inner Traditions/Findhorn Press, 2013.

Fox, Robert J. *Prayer Book for Young Catholics.* Huntington, IN: Our Sunday Visitor, 2004.

Gilchrist, Cherry. Alchemy: *The Great Work – A Brief History of Western Hermeticism*. London, UK: Hodder & Stoughton, 2015.

Haich, Elizabeth. *Initiation*. Santa Fe, NM: Aurora Press, 2000.

Hall, Manly P. *Initiates of the Flame: The Deluxe Edition*. New York: St Martin's Essentials, St Martin's Publishing Company, 2021.

—. *The Secret Teachings of All the Ages*. Los Angeles, CA: The Philosophical Research Society, 1988.

Hemenway, Priya. *The Secret Code: The Mysterious Formula that Rules Art, Nature and Science*. Springwood, SA/Lugano, Switzerland: Evergreen, 2008.

Hurtak, JJ, and Desiree Hurtak. *Pistis Sophia: A Coptic Text of Gnosis with Commentary*. Los Gatos, CA: The Academy for Future Science, 2003.

Jansen, Eva Rudy. *The Book of Hindu Imagery: Gods, Manifestations and Their Meanings*. Havelte, Holland: Binkey Kok Publications, 2001.

Jones, Aurelia Louise. *Prayers to the Seven Sacred Flames*. Mount Shasta, CA: Mount Shasta Lighthouse Publishing, 2007.

Jung, Carl. Edited and with an Introduction by Joseph Campbell. *The Portable Jung*. New York: Penguin Books, 1976.

Jung, Carl, with Marie-Louise Franz. *Man and His Symbols*. Garden City, NY: Doubleday, 1964.

Kalahari, Angelina. *Breathing for Confidence: Your Voice, Your Superpower: 1* London, UK: Flame Projects, 2020.

Lipton, Bruce H. Lipton. *The Biology of Belief: Unleashing the Power of Consciousness, Matter and Miracles*. London: Hay House UK, 2015.

Melchizedek, Drunvalo. *The Ancient Secrets of the Flower of Life, Volume I*. Flagstaff, AZ: Light Technology Publishing, 1998.

—. *The Ancient Secrets of the Flower of Life, Volume II*. Flagstaff, AZ: Light Technology Publishing, 2000.

Moody, Raymond Moody. *Making Sense of Nonsense: The Logical Bridge Between Science and Spirituality*. Woodbury, MN: Llewellyn Publications, 2020.

Moorjani, Anita. *Dying to be Me: My Journey from Cancer to Near Death to True Healing*. London: Hay House UK, 2012.

Picknett, Lynn, and Clive Prince. *The Templar Revelation: Secret Guardians of the True Identity of Christ*. New York: Touchstone, Simon & Schuster, 1998.

Piper, Martha. *Introduction to Vortex-Based Mathematics*. Tyler, TX: The Hammerhead Shark Publisher House, 2017.

Prophet, Mark L., and Elizabeth Clare Prophet. Compiled and edited by Annice Booth. *The Masters and Their Retreats*. Corwin Springs, MT: Summit University Press, 2003.

Pullman, Philip. *His Dark Materials Trilogy: Northern Lights, The Subtle Knife, and The Amber Spyglass*. New York: Scholastic, 2019.

Radin, Dean. *Entangled Minds: Extrasensory Experiences in Quantum Reality*. New York: Paraview Pocket Books, 2006.

Regardie, Israel. *The Golden Dawn: The Original Account of the Teachings, Rites, and Ceremonies of the Hermetic Order*. Seventh Edition. Woodbury, MN: Llewellyn Publications, 2020.

Starhawk, *The Spiral Dance: A Rebirth of the Ancient Religion of the Great Goddess 10th Anniversary Edition*. San Francisco, CA: HarperCollins, 1989.

St John of the Cross, *Dark Night of the Soul*, New Translation and Introduction by Mirabai Starr. Foreword by Thomas Moore, author of *Care of the Soul*. New York: Riverhead Books, 2003.

Strassman, Rick. *DMT: The Spirit Molecule*. Rochester, VT: Inner Traditions / Bear & Company, 2001.

Tesla, Nikola. *The Inventions, Researches, and Writings of Nikola Tesla*. New York: Barnes & Noble, 2014.

Wahbeh, Helané. *The Science of Channeling: Why You Should Trust Your Intuition and Embrace the Force that Connects Us All.* Oakland, CA: New Harbinger Publications, 2021.

Wenman, Alexandra. *Archangel Fire Oracle.* Forres, Scotland: Findhorn Press, 2021.

Online

https://www.shutterstock.com/g/larissa+wenman

The Alexandra Wenman Show - Dr Eben Alexander, science, NDEs & other realities: "I was a speck of awareness on a butterfly wing": https://www.youtube.com/watch?v=EuopePJ1_gU

https://www.ninds.nih.gov/Disorders/Patient-Caregiver-Education/Understanding-Sleep

http://healthysleep.med.harvard.edu/healthy/science/what/sleep-patterns-rem-nrem

https://www.mind.org.uk/information-support/types-of-mental-health-problems/sleep-problems/about-sleep-and-mental-health/

https://noetic.org/research/healing-lucid-dream-pilot-study/

The Alexandra Wenman Show: Karen Newell, Author & Co-founder of Sacred Acoustics: "I wanted to know the answers to everything" – https://www.youtube.com/watch?v=XUKZcNMyNQI

https://www.newscientist.com/article/mg24632881-300-consciousness-isnt-just-the-brain-the-body-shapes-your-sense-of-self/

HeartMath Institute. McCraty, R, Ph.D. Retrieved from https://www.heartmath.org/resources/downloads/the-energetic-heart/

www.britannica.com/art/chromaticism

https://solarsystem.nasa.gov/resources/2559/echoes-of-the-universes-creation/

https://www.newscientist.com/article/dn21653-ancient-sound-waves
-sculpted-galaxy-formation/

https://www.smithsonianmag.com/science-nature/diamonds-unearthed
-141629226/

https://geology.com/articles/diamonds-from-coal/

https://phys.org/news/2017-01-reveals-substantial-evidence-holographic
-universe.html

https://www.independent.co.uk/life-style/gadgets-and-tech/universe-brain
-shape-cosmic-web-galaxies-neurons-b1724170.html

https://www.frontiersin.org/articles/10.3389/fphy.2020.525731/full

https://www.casemine.com/judgement/uk/6155633d2c94e0721071cff6

https://www.space.com/31933-quantum-entanglement-action-at-a-distance
.html

https://www.sciencedaily.com/terms/quantum_entanglement.htm

https://www.extremetech.com/extreme/295013-scientists-capture
-photographic-proof-of-quantum-entanglement#:~:text=Scientists%20
have%20successfully%20demonstrated%20quantum,and%20even%20
very%20small%20diamonds.&text=The%20experiment%20used%20
photons%20in,known%20as%20a%20Bell%20entanglement.

https://noetic.org/profile/dean-radin/

https://www.britannica.com/science/cosmic-ray/Electrons-in-cosmic-rays

https://home.cern/science/physics/cosmic-rays-particles-outer-space

https://www.livescience.com/60842-cosmic-rays-reveal-void-great-pyramid
.html
https://www.nobelprize.org/prizes/medicine/1946/muller/biographical/

https://www.nasa.gov/analogs/nsrl/why-space-radiation-matters

https://journals.plos.org/plosone/article?id=10.1371%2Fjournal
.pone.0006256

https://www.lightstalking.com/
what-is-kirlian-photography-the-science-and-the-myth-revealed/

https://www.verywellmind.com/what-is-an-action-potential-2794811

https://www.newstatesman.com/culture/2016/06/love-affair-between
-science-and-poetry

https://www.frontiersin.org/articles/10.3389/fneur.2015.00003/full

The Alexandra Wenman Show - Raymond Moody: "Near death/shared death
experiences & the existence of life in other dimensions", 2013:
https://www.youtube.com/watch?v=HyQp1cCG8h4&t=23s

The Alexandra Wenman Show - Githa Ben-David: "The note from heaven is
like a bridge to the oneness": https://www.youtube.com
/watch?v=xoKJFggtOl8&t=4s

https://journals.sagepub.com/doi/full/10.1177/2156587216668109

https://www.ncbi.nlm.nih.gov/pmc/articles/PMC4325896/

The Alexandra Wenman Show - Eben Alexander & Karen Newell: "The brain
doesn't create consciousness…Consciousness is primordial":
https://www.youtube.com/watch?v=dL47BIpj_EA&t=2892s)

https://www.youtube.com/watch?v=4vG-mWCP9vA

http://www.goldenmean.info/ophanim/

http://www.goldenmean.info/dnaring/

http://www.soulsofdistortion.nl/SODA_chapter11.html

https://www.universetoday.com/9295/astronomers-find-a-huge-diamond
-in-space/

https://www.bbc.co.uk/news/uk-scotland-edinburgh-east-fife
-46694316#:~:text=Built%20for%20King%20Khufu%20and,9%20
miles)%20down%20the%20Nile

https://noetic.org/publication/energy-medicine-treatments-hand-wrist-pain/

https://noetic.org/blog/ions-researchers-explore-reiki-energy-medicine/

https://www.forbes.com/sites/paulhsieh/2022/02/27/what-happens
-in-the-brain-at-the-moment-of-death/?sh=79a46bb76046

https://www.newscientist.com/article/mg21128294-900-near-death
-experiences-may-be-triggered-by-serotonin/

The Alexandra Wenman Show: Dr Karen Wyatt: "None of us has the power
to fix what's happening right now – love will sustain us" –
https://www.youtube.com/watch?v=KPNXVwSvGVU

https://www.frontiersin.org/articles/10.3389/fnagi.2022.813531/full

https://www.mathsisfun.com/numbers/fibonacci-sequence.html

http://www.mathematicsmagazine.com/Articles
/FibonacciNumbersPineConeandVatican.php#.YjN3pxDP0Xo

https://www.mos.org/leonardo/activities/golden-ratio

Vortex Math, Part 1 and 2: Nikola Tesla; 3, 6, 9: The Key To Universe:
https://www.youtube.com/watch?v=OXbVZc10lnk

http://www.magicmerkabahangel.com/

https://tombedlamscabinetofcuriosities.wordpress.com/category
/metatron-cube/

https://www.the-cma.org.uk/

https://www.resonancescience.org/about-nassim-haramein

https://lynnemctaggart.com/

https://www.judecurrivan.com/

https://hurtak.com/

https://www.simonandschuster.com/authors/Christopher-Dunn/454420315

https://tcche.org/

https://www.gaia.com/

https://www.history.co.uk/shows/ancient-aliens

https://www.gaia.com/series/pyramid-code

https://www.youtube.com/c/DanWinterFractalField

https://www.youtube.com/user/Jain108Mathemagics

https://www.cityofshamballa.net/group/drstoneteachings/forum/topics
/last-activation-meditation-to

https://www.kingjamesbibleonline.org/Bible-Verses-About-Melchizedek/

Scientific Studies

Afshordi, Niayesh, et al. From Planck Data to Planck Era: Observational
Tests of Holographic Cosmology, *Physical Review Letters* (2017). DOI:
10.1103/PhysRevLett.118.041301.

IONS Channeling Update (2016-present) 7/12/2020, noetic.org.uk

Konkoly, K.R., et al. "Real-time dialog between experimenters and dreamers
during REM sleep," *Curr Biol*, doi:10.1016/j.cub.2021.01.026, 2021.

Reddan, Marianne Cumella, Tor Dessart Wager, & Daniela Schiller.
"Attenuating Neural Threat Expression with Imagination." *Neuron*,
2018; 100 (4): 994 DOI: 10.1016/j.neuron.2018.10.047.

Remark made in 1923; recalled by Archibald Henderson, *Durham Morning
Herald*, August 21, 1955; Einstein Archive 33-257.

Response to the editor of a German magazine dealing with modern art requesting a short article, January 27, 1921; quoted in Dukas and Hoffmann, Albert Einstein: *The Human Side*, 37.

Tanaka, Yoshiyuki, and Akira Tsuda."The Role of ikiiki (Psychological Liveliness) in the Relationship between Stressors and Stress Responses among Japanese University Students." *Japanese Psychological Research*, Volume 58, No.1.71-84, 2016.

Wahbeh, Helané. *The Science of Channelling: Why You Should Trust Your Intuition and Embrace the Force that Connects Us All*. Oakland, CA: New Harbinger Publications, 2021.

Wahbeh, Helané, Loren Carpenter, & Dean Radin. (2018). "A Mixed Methods Phenomenological and Exploratory Study of Channeling." *Journal of the Society for Psychical Research*, 82(3), 129-148.

Acknowledgements

When I started writing about the information coming through in my Archangel Alchemy channellings back in 2009–2010, never in my wildest imaginings did I expect anything quite like the journey it has taken me on. Nor did I foresee that it would eventually become the subject of my first major work devoted to the angels. So some very big thanks need to go to all those who have walked this path alongside me…

First and foremost, thanks must go to Spirit – to my beloved higher self, all my angels and guides for setting me on this path, and keeping me firmly there against all the odds. This human shin-dig sure is tricky terrain!

From the outset in my days as editor at *Prediction*, my darling friend Gemma Kala (Shamrang Kaur) was there, both as a soul sister and my deputy editor, and I owe her such a debt of gratitude for her infinite kindness, wisdom, and love. And to my dear friend Kat Slack, who designed the pages for my magazine column back in the day, and has now returned to create the beautiful layouts and covers for my oracle decks. Thanks also to my then Group-Editor at IPC / Time Inc., Garry Coward-Williams for inviting me to head up the magazine re-launch and offering me the opportunity to write my very own angel column.

To the goddesses Lorraine Flaherty and Sarah Katz, who both showed up out of the blue at just the right time as the most divine and supportive sisters, and who continue to be my closest confidantes.

To my beloved husband and rock, Tony; to my family – especially Mum and Dad, and my siblings: Larissa, Alicia, Gabrielle, and Jonathon – and all my loved ones and friends for their unwavering support.

Heartfelt thanks to dear Colm Holland for agreeing to write the beautiful foreword for this book. And for so lovingly and vulnerably sharing his own heart and entrusting us with such a deeply personal story.

Huge gratitude must go to my agent Séverine Jeauneau and my publisher Sabine Weeke, for believing in me. Both these women have become the dearest of friends and offered me unwavering support during the sometimes very intense birthing process of this book.

Thanks to the entire team at Findhorn Press / Inner Traditions, with a special mention for Ashley, who is always a joy and on hand whenever I need her assistance. To my editor Nicky Leach for her careful crafting of the text and her extreme patience when I was dragging the chain. And to Eric Bailey Ladd at Pixywalls, who is an integral part of my publishing team, for his valuable friendship, kindness, and advice.

To my colleagues, friends, and Earth angels, Lorraine, Gemma, Francesca Cairns, Jane Alexander, Andrea Barneveld and John Levine, who were all willing to stand up for me during one of the biggest initiations I have had to face to stay in my truth.

To my incredible legal team, without whose help I would not have been able to use the title I channelled for this book – Sam O'Toole and William Miles at Briffa, and Christopher Hall at 11 South Square.

Thanks also to all the courageous researchers and scientists, who are willing to put their credibility on the line to help bridge the worlds of the physical and metaphysical, helping to prove what the mystics have always known.

So much love and gratitude goes out to all my clients and students, who continue to make teaching and sharing this work so worthwhile. It fills me with pride to see you all step into your true power and take flight.

To all those who have so graciously endorsed and supported my work over the years.

And, lastly, to you dear reader, for having the courage to embark on the magnificent journey to unity love consciousness.

I wish you all Heaven on Earth.

About the Archangel Alchemy Qualifications

Archangel Alchemy has been certified as a professional archangel healing modality by the Complementary Medical Association in the UK. To find out more about how to train in this system and qualify as an Archangel Alchemy practitioner, visit www.**alexandrawenman.com**.

Index

About the Author

As a channel and spiritual teacher, founder of the Precious Wisdom, World Angel and Archangel Alchemy healing systems, and priestess of the divine feminine, Alexandra Wenman is a go-to voice for the cosmically curious. Devoted to normalizing the conversation about spirituality and awakening, Alexandra brings the "out there" in here with her down-to-earth approach to channelling higher wisdom, connecting to Angels and guides, navigating the dreamscape, accessing our soul records, recognizing our true multi-dimensional birthright, and honouring our divinity.

A former journalist, Alexandra was previously the editor of *Prediction*, a national holistic magazine in the UK. She has co-authored *21 Rituals to Connect with Nature* by Theresa Cheung (Watkins) as well as two collections of poetry, *Poems of Precious Wisdom* and *The Poetry of Light*. Her oracle card deck *Archangel Fire Oracle* (Findhorn Press) is the perfect practical accompaniment to this book.

Alexandra grew up in Coffs Harbour, Australia, and lives in London, UK, with her husband, Tony, and cat, Jezebel.

For channelled guidance and expert interviews, watch *The Alexandra Wenman Show* on YouTube, or follow her on Instagram @alexandracwenman.

For more information see Alexandra's website:
www.alexandrawenman.com

FINDHORN PRESS

Life-Changing Books

Learn more about us and our books at
www.findhornpress.com

For information on the Findhorn Foundation:
www.findhorn.org